SYSTEM IN CRISIS

The Dynamics of Free Market Capitalism

James Petras and Henry Veltmeyer

Fernwood Publishing • Zed Books

Editing: Douglas Beall
Cover image: Pavel Eguez, Quito
Design and production: Beverley Rach
Printed and bound in Canada by: Hignell Printing Limited

Published in Canada by: Fernwood Publishing
Site 2A, Box 5, 8422 St. Margaret's Bay Road
Black Point, Nova Scotia, B0J 1B0
and 324 Clare Avenue, Winnipeg, Manitoba, R3L 1S3
www.fernwoodbooks.ca

Published in the rest of the world by Zed Books Ltd.
7 Cynthia Street, London N1 9JF, UK
and Room 400, 175 Fifth Avenue, New York, NY 10010, USA.

Distributed in the USA exclusively by: Palgrave, a division of St Martin's Press LLC
175 Fifth Avenue, New York, NY, 10010, USA.

Zed Books
ISBN:1 84277 364 X Hb ISBN:1 84277 365 8 Pb

Fernwood Publishing Company Limited gratefully acknowledges the financial support of the Department of Canadian Heritage, the Nova Scotia Department of Tourism and Culture and the Canada Council for the Arts for our publishing program.

A catalogue record for this book is available from the British Library.
National Library of Canada Cataloguing in Publication

Petras, James F., 1937-
System in crisis: the dynamics of free market capitalism / James Petras, Henry Veltmeyer.

Includes bibliographical references and index.
ISBN 1-55266-115-6

1. Capitalism — History — 20th century. 2. Globalization — Political aspects. 3. Globalization — Environmental aspects. 4. Developing countries — Economic conditions. 5. Latin America — Economic conditions — 1945-. 6. Anti-globalization movement. I. Veltmeyer, Henry II. Title.

HB501.P4159 2003a 330.9'049 C2003-903819-X

Contents

Part II
POLITICAL DYNAMICS OF ANTI-GLOBALIZATION

Acknowledgement and Dedication

The authors acknowledge with appreciation the financial support provided by the Social Sciences and Humanities Research Council (SSHRC) of Canada for the field research involved.

The authors dedicate this book to their respective partners in life, Robin Eastman-Abaya and Annette Wright, as well as the many peoples and workers all over the world who have to live and struggle against the conditions that we describe and analyze in this book. May they be successful in their long and difficult revolutionary struggle to help bring about the overthrow on an unjust and exploitative capitalist system. In this regard we wish to pay particular homage to the long and heroic struggle, and the years if not centuries of resistance, of the aboriginal peoples of the Americas, both in the North (Canada, Mexico and the United States, to be precise) and in the South. As an aside, we would like to draw attention to the long struggle of the Armenian people and nation to ensure that the Armenian genocide not be forgotten nor forgiven; that the Turkish state be held to account for this genocide, the subsequent usurpation of Armenian national territory and their continued denial of one of history's holocausts.

Introduction

In the 1930s, in the throes of a major international depression, there was fear in some circles (and jubilation in others) because the capitalist system that dominated the lives of people and countries all over the world appeared to be on its last legs, fated to collapse or be overthrown. Since then, at critical junctures in the history of what Eric Hobsbawm (1994) termed the "short twentieth century," similar fears and apocalyptic predictions of the system's collapse would resurface. The system itself, however, managed to offset its obvious propensity towards crisis and weather the various storms that beset it, invariably tacking with the winds of change. The first such tack involved a series of state-led, socialist-type reforms, introduced from the 1930s to the 1950s that, in effect, created a mixed economy and a more human form of reformed capitalism. In the early seventies, however, this system began to fray at the seams and almost fell apart. The "last great offensive" of the working class in Europe (and to some extent in North America and elsewhere), which was initiated in 1968, exposed serious cracks in the foundation of the world capitalist system that once again threatened its very survival. But once more the system rallied. In 1973 and 1974 the capitalist class in various countries in the North and South of a growing divide in the world system launched a major counteroffensive in the class war between capital and labour. The following twenty-five years or so can be best understood as a response to systemic crisis; as a series of efforts to restructure the system, including a direct assault on labour; a technological restructuring; the shift towards a new mode of regulation — post-Fordism; a new international division of labour; and, since the 1980s, a process of structural adjustment to the requirements of a globalized economy based on the workings of market forces freed from regulatory and political constraints.

The epoch-changing transformations associated with what has been widely termed "globalization" can be understood in this context. However, globalization so understood — as the latest response to a propensity towards systemic crisis — does not describe well the nature and scope of the developments unfolding across the world. We argue that the process of these changes can be better understood through the lens of the word "imperialism." Using this term it is easier, for example, to identify the players on the stage of world development, the game that is being played, the seriousness of the stakes, and the dynamic forces being released in the struggles of supporters and opponents of the capitalist system at its present conjuncture.

Part I of the book explores diverse dynamics of the crisis that have beset the capitalist system in its global and imperialist projection. Chapter 1 provides an overview of the most critical dimensions of the crisis. In Chapter 2 the focus is on the strategies pursued by the United States in its efforts to reverse the conditions of economic crisis and reassert its political hegemony over the system. Chapter 3 examines the dynamics of this process in the context of developments arising out of 9/11. The focus of this chapter is on the War Against Terrorism and on the opportunities this war has created for the US to advance its imperialist designs elsewhere in the world.

Chapter 4 turns to the economic and political crisis that is unfolding on the Latin American periphery of the system. No head of state was as assiduous in prostrating himself and his country in face of the power projected from the United States as Carlos Menem, president of Argentina for much of the 1990s. The legacy of the Menem regime is examined in terms of the worst economic and political crisis in Argentina's history. Early on in the twentieth century, Argentina had the seventh highest per capita incomes in the world, and in many respects had the structure and conditions of a developed society. However, for a number of reasons — one being its location on the margins of the world capitalist system — Argentina did not share in the economic growth, capitalist modernization and transformation undergone by the countries at the centre of the system and, after the Second World War, by a number of countries in the world of developing nations. Nevertheless, by the 1970s Argentina still retained its status as the most developed economy and society in Latin America, a status eroded by the neoliberal experiment in economic policy indulged in by the military regime in the context of a war against subversives that cost the lives of thirty thousand workers, unionists and activists. Even worse, by the late 1990s, after two decades and several permutations of this "experiment," first under a military regime and subsequently under the facade of several constitutionally elected or democratic regimes, Argentina was pushed to the brink of disaster. Since 1998, Argentina has been in the throes of a deep economic crisis that has exceeded the capacity of the political class to solve or even manage. Today the system is embroiled in a crisis without any apparent solution within the framework of the existing capitalist system and neoliberal model in place. The chapter explores the various dimensions of this economic and political crisis, which prefigures trends likely to unfold in other parts of the region and the world in the thrall of capitalism.

In Chapter 5 the focus turns from Argentina's economic crisis to the broader political crisis that has infected much of the region and that might well be endemic to the electoral system generally. As a point of fact, as well as theory, democracies in the region have tended to be fragile or unstable, undermined by neoliberal policies of structural adjustment, liberalization, deregulation and privatization — an economic process put into motion ostensibly to strengthen and support democracy in the region. The dynamics of this electoral crisis are explored in some detail not only in the Latin American context but in Europe.

In Chapter 6 the focus shifts towards the ecological crisis of the capitalist economic system. The conditions of this crisis are omnipresent. A number of authors, such as Joel Kovel (2002), have argued that the logic of capitalist development includes a propensity towards ecological disaster, with the incessant search for accumulation and profits pushing the system beyond the carrying limits of the ecosystem on which economic activity, and indeed life, depends. There are multiple dimensions of this process of environmental degradation, which is truly global in scope, as its effects push economy after economy, and society after society, to the brink of collapse. The chapter takes one particular case that provides a glimpse into the environmental crisis that is threatening to engulf the world. The chapter focuses on developments associated with the cod fishery in the Northern Atlantic, which like many fisheries has been pushed beyond the carrying capacity of the system to the critical point of collapse of the resource and the way of life built upon it. The repercussions have already destroyed the livelihoods of many thousands of people in the coastal communities of Newfoundland and hundreds of these communities themselves. The chapter explores the conditions behind this story.

Part II of the book turns away from the macro- and meso-dynamics of crisis towards the political dynamics of alternative development, anti-globalization and anti-capital — the forces of opposition and resistance mobilized in a growing global civil society. Appearances (and some arguments) to the contrary, so-called "globalization" is neither inevitable nor immutable. Diverse groups of people in an increasingly organized, albeit divided and fragmented global civil society are, in fact, coming together to mobilize the forces of resistance and opposition into an anti-globalization movement. The four chapters in this part of the book bring into focus and place into theoretical and political perspective the diverse forms of struggle associated with this movement.

Chapter 7 examines the protracted struggle of peasant farmers for survival and change and against the state. The context for this analysis is Latin America, but the issues that surround the peasant-state relation are found in other parts of the world and have a broader relevance. Many analysts have given up on the peasantry as a force for change, viewing it as a spent social force, doomed to disappear into the growing urban slums — and into the dustbins of history. We disagree. In fact, we see the Latin American peasantry as major force of rural development and revolutionary change — in the forefront of the broad struggle against the neoliberal form of capitalist development.

In Chapter 8 the authors turn towards another social group that has been at the receiving end of various centuries of capitalist development, imperialism, colonialism, exploitation and oppression. In Latin America, as elsewhere, diverse nations of indigenous people have been decimated by these forces — more than five hundred years of "primitive accumulation" (dispossession of their means of production), enslavement, exploitation and class oppression. However, as demonstrated in Chiapas and Ecuador, indigenous people also constitute a repository of forces for alternative development and revolutionary change. In fact, the uprising of indigenous people against the state in Ecuador — given the economic model of neoliberal capitalist development and globalization behind it — provides an exemplary case study of the global struggle against capitalism and imperialism. The chapter provides a brief gloss on, and analysis of, the recent history of this struggle waged in the form of a social movement that has shaken the political class of the country to its roots and created the spectre of an impending political crisis. The indigenous peoples of the world are on the move — against capitalism.

Chapter 9 documents and analyzes the Unemployed Workers Movement in Argentina, an exemplar of the new forms taken by the labour movement in recent years. This movement represents a new wave of struggles for social change in the region and is analyzed in these terms. The political dynamics of the ongoing struggle by unemployed workers in Argentina are analyzed in the context of the economic and political crisis discussed in Chapter 4.

The concluding chapter looks at developments associated with what is known as the Anti-Globalization Movement (AGM). Unlike the movements discussed in the previous chapters. this movement is unfolding for the most part in societies on the north side of the global divide — in the capitalist societies of Europe and North America. And its main social base is found not in the producing or working class but in the middle class of the major urban centres of these societies. At the moment, however, the Anti-globalization Movement is divided along class lines that are blurred by ideology and other factors. The final chapter focuses on the nature of this division and its political repercussions. This analysis provides a more general perspective on the broader Anti-Globalization Movement and the possibilities for unifying the diverse forces of resistance and opposition to neoliberalism, capitalism and imperialism — and the prospects for an alternative, more human, socialist form of development. The book ends on this note.

Part I

THE CRISIS OF FREE MARKET CAPITALISM

1. The Dynamics of Systemic Crisis

That countries and most people of the world are inextricably bound up in one set of interconnected structures, or system, is by now common knowledge. Equally clear is that this system is in crisis and has been so for at least three decades. A propensity towards crisis is one of the defining features of the operating economic system, which since its inception has lurched from one crisis to another.

In the late 1960s the operating world capitalist system hit a snag, exposing cracks that went to its very foundations. At first this crisis was viewed as merely episodic, part of a normal business cycle with its ebb and flow pattern of capital accumulation in which markets are saturated and capitalists unable to realize profits on their investments are compelled to disinvest and slough off labour, thereby increasing the mass of unemployed workers, reducing purchasing power and consumption capacity, and initiating a further downward cycle of disinvestment and recession. On the downside of an unusually long growth cycle, and in the context of what in retrospect might be seen as the last great offensive of workers in Europe and elsewhere in their struggle for higher wages and improved working conditions, the system ran out of steam. Cracks in the system appeared, reviving the spectre of crisis that haunted the system in the 1930s and giving rise to serious concerns about both the viability of the international order put into place at Bretton Woods a quarter century before and the very survival of capitalism. By 1973, in the midst of a serious downturn in world production and a significant hike in the world price of oil, the systemic nature of the crisis was all too evident.

By the end of the 1990s it was clear that, despite tremendous advances in technology and a series of efforts to restructure the system, capitalism was still in crisis — very much so. These efforts, which can be viewed in strategic or structural terms, included: (1) a restructuring of world production, creating a global production system and a new international division of labour; (2) new computer- or information-based technologies designed to revolutionalize the structure of production — productive transformation; (3) a new mode of capital accumulation and regulatory regime — post-Fordism; and (4) and a program of policy reforms and structural adjustments, to facilitate a process of globalization and the renovation of the world order — a new economic order in which capital and commodities could move freely on a global scale.

But despite epoch-defining changes wrought in the structure of the dominant relations of production (and power), the world economic system could not avert its propensity towards crisis. Nor — despite the enormous expansion of world production since the 1970s and revolutionary technological advances — have there been a halt to and reversal of a system-wide tendency towards sluggish productivity growth. The growth dynamic in the area of computer hardware and software has not translated into system-wide productivity growth (Jorgenson and Stiroh 1999).

Even in the United States, the world's largest economy and the dynamic centre of world production, the economy is in crisis, having lost thousands of billions of dollars in capital invested in high-tech fibre optics, telecommunications and biotechnology, the most dynamic sectors of economic growth. From March 2000 to March 2001 the NASDAQ lost 62 percent of its value. And at this point the stock market collapse hit stocks in other sectors as well: from March 2000 to March 2002 the S&P500, the index of the strongest stocks on Wall Street, fell 50 percent (Passet 2002: 16).

From the mid- to late- 1990s a speculative bubble of unprecedented size masked the depth and persistent nature of the crisis, but in 2000 it sparked a twenty-one-month period of decline in the level of US industrial production. In the second half of 2002 the US economy finally showed some signs of recovery, but indications were that the apparent improvements in the real economy were temporary and could not be sustained. GNP growth in 2001 was only 0.3 percent and it was anticipated that 2002 would show a similar or deeper decline. As it turned out, the economy continued on its sluggish path well into 2003. In March 2003 the Bush administration launched its offensive against Iraq, in part because of geopolitical considerations, but also as a means of reactivating the ailing US economy. The crisis is indeed endemic, and it is global, as the system is pushed towards (and beyond) its functional limits at a number of levels — economic, ecological, social and political.

The economic dimension of this crisis includes unmanageable external debts contracted by a large number of developing countries in their turn towards international capital markets to finance their development projects and keep afloat. Most of this debt financing went to three large economies in Latin America — Argentina, Brazil and Mexico — that by themselves accounted for one-half of all third world debt in 1982. In the

1980s the level of debt in both Latin America and sub-Saharan Africa reached crisis proportions, precipitating a decade lost to development in both regions. However, by the end of the decade, according to the World Bank, the debt crisis was virtually over, most countries having been brought back from the brink of collapse or bankruptcy, and able to service their debt obligations within manageable limits (less than 50 percent of export earnings). Nevertheless, over the course of the next decade, total developing-country external debt would grow to an astronomical level — to more than $4.5 trillion in 2000, three times the level at the end of the 1980s, at the height of the debt crisis. By 2002 in Argentina alone the external debt climbed to close to a trillion dollars ($805 million). In Latin America, where the World Bank has noted the greatest improvement in the area of external indebtedness, more than half of all countries still approach or exceed the Bank's own crisis indicator vis-à-vis external debt (payments at or over 50 percent of export earnings). In Brazil, from 1994 to 2002, the external debt doubled, while in Argentina the external debt reached a level that would precipitate the greatest and deepest economic — and political — crisis in its history (see Chapter 4 below). In sub-Saharan Africa, despite the global Jubilee campaign to have creditors "forgive" the crushing debt of the poorest and most highly indebted countries on the continent, many countries are still mired in a crippling debt load that has totally undermined any plans for economic reactivation. And, more generally, the World Bank (2002) notes that developing country debt has surged.

Social Dimensions of the Crisis

The social dimensions of the systemic crisis can be found in the rapidly growing gap in the distribution of wealth and income, and the associated conditions of unemployment and poverty. Two hundred years ago the gap between the richest and the poorest countries was not very large. Economic historian Angus Maddison (1995) estimates based on GNP per capita around 1820 that the richest countries were about three times richer than the poorest. This ratio rose to fifteen to one in 1950 and then dropped to thirteen to one in 1973, after two decades of international economic development and the onset of a worldwide production crisis. It then increased to twenty to one by 1998.

The United Nations Development Programme (UNDP 1996) calculated that the top 20 percent of the population in the world's richest countries had thirty times the income (in terms of total GDP) of the poorest 20 percent in 1960. This grew to thirty-two times in 1970, forty-five times in 1980 and fifty-nine times by 1989. By 1997, after five decades of development and fifteen years of structural adjustments — a period in which world production grew 600 percent (and trade three times as fast) — the top quintile received seventy-four times the income of those at or close to the bottom. Within the neoliberal order of capitalist development and globalization, just 358 individuals disposed of the same income as 45 percent of the world's poorest, that is to say, the 2.4 billion people who subsist on less than two dollars a day, the World Bank's international poverty line. According to the UNDP (2002), the world's richest one percent receive as much income as the poorest 57 percent, and the income of the world's three richest individuals is greater than the combined GDP of all the least developed countries. The UNDP characterizes these and similar facts about income levels as "grotesque."

Comparing the 1960–80 period (under the old model of state-led development) to 1980–2000 (under the neoliberal order), the Washington-based Center for Economic and Policy Research looked at changes in economic growth, plus health, education and other social indicators, for 116 countries. After sorting countries into five categories based on common starting points, they found that economic growth rates for all five groups were much lower in the second period than the first. In fact, the poorest group went from average per capita GDP growth of 1.9 to -0.5 percent a year. The second poorest group dropped from 3.6 percent a year to less than one percent. The study also found that progress in health and education indicators, so marked in the first period (see Patel 1995) was reduced for most countries, especially those subjected to neoliberal policy and structural reforms. In this connection poverty is bound to rise. and has done so, as the state retreats from its economic development and social welfare role, and social programs are privatized. Significantly, the latest edition of the World Bank's *World Development Indicators* (WDI) shows that the developing country that surpasses all others in levels of health and education is Cuba, the one developing country that has been excluded from the neoliberal world order, and the only country other than North Korea that has received no World Bank loans for the past forty years. Saxe-Fernandez (2002) shows what happens to countries such as Mexico that come to depend on such loans: dramatic increases in social inequalities and poverty, and dramatically reduced capacity to benefit from exploitation of domestic productive assets.

Like the pattern of inequality between countries, within-country inequality fell in a large number of countries during the golden age from the 1950s to the early 1970s. Since then, however, this inequality has increased in forty-nine of the seventy-three countries for which high quality data are available (Lee 2002). These forty-eight countries represent 59 percent of the population and 78 percent of the GDP within the seventy-three-country sample. Sixteen countries had constant levels of inequality, while nine experienced decreasing inequality over this period, a trend that was dramatically reversed under the conditions of the financial crisis that hit Asia in 1997.

The regional distribution of this pattern of growing inequalities reveals the fundamental workings of the dominant model of capitalist development: rising inequality is strongly linked to neoliberal policy reforms adopted in industrialized, transitional and developing countries alike. All of the low-income countries in sub-Saharan Africa and middle-income countries in Latin America that have been structurally adjusted — some, such as Mexico and Ghana, for close to two decades — have experienced deteriorating economic conditions and increased social inequalities. At the same time, those countries (mostly in Asia) that were not subjected to International Monetary Fund (IMF) reforms and the World Bank's regime of neoliberal reforms experienced higher rates of growth or decreasing inequalities in the distribution of wealth and income. China, with a quarter of the world's population, and on the margins of the global world economic order, has also experienced an upsurge of inequality since the mid-1980s. In this context we need hardly mention the drastic deterioration in economic conditions and the rapid rise in social inequalities that have accompanied the process of transition in Russia and the other countries that constituted the socialist bloc of former times. Under these conditions, the rate of poverty in many countries, particularly in what the World Bank categorizes as least developed (with low per capita income), has grown in both extent and depth. In Indonesia, for example, poverty has increased by 50 percent since the onset of the financial crisis in 1997. In South Korea, until the 1990s a paradigmatic case of rapid economic growth and relatively equitable development (growth with equity), poverty doubled over the same period. And in Latin America, according to the UN Economic Commission for Latin America and the Caribbean (Campos 2000), under a generalized policy regime of neoliberal economic structural reforms an additional 20 million new poor were produced in just a few years (from 1998), adding up to 223 million people suffering from poverty, 43.8 percent of the total population.[1] As for Russia, under different conditions (with the collapse of its economic model and transition towards a neoliberal form of capitalist development) poverty rose from 2.9 percent to 32.7 percent between 1986 and 1998 (Goldsmith 2002: 32).

As for the rich countries in the Organization for Economic Co-operation and Development (OECD) and the Group of Eight (G-8), rising inequality has been driven by greater disparities in market-generated incomes and a political class struggle in which capital has managed, through diverse mechanisms, to bring about a reduction of salaries and wages. In this connection, in the United States — and the same pattern can be found in the other OECD countries, particularly in the UK and Canada, which are oriented towards the Anglo-American model of capitalist development — the value (purchasing power) of wages dropped some nine percentage points between 1974 and 1983 and has dropped at least ten points since. In this context, it is estimated that the wealthiest one percent of the population in the United States has managed to capture virtually all of the wealth generated over the past two decades.

Another social dimension of the systemic crisis is reflected in statistics on unemployment and underemployment, which, like low incomes and poverty, can be viewed alternatively as a form of social exclusion or exploitation.[2] In the Latin American context, the statistics are staggering, pointing towards a problem that has reached crisis proportions. In 2002 the official rate of unemployment regionwide was 9.3 percent (ILO 2002), which meant that more than seventeen million people in the region were actively seeking but could not find employment in any form, not even on a part-time or short-term basis. What this means in Argentina, until recently the most highly developed society in Latin America, is discussed in Chapter 4. According to the International Labour Organization (ILO) the drop in the regional unemployment rate over the last trimester of 2002 was even greater than that registered in previous periods of crisis — the debt crisis of 1983, Mexico's financial crisis of 1994 and the Asiatic crisis of 1997. Not only are many of the unemployed pushed to the brink and into a state of impoverishment, with all of its critical dimensions, but the official statistics of the number of unemployed tell only a very small part of the story, that of the desperate plight of so many individuals and families in the working class. In addition to these unemployed the ILO estimates that up to 93 million people in Latin America cannot find decent work, that is, they are underemployed. Furthermore, at least 47 percent of Latin Americans work in the ubiquitous informal sector without social security of any sort, neither unemployment insurance, a pension nor health plan. This situation reflects close to twenty years of the workings of the new economic model (of structural adjustment) in the region.

The Ecological Crisis

Notwithstanding the depth and severity of the social crisis, an even worse crisis is looming, threatening to knock down the basic pillars of the economic production and development process. This crisis has to with the ecological foundations of not only the economic production process but life itself. The logic of capital accumulation and the economic processes of industrialization and modernization have pushed the system well beyond its ecological limits. Ecologists of various persuasions have raised their voices in unison about an impending ecological crisis evident in clear signs that the carrying capacity of the Earth's ecosystem has been stressed well beyond its limits, with irreparable and irreversible damage to the systems that sustain human life and livelihoods. The collapse of fish stocks profiled in Chapter 6 is but one small part of this process, which has been well documented and analyzed in depth but to little avail (and, in any case, too little, too late).[3]

However, all the warning signs and critical voices, and the growing environmental movement, have been ignored as the guardians of government policy and international organizations travel from one workshop and conference to another in search of a quick solution that does not require any substantive change in the operative system. The framework for such a solution was found in the notion of "sustainable development" (WCED 1987), which presupposes the ability to extend the limits to growth via technological advances and to support this process with appropriate government environmental legislation and better resource management. But, for more than two decades now, this approach has been implemented with only marginal results — new green technologies, community-based regimes of resource management, diverse strategies and government policies to sustain both the environment and livelihoods in partnership with the community, local governments and, in the 1990s, the private sector.[4] Notwithstanding the eternal optimists and those who have stuck their heads in the sand, there is an emerging consensus that the world is still very much on the road to ecological disaster, a fast and short road at that. This point is illustrated in Chapter 6 with regard to the collapse of one of the world's most valuable fish stocks, the North Atlantic cod, one of many natural and renewable resources that are being pushed towards and beyond the brink of collapse. Examples of impending or incipient ecological disaster are everywhere. It would take a huge volume just to catalogue them.

Within the mainstream of development thought and practice the dominant response to this ecological crisis has been "sustainable development," to extend the ecological limits to economic growth via a technological fix, appropriate government environmental legislation and better resource management, and requiring, it is now argued, community-based resource management as well as partnerships between governments and the "private sector" of global corporations.[5]

The strategy of sustainable development, however, has proven difficult to implement in practice and has been surrounded by dispute and criticism. One school of thought sees the notion as entirely misbegotten, in that it fails to recognize the inherent ecological limits to economic growth and industrialization (Kovel 2002; Sachs 1999). Another school of thought sees the problem as capitalism itself, viz. its built-in drive towards incessant capital accumulation. There are a number of permutations of this approach (Foster 1999, Kovel 2002, O'Connor 1998, Sachs 1999), but these critical perspectives are unified by the beliefs that (1) no real development is possible within the system; that (2), as Kovel (2002) and O'Connor (1998), among others, see it, capitalism cannot help but shit on the plate it eats from and that (3) an alternative system is the *sine qua non* for resolving the ecological crisis and securing any hope for saving the planet from impending ecological disaster.

The Crisis in Development Finance

One of the critical components of the liberal "world economic order" set up at Bretton Woods in 1944 was a set of institutions (the IMF, the World Bank and a fixed currency exchange mechanism) that provided the "financial architecture" for the system as a whole. The system was set up as early as 1944, but it was not until well into the 1970s, facilitated by new information technologies, that it began to operate on a major scale, circulating hundreds of billions of dollars, the reserve currency of the system. By 1980, transactions in the diverse international capital markets set up were so gigantic in scale as to dwarf operations in the real economy. It was estimated that the transactions in just one capital market, the Eurodollar exchange, exceeded by a factor of twenty-five the annual value of world trade. In addition, it was calculated that less than five percent of all financial transactions were connected to the real economy, that is, invested productively.

Fuelled by this enormous expansion of speculative capital, the real economy began to swing from crisis to crisis before almost wrecking itself on the reef of the Asian Miracle in 1997. The first major crisis in the system, however, was associated with, if not triggered by, the dramatic increase in the price of oil engineered by the Organization of Petroleum Exporting

Countries (OPEC) in 1973, as well as problems associated with excessive liquidity in the Eurodollar market.

As to the developing world, the initial crisis took the form of an unsustainable level of debt on money extended by multinational banks to governments (and private firms)[6] that borrowed so much and so freely that, by 1982, caught in the scissor-squeeze of rising interest rates and falling world prices for their exports, they were forced to default on their debt payment obligations. The rest, as they say, is history — that of an entire decade lost to development in both Latin America and Africa.

Fortunately for the newly industrializing countries of Asia, an alternative (Japanese) model of capitalist development, in which the state played a predominant role at the level of strategic investments was available. Under this model the predicament of Latin American and sub-Saharan African states was averted and history took a very different course — rapid economic growth for the eight leading economies in the region. However, it turns out that as governments in Asia sought to incorporate their economies into the globalization process, particularly at the level of capital markets and production, East and Southeast Asia would not remain immune from the propensity towards systemic crisis.

The first major financial crisis occurred in Mexico, in December 1994, when the bottom fell out of the stock market, threatening billions of dollars of US investments in government bonds. In this instance, as in the savings and loans fiasco at home, the US government bailed out these investors in the form of a $40 billion financial aid package to Mexico. In the context of this crisis, an estimated one million Mexican workers lost their jobs and hundreds of thousands of small and medium-sized firms were pushed into bankruptcy while all of the major US investors were saved and protected. With the destruction of local capital, physical as well as financial, and a loss of up to 60 percent of the value of assets, salaries and wages, the country's middle class was also seriously affected. The system, however, was saved, at least temporarily. American investments in Mexican government bonds and stocks were rescued. But by 1997, a few years later, financial crisis hit country after country in Asia, before hitting Russia and infecting Brazil, and then Argentina.

The contagious "flu" of financial crisis (the tequila effect) hit Asia with a vengeance, first in Malaysia, then Indonesia, Thailand and South Korea. Japan was already in crisis, its economy having run out of steam in 1989. The dimensions of the crisis were so momentous that it brought the whole system into question, raising the spectre of economic collapse (Stiglitz 2002). With so much foreign capital invested in the emerging markets of these economies, it was feared that the "Asian flu" would eventually infect the economies of North America and the European Union (EU) that depended on Asia for markets, returns on their investments and the production of cheap goods. In any case, the Asian financial crisis stilled any notion of an "Asian miracle." It also generated diverse arguments about the need for a new financial architecture, or at least some means of regulating and controlling cross-national flows of volatile speculative capital.

Explaining the Crisis

There is no shortage of explanations of the crisis in its diverse dimensions — financial, economic, social, environmental and political. The self-appointed guardians of the world economic order have convoked forum upon forum to discuss the problem, and a bibliography of attempted explanations and proposed solutions would fill an enormous volume. Theories as to the underlying cause and contributing factors range from domestic factors such as lack of leadership, poor management, or the dominant form of production being forced to its technological or environmental limits, to arguments about a built-in tendency for profits to fall, or structural-political conditions for a profit crunch.

With regard to the recent financial crisis, the conditions of which have spread from Mexico to Asia to Russia and to the very centre of the global economy, most explanations have focused on a lack of regulatory control over the volatile global movements of investment capital that have been facilitated by new technologies that dramatically increase the pace and volume of transactions on world markets. Of particular salience is the movement of speculative or parasitical capital in search of quick profits on hourly, and even minute to minute, changes in exchange rates or in futures trading etc. The volume of these transactions is such as to dwarf the real economy.

Under these conditions, rapid movements of large pools of short-term speculative capital undermined production processes in most of the countries that had constituted the "Asian miracle." However, for a solution to the problem, most analysts turned towards a search for new mechanisms of capital control — reforms to the financial architecture within which the flow of capital could be regulated. In effect, the problem was thought to be not "structural" but not systemic, requiring a new financial architecture that would establish some level of control and form of governance. In this context, a number of well-known analysts and theorists such as Dan Rodrik, Joseph Stiglitzl, even the financier (speculator, to be exact) par excellence George Soros, and Carlos Slim, the richest industrialist and financier in Mexico[7] — all regarded as somewhat soft on the dominant US (neoliberal) model of capitalist development[8] — turned towards the IMF as the culprit, viewing its policies as throwing oil on the fire, seriously aggravating the situation, and absolutely the wrong medicine for curing the ills of the system (see, for example, Stiglitz 2002).

By the end of the decade the worst seemed to be over, as the problem was evidently contained if not cured. Indeed, it was even suggested that the Asian crisis was engineered by interests in the US, seeking to restructure their position in the world market and offset a trade imbalance that was threatening to reach crisis proportions. In any case, a number of economies in the region showed signs of slow recovery, even as the US economy itself, as well as Brazil and then Argentina, slipped into economic crisis.

The Crisis in Sub-Saharan Africa

As the 2000s progress, the day of reckoning for the system may have continued to be averted, but it is clear that the propensity towards crisis is both systemic and multi-dimensional. We have briefly examined dimensions of this crisis as they relate to Latin America and Asia. Sub-Saharan Africa, however, has been even more affected by the crisis of the world capitalist system. To speak of a continent in crisis would be no exaggeration. It has been in crisis for decades, ever since it jumped (or was pushed) from the frying pan of colonialism into the fire of integration with the world capitalist system. The dimensions of this crisis are staggering in terms of their human and social costs. Almost all of the least-developed, low-income countries of the world are found on the continent, with conditions of poverty that had long ago been eradicated in other parts of the world. The United Nations Development Programme (UNDP) calculates that close to half of the population — 46.7 percent — are forced to subsist on less than a one dollar a day. The conditions of poverty include inordinately high rates of birth and child mortality, killing within the first five years of life nearly a fifth of all African children (175 out of every 1,000); an equally high rate of poverty-related illnesses and HIV/AIDS, undermining and cutting off the human potential and shortening the lifespan of perhaps 40 percent of the population. The UNDP estimates that 75 percent of all HIV/AIDS victims are found in sub-Saharan Africa and that the incidence of AIDS in the 1990s has shortened life expectancy in the region by eight years, down to age forty-seven. In Botswana, life expectancy has been reduced by 50 percent (UNDP 2002: 27). The quality of life of the vast majority of the population in sub-Saharan Africa, which includes some of the most resource-rich countries in the world, has been drastically altered for the worse over the past three "development" decades.

Under the conditions of the old economic model, several decades of both bilateral and multilateral development assistance have failed to lift the continent out of its colonial legacy of underdevelopment and poverty. Indeed, it could be argued that this massive development effort has worsened the situation. As a condition of foreign aid, most countries in the region have been forced to adopt policies that have left them vulnerable and worse off. In fact, these policies have encouraged rentierism, corruption and mismanagement, not to speak of conflicts over natural resources and spoils of empire. In this connection, each of the three major geopolitical projects of the post-Second World War period — development, globalization and the new imperialism — has worked in this way, forcing the continent deeper into a crisis of gigantic proportions. The conditions of capitalist crisis are widespread and endemic, but in no region has the process of capital accumulation wreaked so much havoc. Capitalism, as Marx recognized a century ago, is two-faced, creating at one and the same time conditions of economic progress and underdevelopment and immiseration — the social costs of progress. Unfortunately, for the people living in Africa, the uneven development of capital has resulted in the continent receiving a grossly disproportionate share of both the benefits and the costs of development and globalization.

Of course, the conditions of crisis are rooted in not only Africa's connection to the capitalist system but also the internal structures of its societies. There is an ongoing debate on this issue, with a lot of weight given to internal, non-systemic factors such as corruption, rentierism, mismanagement and poor leadership, as well as political conflict and war. However, notwithstanding the relevance of some of these conditions as factors of an endemic crisis, there is an undoubted systemic factor at work. For example, one of the ways in which the system has been restructured as a solution to the crisis has been to change the structure of international relations within the global economy and, in the process, to weaken the position and worsen the situation of many sub-Saharan countries. In this regard, a system-wide study of trade reform in 1998 determined that with global reform of trade, achieved by degree through a round of General Agreement on Tariffs and Trade (GATT) negotiations, every region in the world economy would benefit, with the exception of sub-Saharan Africa. Not only has the continent received a scant share of the benefits of global integration, but anticipated reforms of the system would negatively impact the economies of countries in the region, deepening and extending the conditions of a multi-faceted crisis.

The Development Project: Dynamics of a Theoretical Impasse

In strictly intellectual terms, responses to systemic crisis can be placed into three categories: liberal reform, social revolution and anti-development (globalization and structural adjustment).

Various schools of thought, or paradigms, provide alternative toolboxes of ideas that can be used to explain, describe or prescribe developments associated with the crisis of the system. However, most of these approaches are associated with the idea of development and the associated project launched in the aftermath of the Second World War and reformulated in the context of the system-wide production crisis of the late 1960s and 1970s.

Development as an idea, area of academic study, and project taken up by governments in the countries that made up the rich industrialized countries in the West, can be traced back to the immediate post-war context of the late 1940s. For Wolfgang Sachs and his associates in grassroots postmodernism (Esteva and Prakash 1998; Sachs 1993), the idea of development was invented, as it were, and launched by US president Harry Truman in his four-point program designed to assist economically backward countries, recently liberated from the yoke of colonialism, in their struggle against poverty — and to elude the lure of communism. For the next quarter century, the so-called "Golden Age of Capitalism," the study (and practice) of development was approached from the theoretical perspective of economic growth and modernization, and with the analytical tools of economics, sociology and political science. The goal of the development process was economic growth, to create conditions of both economic and social development. Within the framework of the prevailing theory this conditional advance and improvement in economic conditions required and was predicated on structural change in the form of industrialization, modernization and expansion of the capitalist nucleus (Hunt 1989).

In the 1970s the development project fragmented under conditions of a worldwide systemic crisis and in a double context of pressures for revolutionary change and a counter-offensive of capital to halt and revert the advances of labour (Davis 1984; Crouch and Pizzorno 1978). Within the mainstream of development thought and practice, these pressures from the Left and the Right brought about an involution of the development project in the direction of liberal reform. In this context there occurred a major shift towards a belief in the need for structural reform and the need for government policies that would ensure a process of growth with equity and a meeting of the basic needs of the poor, estimated by the World Bank in 1973 to make up some 40 percent of the world population.

This orientation towards liberal reform constituted one ideological and intellectual response to evidence of systemic crisis, an involution of the processes of economic growth, industrialization and modernization. A variation of this response was advanced and represented by CEPAL: Latin American structuralism. However, responses to the growing crisis of the Bretton Woods international economic order went well beyond these two mainstream approaches. Another response can be found in the evolution of an interdisciplinary approach towards development, capable of conceptualizing, theorizing and dealing in practical terms with the multi-dimensional nature of the development process.

A second intellectual response to systemic crisis and the growing development divide between the poor and the rich occurred within a sidestream of development thought and practice. It was characterized by a radical orientation towards change, a political-economy type of structural analysis, and various theories predicated on the need for systemic change. In the 1970s there was a decided shift of thinking, if not practice, towards this radical line of structural analysis, the political economy of development, informed by various and diverse theories that were predicated on and prescribed radical change in the operating structures of the world capitalist system.

Within the mainstream of development thought, however, the dominant trend was towards systemic (structural) reform — of international trade, ownership of land and other productive resources (physical capital, technology), enterprise and industrial development (nationalism, nationalization) and the institutions of social development (programs of health, education and social welfare). In the absence of, or with a weak, capitalist class in many developing countries vis-à-vis the economic functions of investment, entrepreneurship and management and marketing, the state was viewed as the primary agent of development, taking on the role assigned in theory to the capitalist class. However, after a decade of reforms and negligible results, if not total failure, in closing the development gap, the proponents of liberal reform lost confidence in their analysis and prescriptions, and their nerve.[9] Under attack from both the Left and the Right, the liberal reformers withdrew from or abandoned the field, providing theoretical and political space for the emergence of what Toye (1987) among others termed "a counter-revolution" in development thinking and practice. In intellectual terms, this counter-revolution was a third category of response to evidence of a systemic crisis. In political terms this counter-revolution was supported by a neo-conservative ideology and the emergence of neo-conservative political regimes. In economic terms, however, it was based on a neoliberal model of capitalist development: the world market as the engine of growth, the private sector as the driver of this engine, and the untrammelled freedom of individuals to pursue their self-interest, accumulate capital and profit from their investments as the fuel and catalyst of the development process.

The World Bank assumed the responsibility for designing the new model of capitalist economic development. This model was based not on the idea of development but on "globalization." On this basis, the bank designed a series of structural reforms in economic policy designed to adjust economies to the requirements of the global economy in the new economic order, allowing each country to insert itself or be integrated into the new neoliberal world order. As designed by the Bank, this model had six components: (1) *measures to stabilize the economy* — tight fiscal and monetary policies (balanced accounts, low inflation etc.); (2) *privatization of the means of production and state enterprises*, reverting the earlier process of nationalization of strategic industries and selling public assets to the private sector; (3) *liberalization of capital markets and trade*, reversing the earlier policy of state protection and opening up domestic firms to the forces of free competition and market prices; (4) *deregulation of private economic activity*, reducing the impact of government regulations on the operations of market forces; (5) *labour market reform* — reduced regulation and employment protection, erosion of minimum wages, restrictions on collective bargaining and reduced public expenditures — and (6) *downsizing of the state apparatus*, modernizing it and decentralizing decision-making powers to provincial and local levels of government, allowing a more democratic and participatory form of top-down development. The last in these various "steps to hell" — to quote Joseph Stiglitz (2002), former head economist at the World Bank (WB) but now a major critic of the IMF's neoliberal policies, is the creation of a free trade area, first regionally and then worldwide.

A neoliberal model of capitalist development is the fourth intellectual response to systemic crisis. However, although dominant, it is by no means hegemonic, generating as it has not only a search for alternative means of development but forces of opposition and resistance to its implementation. Associated with these forces are three other intellectual responses to the systemic crisis: one in the mainstream of development thought, and the others in two sidestreams, one on the right and one on the left of the political spectrum.

In the mainstream of the development project, the fifth in our catalogue of intellectual responses is given in the search for an alternative form of development — "Another Development" — that merged in the 1970s. Growing out of the liberal reform approach towards development, it took the form of development that is initiated *from below and within* civil society rather than *from above and the outside*; *socially inclusive* (in terms of gender, indigenous people, ethnic minority groups and the poor); *human* in form and scale; *participatory* and *empowering*; and *sustainable* in terms of the environment and livelihoods.

There are numerous permutations of this approach. The most recent is based on the "sustainable livelihoods approach" (SLA), the latest form of "other development" in two decades of twists and turns in what has emerged as an international movement. The advantage of this approach (to the guardians of the neoliberal order, if not the poor) is that it focuses its strategic response to the problems of social exclusion and poverty on building social capital, a productive resource (or asset) which the poor have in abundance, namely the capacity to organize and form social networks, act collectively and create their own future with their own resources. The other major forms of capital — natural, physical and financial — that have always been at the centre of development theory entail a political process fraught with contestation and conflict.

The issue in the case of these productive resources is how to improve access to them or create a more equitable distribution, neither of which is easy given the fact that they tend to be highly concentrated or in the hands of the rich and powerful, who are loath to reduce their control over productive resources or share their power to decide how they are to be allocated by the market or the government. The beauty of the SLA is that it can be implemented without making any of the structural changes that a redistribution of natural, physical or financial forms of capital calls for. Thus it is possible to avoid a confrontation with the power structure, and to empower the poor without disempowering the rich. Thus, it might be possible to orchestrate, via a politics of dialogue and negotiation rather than confrontation and direct action, what the guardians of the neoliberal order need and so fervently desire — solidarity between the rich and the poor.[10]

Various schools of thought have emerged on the Right, particularly the "new political economy" (NPE), which focuses on the predatory nature of the state and its capture and use by private interests to advance their own aims. In this context the focus of analysis is on rentierism and corruption, on the misuse of foreign aid for personal enrichment and on heightened conflict over, and the squandering of, society's productive resources. So goes the World Bank's diagnosis of the failure of Africa to realize its potential, and the steps that continent must make to take advantage of the opportunities provided by the new world order, by adopting good policies and good governance.

The NPE has had some resonance in certain academic and policy-making circles. However, the dominant trend on the Right has been towards rejection of development, substituting instead the idea of globalization, or, more recently, and in a different context, the resurrection of imperialism. Thus it is that Latin American economists such as Roberto Campos (2000) can identify four phases of globalization, the third of which corresponds to capitalism's Golden Age and the fourth to the neoliberal world order of the 1980s and 1990s. This conceptualization differs somewhat from the model advanced by proponents of regulationism — a new form of political economy on the left of the political spectrum, with a more critical stance on the changes wrought by the neoliberal order. According to the regulationists, the source of systemic crisis can be found in the structure of production, in the expansion of a particular regime of accumulation and mode of regulation (Fordism) and in its replacement by another (post-Fordism). Whereas Marxists, in their analysis of systemic change, place emphasis on *technological restructuring* — the substitution of dead for living capital — as the primary means by which capitalism adjusts to the forces of change and maintains stability, and on the *exploitation of labour* by capital, regulationists emphasize the *regulation of labour* — an historic shift towards a new regime of accumulation based on a post-Fordist mode of regulation. Political ecologists, in contrast, focus their analysis on the environmental damage and ecological crisis created by the growth and accumulation imperatives of the capitalist industrialization process.

Ironically, the rejection of the development project — a fourth intellectual response to systemic crisis — was aided and abetted by a radical critique of the dominant model (of neoliberal capitalist development and globalization) launched from the Left on the basis of a post-structuralist, grassroots postmodernist perspective (Esteva and Prakash 1998). From this perspective, the overarching ideologies and metatheories that had been constructed over the years to explain the process of historic change, and to fuel one project for social transformation after another, have all lost their relevance.[11] There are no longer any systemic forces at work, and people have the capacity, and the need and opportunity, to construct their own futures from the fabric of their own political imagination and cultural resources (Esteva and Prakash 1998).

However, it was not the people that responded to this situation, filling in the theoretical and political vacuum created by the theoretical impasse, or intellectual crisis, and creating a new ideological and geopolitical project. Nor was it the Left. The forces of opposition and resistance on the Left are for the most part still in disarray or chasing the chimera of alternative development — a reform of the neoliberal model and the globalization project. Or they continue to wallow in a theoretical impasse with nonsensical notions such as "anti-power" (Benasayag and Sztulwark 2000; Holloway 2001; Negri 2001) or of an "empire without imperialism" (Hardt and Negri 2000). As for the political Right, the forces of reaction and defence of the system have gravitated towards two new projects: *globalization*, based on a neoliberal model of capitalist development, and *a new form of imperialism* that would allow the United States to re-establish its hegemony over the world economic order. Chapters 2 and 10 examine the political dynamics of these two projects.

The Crisis of the Left: Postmodern Illusions and Imaginaries

In the wake of both the postmodernist attack on all forms of structural analysis in the 1980s and the collapse of the socialist project, the Left has been engulfed in a deep intellectual, and ideological and political, crisis. This crisis is manifest with regard to the projects of development and globalization but is particularly sharp as concerns the new imperialist project.

With regard to the development project, the crisis of the Left is manifest in the turn many leftists have taken away from the realities of class and state (and the need to confront this power through direct, collective action) and towards alternative forms of development and local power. In this turn, the social Left, in the form of non-governmental organizations (rather than political parties or socio-political movements) has knowingly or unwittingly abandoned the confrontationalist politics of direct action in exchange for an intermediary role vis-à-vis the poor. In this exchange the poor are empowered in their local communities to participate in decisions that are local in scope, for example, how to spend the poverty alleviation funds directed to the communities from the outside, by the World Bank etc. In exchange for this power the poor are encouraged to abandon confrontationalist politics and direct action to challenge the greater structure of economic and state power, and to adopt instead the pacific politics of dialogue, negotiation and local development. In this political context a number of intellectuals, with a leftist orientation but a postmodernist sensibility (who believe there are no operating structures or systemic forces), have abandoned any form of class analysis and participation in class struggle in favour of a new way of doing politics — anti-power (Negri 2001).[12]

The imperialist project launched by the regime of George (H.) Bush the elder in the context of a collapse of the socialist project in the Soviet Union, and relaunched in the wake of 9/11 with a vengeance by George (W.) Bush the younger (see Chapters 2 and 3) — has created an even sharper crisis on the political and intellectual Left. At a time when the political Right has come out openly in favour of the need to re-establish the dominance of capital and the projection of state power, the Left has retreated to notions of a powerless state and an empire without imperialism. A clear and notable embodiment of this intellectual failure can be found in a book by Michael Hardt and Antonio Negri, called *Empire* (2000).

Empire is a strange if not silly book. At a time when the US is the only superpower, when almost 50 percent of the top 500 TNCs are US-owned and headquartered, and Washington has launched a war of unilateral military intervention against the peasants and workers of Afghanistan and is planning a series of campaigns against Iraq and other "axes of evil" — after previous wars of intervention in the Balkans, Central America (Panama) and the Caribbean (Grenada), and proxy wars in Colombia (Plan Colombia) and earlier in Angola, Mozambique and Nicaragua — the authors of this widely praised book tell us that imperialism is a thing of the past. They argue that "Empire" is a post-imperialist phenomenon in which power is dispersed and no single nation can control the empire. Even worse, they argue that empire is a positive advance in world history: "The thing [sic] we call Empire is actually an enormous historical improvement over the international system and imperialism" (190).

After 413 pages of text and 57 pages of notes, the best the authors can do is tell us that, "In this smooth space [?] of Empire there is no place of power — it is everywhere and nowhere. Empire is an Ou-Topia or really a non-place" (190). Without providing a clear notion of the agents of "empire" or of its dynamics in the actually existing imperial states and their corporations, we are told that Empire is imperial but not imperialist; that the US state is imperial but not imperialist. From this we learn that the US Constitution is imperial because — in contrast to imperialism's project to always spread its power linearly in closed spaces and invade, destroy and subsume subject countries within its sovereignty — the US constitutional project is constructed on the model of rearticulating an open space and reinventing incessantly diverse and singular networks across an unbounded terrain. The contemporary idea of Empire is born through the global expansion of the internal US constitutional project (182). In other words, this celebration of Empire is also a celebration of US constitutionalism (to be exact), which is a model for democratizing the empire.

Having disposed of imperialism the authors proceed to abolish the reality of classes and class conflict (and with them peasants and labourers) from the map of social analysis, viewing these categories as outdated and imprecise. They substitute for these categories of class analysis the notion of "biopolitical production multitudes," a concept which is never clearly defined or given historical or empirical specificity. Apart from these multitudes there are no designated agencies for the announced but unspecified revolution they envisage. And the program of this novel revolution is not very different from that embraced by welfare-state social democrats.

Much has been written about the sweep of the book and its theoretical grandeur. Unsurprisingly, postmodern theorist Frederic Jameson (Hardt's colleague at Duke University) calls it the first great new theoretical synthesis of the new millennium, and *Time* and *Newsweek* have similarly lauded its significance. However, hyperbole aside, few literary reviewers have commented on the book's lack of historical and empirical evidence to buttress its innumerable, unsubstantiated assertions.

We argue this point and elaborate on it in various chapters that follow, but here we can point towards *Empire* as a clear expression of the current state of crisis on the Left. And the crisis is not only intellectual, but also political. For example, the argument of *Empire*, like so much postmodernist theorizing (or discursive imagining), in effect, if not by design, works to demobilize the social and political forces of resistance and opposition to the neoliberal order and the capitalist system (Veltmeyer 2001b). Where it does not demobilize these forces, it leads popular movements into one blind alley after another, effectively stalling social transformation or progressive change.

Conclusion

Capitalism is a system in crisis. The dimensions of this crisis range from the economic and ecological to the political and intellectual. The diverse conditions of this crisis are affecting more and more people and countries as the system extends its operations to become truly global. However, as capitalism globalizes its operations and hold on people the inbuilt contradictions of the system generate forces of opposition and resistance along the fault lines of emerging crisis. As people become more and more aware of their situations, these forces are mobilized against those that rise in support of the system. As a result, the struggle between capital and labour takes on diverse forms, such as the struggles of workers against capitalist exploitation (anti-capital) and to improve wages and working conditions; the protest movement of an emerging global civil society against capitalism in its neoliberal form (anti-globalization); the struggle and social movement of environmentalists and indigenous peoples against the environmental destructiveness of corporate capital; socio-political movements against privatization and other neoliberal policies of structural adjustment and the predations of corporate capital; movements of indigenous peoples, women and the poor against their exclusion from the processes of economic and political development. The dynamics of these struggles are complex and diverse and require documentation and further study as a prelude to informed collective action. The essays in this book have been constructed for this purpose.

2. The Imperial Counteroffensive

Contradictions, Challenges and Opportunities

The attacks on Afghanistan and Iraq were efforts on the part of the US to reverse the relative decline of its empire and re-establish its hegemony in regions of conflict. The wars in Afghanistan and Iraq are only part of a general imperial counteroffensive which has several components: (1) to re-establish the subordination of Europe to Washington; (2) to reassert US control in the Middle East and Persian Gulf region; (3) to extend military penetration in Asia; (4) to increase military warfare in Colombia and project power throughout the rest of Latin America; (5) to restrict and repress protest and opposition to transnational corporations (TNCs) and international financial institutions (IFIs) such as the World Bank, International Monetary Fund and World Trade Organization (WTO) by replacing democratic rights with dictatorial powers; and (6) to use state funds on weapons and subsidies for near-bankrupt TNCs (airlines, insurance companies, tourist agencies) and regressive tax reductions to halt a deepening recession that would undermine public support for the empire-building project.

The preparations for the first imperial counteroffensive involved a three-part plan: First, September eleventh (9/11) was followed by a massive propaganda effort that magnified and distorted the nature of the attack on the World Trade Centre and the Pentagon in order to secure world political support. The anti-terrorism campaign created the appearance of a world consensus in favour of Washington. Second, on October seventh (10/7) the George W. Bush administration launched a massive defensive military attack on Afghanistan, targeting the international terrorist network al-Qaeda put together by Osama Bin Laden and supported by the Taliban regime. The US was actively supported in this first war by hard-core allies England, Turkey, Pakistan, France, Italy, Japan and Spain. At the same time, political, psychological and legal barriers to the war were demolished in the United States, Japan and Germany, setting the stage for a new phase of military interventions, heightened domestic repression and increased profiteering, all under the pretext of permanent war conditions. The third phase of the imperial offensive involved an extension of the Afghan offensive into a generalized military offensive against international terrorists and those who would aid and abet them. It was signalled by a speech on the "axis of evil," in which George W. Bush identified Iraq, Iran and North Korea as the most immediate enemies of a US-led world alliance of the "forces of freedom" against "terrorist" and "rogue" states. This phase of the imperial offensive has involved operations against real or potential adversaries and critics, using intimidation (the threat of massive bombing, as in Afghanistan and Iraq) and increased military presence to extend and deepen control in regions or countries such as Colombia that are crisis-prone or in crisis.

There are three dimensions of an unfolding international crisis:

1. *military-political* — the open-ended war declared by Washington, which seeks to unilaterally restore its power by imposing new client states,
2. *economic* — the decline and challenge to Euro-American imperial power derived from the world recession (and possible depression) and
3. *opposition movements* inside and outside of the imperial states to the forces of globalization and imperialism.

The US counteroffensive has placed a new set of issues before the popular and anti-globalization movements: more repression, increased aggressive militarization, a monolithic and massive propaganda effort, and actions designed to instil fear and provoke anger.

The new imperial order creates many challenges, dangers *and* opportunities for the forces of resistance and opposition if they can overcome the widespread disorientation. The multi-dimensional crisis affecting both pro-empire and oppositional forces is creating an open-ended situation that allows several possible outcomes, depending on the nature and strength of political responses to the contradictions of the system. The argument that follows proceeds by first identifying the context for the imperial counteroffensive, namely the relative decline of US power. We then examine the imperial advantages of extended, open-ended war as a way out of the crisis and its contradictions. Finally we look at the anti-terrorist war as a part of the crisis, its impact on popular opposition and the potential for a resurgence of popular power.

The Relative Decline of Empire and the Need for a New Imperialism

The commonly heard expression, "Since September 11 the world has changed," has many different meanings. The most frequent meaning, given by Washington, echoed by the European Union and amplified by the mass media, is that 9/11 has ushered in a whole new era with new sets of priorities, alliances and political relations.

However, Washington's desire to mark the beginning of the new historical era as September 11 involves a particular perspective that reflects its own losses and vulnerabilities in the search for hegemony. From the perspective of the third world (and perhaps beyond) the new era actually started on October 7, 2001, the date of the massive US intervention and carpet-bombing of Afghanistan. October 7 is important because it signals the start of a major worldwide offensive against adversaries of the United States under the very elastic and loose definitions of "terrorism," "terrorist havens" and "terrorist sympathizers." It clearly marks a new military offensive against competitors and opponents of US imperial power, both abroad and within.

It is important to understand the meaning of the term "new era" because much of what has transpired is not new but rather a continuation and deepening of ongoing imperial military aggression that preceded September 11 and October 7. Likewise, popular liberation struggles in many parts of the world continue unabated despite September 11 and October 7, and despite some significant changes in context.

In short, while September 11 and October 7 are significant events, it is an open question whether the events following either of these dates mark a qualitatively new historical period. In this connection it is more useful to analyze the interrelationship between events and historical processes before October 7 and after, in order to separate what is new and significant from what is neither. Several significant factors establish the parameters and context for this argument. The first is the relative decline in US political and economic power throughout the 1990s in key areas of the world, particularly in the Middle East/Persian Gulf region, Latin America, Asia and Europe — a decline accompanied by an increase in US influence in the less important Balkan states of Kosovo, Macedonia and Serbia, and relative success in its strategic direction of political developments in Central America.

The second factor is the vast expansion of the economic interests of the United States in the third world via its transnational corporations and banks, and the gradual weakening of client regimes that have supported this expansion. International financial institutions such as the World Bank and the International Monetary Fund, through their structural adjustment policies, free trade doctrines and privatization directives, had so drained the wealth of local economies that client states were weakened and rife with corruption, as private-sector elites and politicians pillaged the treasuries. We need but look at Argentina, but it is by no means alone, as regime after regime in Latin America, in the context of implementing unpopular structural adjustment programs and neoliberal policies, has fallen prey to forces of economic recession and political instability. The weakening of the imperial control structure meant that the traditional, almost exclusive, dependence on the IFIs for surplus extraction was becoming inadequate. As noted by journalist Martin Wolf (*Financial Times*, 10 October 2001: 13), the diminution of indirect imperial control over impoverished and devastated third world states (the "failed states") requires a new imperialism — not pious aspirations, but an openly organized coercive force. In other words, imperial wars, as in Afghanistan, Yugoslavia and Iraq, must be accompanied by new imperialist conquests, by recolonization. To ensure the subordination of premodern or modern states in the third world, bombs and marines should be used to supplement the economic restructuring policies of IMF and World Bank functionaries. The "new imperialism," according to Robert Cooper (2002b: 7), foreign policy advisor to Tony Blair, should revert to rougher methods of earlier eras — force, pre-emptive attacks, deception or whatever is necessary. Blair himself, in an address to Canada's Parliament in 2001, spoke in this connection of the need for force and determination in the war against international terrorism — and against protesters who stand in the way of rational argument.

From the end of the first Gulf War and the Bush (the elder) presidency to October 7, 2001, the US won military conflicts in peripheral regions (the Balkans and Central America) but suffered a serious loss of influence in more strategic areas. At the same time the US economy experienced a miniature speculative bubble before entering a deep recession in manufacturing and a major meltdown in the financial sector. The combined effect of the peripheral military victories and the speculative bubble was to hide a deepening structural weakness.

The decline in US influence and military losses can be briefly summarized. In the Middle East, the US strategy of overthrowing or isolating the Iranian government and the Iraqi regime of Saddam Hussein had been a total failure. The regimes had not only survived but also effectively broken the US boycott. US sanctions against Iran were broken by most US allies, including Japan, the EU, the Arab states etc. Iran was accepted among the revitalized OPEC countries and signed nuclear power agreements with Russia and oil contracts with Japan. It signed investment and trade agreements with every major country except the US, and even US TNCs, working through third parties, became involved in Iranian trade. Iraq was reintegrated into OPEC and was accepted at meetings of the Gulf States, at Arab summits and at international Islamic conferences. Iraq sold millions of clandestine barrels of oil via contrabandists through Turkey and Syria, clearly with foreknowledge of transit regimes and Western European consumers.

The Palestinian uprising and the unanimous support it received from Arab regimes (including US clients) had isolated the US, which remained closely tied to the Israeli state. In North Africa, Libya developed strong economic ties with the EU and their oil companies, particularly with Italy, and diplomatic relations with many North Atlantic Treaty Organization (NATO) countries.

Thus, following the first Gulf War, three strategic oil-producing countries labelled as prime targets of US policy increased their influence and ties with the rest of the world, weakening the US stranglehold on the region. Clearly Bush the elder's "New World Order" was in shambles, reduced to mini-fiefdoms in the backward, mafia-infested Albanian provinces of the Balkans.

Another major sign of declining US power was found in the massive trade surpluses accumulated in Asia and the EU at US expense. In the year 2000 the US ran up a $430-billion trade deficit. Western Europe's 350 million consumers increasingly purchased European-made goods — over two-thirds of EU trade was inter-European. In Latin America, European TNCs, particularly Spanish, outbid US competitors in buying up lucrative privatized enterprises.

Politically, especially in Latin America, US dominance was being severely tested, particularly by the formidable guerrilla movements in Colombia, by Venezuela's President Hugo Chavez and mass movements in Ecuador, Brazil and elsewhere. The collapse of the Argentine economy, general economic crises in the rest of the continent and the significant loss of legitimacy of US client regimes were other indicators of weakening US power in its neo-colonized provinces.

The massive growth of the anti-globalization movement, particularly its anti-capitalist sector, throughout Western Europe, North America and elsewhere challenged the power of Washington to impose new, empire-friendly investment and trading rules.

Faced with its declining influence in strategic regions, a growing economic crisis at home and the end of the speculative bubble (in IT, biotech, fibre optics), Washington decided to militarize its foreign policy (via Plan Colombia) and to aggressively pursue comparative advantages via unilateral state decisions: abrogating treaty agreements, such as the anti-ballistic missile (ABM) agreement with Russia, the Kyoto Protocol, the International Court of Justice, anti-biological warfare and anti-personnel/mining agreements etc. Unilateral action was seen as a way of reversing the relative decline, by combining regional military action and economic pressure. To counter the decline of US influence in Latin America and increase its control, Washington pushed the Free Trade Agreement of the Americas (ALCA in Spanish) to limit European competition and increase US dominance. However, opposition was strong in four of the five key countries in the region: Brazil, Venezuela, Colombia and Argentina.

Following the bombing of the US battleship *Cole* in Yemen, the attacks on the embassies in Kenya and Tanzania, and an earlier attempt to bomb the World Trade Centre, September 11 was another indication of the relative decline in US power — this time of Washington's incapacity to defend the centres of financial and military power within its empire.

September 11 *is* and *is not* a significant date. It *is not* because it continued to mark the relative decline of US influence. It *is* because it has become a turning point for a major counteroffensive to reverse this decline and reconstruct a new US-centred world order.

The Counteroffensive of October 7

Washington's declaration of war against Afghanistan had two important phases: (1) the engineering of a broad, US-dominated alliance based on opposition to the terrorist attack on the World Trade Centre and the Pentagon; and (2) the conversion of this anti-terrorist front into a political instrument to support US military intervention in Afghanistan and beyond. The clear intent of the Bush administration was to launch a worldwide crusade against opponents of US power and, in the process, to rebuild a new imperial order. From the onset, the massive bombing attacks and the invasion by hundreds of Special Forces on kill-and-destroy missions were intended to obliterate domestic objections to future ground wars and new military interventions. Equally important, the massive slaughter and displacement of millions of civilians served the explicit purpose of political intimidation, directed at forcing real or imagined state adversaries to accept US dominance and control over their foreign and domestic policies, and to warn social movements that the same violence could be directed against them.

The declining effectiveness of the IFIs as instruments of US hegemony has led Washington to increasingly rely on raw military force and to move from low- to high-intensity violence. The threat of a series of military assaults was explicitly contained in the Bush administration's reference to the Afghanistan invasion as phase one, clearly implying that other imperial wars would follow. Most prominent was Washington's threat to launch another full-scale military assault against Iraq and other safe havens for terrorists. In mid-June 2002, Bush signalled a move towards a second phase by authorizing the CIA to use any and all means to oust Saddam from power, including lethal force. Try as it might, the George W. Bush regime could not make a clear connection between the Saddam regime in Iraq and the purveyors of international terror. It subsequently made issue of Iraq as a "rogue country armed with weapons of mass destruction." In March 2003 the US made its move against Saddam and launched what it regarded as an object lesson to other recalcitrant "rogue" regimes.

In this transition the so-called "anti-terrorist alliance" was effectively melded into a "coalition of the willing." Significantly, all the major military and political decisions in this "war," from general strategy down to operational tactics, are made by Washington with only a minor pretence of consultation. In other words, the war alliance is a continuation of Washington's prior unilateralism; only now the Bush administration has successfully reasserted its dominance over the EU. While Tony Blair's hyperkinetic activity on behalf of Washington's wars elicited praise from the US president and media, it has not led to a sharing of decision-making power.

At least in this phase of the US counteroffensive, Washington has reasserted its domination over Europe. Taking advantage of its strongest card in the interstate system — military power — Washington has sought to militarize political-economic realities. By making anti-terrorism the dominant theme at international and regional forums, Washington hopes to undermine the horizontal divisions between rich and poor countries and classes and replace them with a vertical ideological-military polarization between those who support US-defined terrorist adversaries and resist US military intervention and those who don't.

Many regimes have already seized upon this military definition of socio-economic realities to repress popular and left movements and liberation organizations in the Middle East, Latin America and Central Asia. The multiplication of "anti-terrorist" purges by client regimes serves

Washington's policy perfectly, as long as the newly labelled terrorist movements also oppose US policy and America's authoritarian clients accept the new imperial order.

Washington's threats of indefinite and extended wars of imperial conquest have predictably been accompanied by repressive legislation that in effect confers dictatorial powers on the US president. In this legislation, all constitutional guarantees are suspended and all foreign-born terrorist suspects become subject to military tribunals in the US — no matter where their geographical location. There is a broad consensus that the war-making powers assumed by the executive violate the letter and intent of the US Constitution and the norms of a democratic regime, but this consensus has been to no avail. The argument by the defenders of authoritarianism that these clearly dictatorial measures are temporary is not convincing, given the president's position that we are in for a long and extended period of warfare. Authoritarianism and engagement in aggressive imperialist wars are seen to go together, obliterating the democratic republican vision of the American Revolution.

History teaches us that imperial wars are always costly, their economic benefits are unequally distributed and the burdens are borne by the waged and salaried workers. The authoritarian measures act to repress or intimidate those who question the patriotic rhetoric, who interpolate the war slogan "United We Stand" by adding "Divided We Benefit."

The resurgence of empire building at a time of deepening economic recession is a problematic strategy. While the Bush administration slashes taxes for the rich, the war increases expenditures, putting deep strains on the budget and less affluent taxpayers. Military Keynesianism might stimulate a few sectors of the economy, but it has not reversed, and will not reverse, the sharp decline in profits for the capitalist sector as a whole. Moreover, stretching the repressive apparatus of client regimes to secure their acquiescence with the global empire-building project will not expand overseas markets for US exports. In fact, overseas conflicts will shrink markets, deepening the negative external accounts of the US economy.

More significantly, the current military approach to empire building in the post-Afghan period (phase 2) is designed to reassert the hegemony of the US state and capital over the system as a whole and will undoubtedly destabilize the economies of Europe, Japan and the US's Middle Eastern client states in the process. The military attack and occupation of Iraq has to some extent disrupted the flow of oil to Europe and Japan and is threatening to destabilize domestic politics in Saudi Arabia and other Gulf and Middle Eastern countries. Fear of the destabilizing effects of this phase of empire building has already led to dissent, even among Washington's most servile European followers in England, and certainly in France and Germany. Nevertheless, given Washington's imperial vision, its unilateral approach and its access to alternative sources of oil (in Mexico, Venezuela, Ecuador, Alaska, Canada etc.), a military attack on Iraq served three strategic objectives: (1) to weaken European competitors in the battle of the world marketplace; (2) to eliminate Iraq as a potential regional rival; and (3) to acquire strategic and operational control over the second-largest oil reserves in the world. In the military conquest of Iraq, the US state was quite prepared to damage the economies of the EU, alienate its two major Arab clients (Saudi Arabia and Egypt) and risk both an involution of capital markets all over the world and the consolidation of an anti-American clash of civilizations — a war between Islamic fundamentalism (and its associated "terrorism") and the non-Islamic capitalist "West." A secondary objective of the conquest was more symbolic than real: to assert US hegemony and demonstrate its capacity and willingness to assert power. Washington also demonstrated it can brush off Europe's objections and still secure its acquiescence.

It is still too early to judge the fallout, but the war on Iraq and moves against other rogue regimes, such as North Korea, have created uncertainty among investors worldwide, and the weakening of Europe will have negative repercussions for the US economy at a time of negative growth. A war-induced European decline might improve the *relative* position of the US, but its economy would decline in *absolute* terms.

In focusing exclusively on pursuing a handful of supposed terrorists, President Bush strains at gnats and swallows camels. The overall damage to both the EU and US economies resulting from war far exceeds any possible losses resulting from terrorists. To make matters worse, the imposition of the Bush administration's military definition on political and economic conflicts in the third world resonates with the state terrorist policies of Israel (against the Palestinians), Algeria (against the Berbers), Turkey (against the Kurds), China (against its western Muslim rebels), Russia (against the Chechens) etc.

The "Ariel Sharons" in Washington, advocates of permanent war for empire building, have given virtually no thought to the *economic* consequences of military intervention in the Middle East. The collapse of financial architecture and energy supplies can bring down an empire far more quickly and with greater certainty than any real or imagined terrorist network.

The Counteroffensive in Latin America

The imperial counteroffensive is worldwide. In the hierarchy of regions to reconquer, Latin America stands out as second after the Middle East. It is Latin America that has provided the United States with its only favourable trade balances. Its ruling and affluent classes have drained hundreds of billions in illegal transfers to US banks, and the US economy has received almost a trillion dollars in profits, interest payments, royalties and other transfers over the past decade. Latin America's client regimes usually follow US positions in international forums and provide nominal military forces for its interventionary forays, thus providing a fig leaf for what are in effect unilateral actions.

Washington has identified the Colombian peasant-based guerrilla movements such as the Revolutionary Armed Forces of Colombia (FARC) and the Army of National Liberation (ELN), which pose the most powerful challenges to its dominance in the hemisphere, as terrorist groups. Controlling or influential in more than 50 percent of the country's municipalities by the mid-1990s, the advance of the FARC/ELN, together with the independent foreign policy of the Chavez regime in Venezuela and the revolutionary government in Cuba, represents an alternative pole to the peon presidents of the continent who serve "the Empire."

Since the late Clinton presidency and with more emphasis during the Bush administration, the US has declared total war on this popular insurgency. Plan Colombia, and later the Andean Initiative, were essentially war strategies which preceded the Afghan war but served to highlight the new imperial counteroffensive. Washington allocated $1.5 billion in military aid to the Colombian military and its paramilitary surrogates, and hundreds of Special Forces were sent to direct operations in the field. US mercenary pilots were subcontracted from private firms to engage in chemical warfare in the poppy fields of Colombia, and paramilitary forces multiplied under the protection and promotion of the military command. Airspace, seacoasts and river estuaries were colonized by US armed forces. Military bases were established in El Salvador, Ecuador and Peru to provide logistical support, and US officials established a direct operational presence in the defence ministry in Bogota.

The worldwide counteroffensive of October 7 deepened the militarization process in Colombia. Under US direction the Colombian air force violates the airspace over the demilitarized zone where the FARC and the Pastrana regime negotiate. Illegal cross-border forays into the zone have led to conflicts. The US State Department's labelling of FARC/ELN as terrorists puts them on the list of targets to be assaulted by the US military machine. Under the Bush-Rumsfeld doctrine, half of Colombia is a haven for terrorists and thus subject to total war.

War fever caused the State Department to send an official delegation to Venezuela to bludgeon the Chavez government into supporting the imperial offensive. According to officials in the Venezuelan foreign ministry, when Chavez condemned both terrorism and the US war, the State Department threatened his government with reprisals in the best tradition of mafia dons.

The key dimension of Washington's empire-building project in Latin America is the proposed Free Trade Agreement of the Americas (FTAA). This proposal will give US-based TNCs and banks unrestrained access to markets, raw materials and labour, while limiting European and Japanese entry. This neomercantilist imperialist system is another unilateral initiative, taken in agreement with satellite regimes in the region, without popular consultation. Given the high levels of discontent already present in the region, under neoliberal regimes, the imposition of neomercantilist imperialism will likely lead to explosive social conditions and the re-emergence of nationalist and socialist alternatives. Washington's anti-terrorist military doctrine, with its threats of violent intervention and its active and direct military presence, is a useful ideological weapon to extend its empire.

Latin America today is half colonized: its bankers, politicians, generals and most of its bishops stand by and for the US empire. They want deeper "integration." The other half of Latin America — the vast majority of its workers, peasants, Indians, lower-middle-class public employees and, above all, its tens of millions of unemployed who are exploited by the empire — rejects and resists it. The imperial counteroffensive is directed at intervening to sustain colonial clients and cower the other half of Latin America, which owns no property but represents the historical interests of the region.

We are entering a period of intensified warfare, continual military threats, savage bombings, wholesale massacres and tens of millions of displaced persons. The sites of violent social conflict are no longer confined to the third world, though that is where humankind will pay the heaviest price. Will this period of war also be a period of revolutions, as in the past? Can the US economy sustain a sequence of wars without undermining its own economy? Can it survive by destabilizing its European and Japanese competitors, who are also its trading and investment partners?

The Centrality of the Imperial State

There are clear indications that the economic bases of the US empire are weakening for economic and political reasons. At the economic level, in 2002 the US manufacturing sector finally began to pull out of an eighteen-month-long recession but there was every indication of propensity towards crisis. Over the same period (after the 1995–99 speculative boom masked an underlying trend towards recession), hundreds of billions of dollars invested in information technology, fibre optics and biotech ventures were lost. As revenues have plummeted, thousands of firms have gone bankrupt. Both the old and new economy are having great difficulty in pulling out of a deep and prolonged crisis. The financial and speculative stock market sectors are heavily dependent on volatile political-psychological circumstances in the US and in the world economy. The vertical decline in the stock market following 9/11, and its sharp recovery following 10/7, reflected that volatility. Specifically, US stock and bond markets depend heavily on overseas investors, as well as local speculators. These wealthy investors and their US counterparts tend to invest in the US as much for political as economic reason, seeking safe and stable havens for their private fortunes. But September 11 shook their confidence because it demonstrated that the centres of economic and military power are vulnerable to attack and destruction. Hence the massive flight of speculative and productive forms of capital and the continued vulnerability of financial markets.

However, the 10/7 counterattack, the massive worldwide counter-offensive of the US empire, and the destruction of Afghanistan, restored investor confidence and led to a significant influx of capital and a temporary recovery of the stock market. The "total war" strategy adopted by the Pentagon was as much about restoring investor confidence about the invincibility and security of imperial power as it was about political aims or future oil pipelines. Stock market behaviour, particularly that of large, long-term foreign investors in the US market, seem to be influenced as much by security and safety reasons as the actual performance of the world economy. Hence the paradox of an inverse relation between the stock market and the real economy: while all the economic indicators of the real economy declined toward negative growth, the stock market temporarily recovered its pre-9/11 levels.

Nevertheless, there are limits to this political basis for investment. Prolonged negative growth and declining profits (or increasing losses) will eventually end the recovery and produce a sharp decline in the stock market.

As the economic foundations of empire weaken, the role of the imperial state increases. The empire becomes more dependent on state intervention, revealing the close ties between the imperial state and investors, including the TNCs. Equally significant, the military components of the imperial state come to play an increasingly dominant role in re-establishing investor confidence by smashing and intimidating adversaries, buttressing faltering neo-colonial regimes, imposing favourable economic accords such as the FTAA, which benefit US investors and are prejudicial towards European and Japanese competitors.

The old imperialism of the 1980s and 1990s that depended more on the IFIs is being supplanted and/or complemented by the new imperialism of military action — the Green Berets come to replace the bow-tie functionaries of the IMF and WB.

Washington-led NATO has extended its dominion to include its Baltic client states and Balkan satellites, and beyond Turkey and Israel to the Central Asian (ex-Soviet) republics. The missing link in this imperial chain was the strategically important Gulf state of Iraq. (And Iran still resists compliance.) While this imperial chain is militarily significant, it is more a cost to empire than a source of revenue: it borders great riches but does not produce them, at least as yet. This is clear to the Bush administration, which is more interested in destroying regional powers than in large-scale investments in colonial states, as is seen in the meagre resources invested in the Balkans, Central Asia and Afghanistan.

The centrality of the imperial state in expanding US power through military means has refuted the assumptions of leading theoreticians of the Anti-globalization Movement, such as Susan George, Tony Negri, Ignacio Ramonet, Robert Korten etc., who think in terms of the autonomy of global corporations. Their emphasis on the central role of the world market in creating poverty, dominance and inequality is in the present context an anachronism. As the Euro-American imperial states send troops to conquer and occupy more countries, and destroy, displace or impoverish millions, there is a great need to shift from an anti-globalization to an anti-imperialist movement, away from false assumptions of autonomous multinational corporation (MNC)-dominated superstates to the reality of TNCs tied to imperial states.

The worldwide counteroffensive led and directed by the US imperial state has had as its goal the reconstruction of the failed "New World Order" of the first post–Gulf War period. Today, in the face of economic crisis and growing popular resistance, the TNCs do not have the will or resources to act "autonomously" via market forces. The new imperialism is based on military intervention (Afghanistan, the Balkans), colonization (military bases) and terror (as in Colombia). From the wars in Iraq and the Balkans to Afghanistan, the imperial juggernaut advances, each new and even more horrendous human catastrophe justified by an even greater barrage of propaganda about humanitarian missions.

The imperial offensive after October 7 is based on strategic and economic imperatives and has nothing to do with a "clash of civilizations." The US empire includes Muslim states (Pakistan, Saudi Arabia, Egypt, Turkey, Morocco, Bosnia, Albania etc.), the Jewish state of Israel, and secular, nominally Christian, regimes. What defines the US imperial offensive is not permanent allies of one religion or civilization or another, but permanent interests. In the Balkans, and earlier in Palestine and Afghanistan, Washington promoted fundamentalist Muslims and drug traffickers against secular nationalists and socialists. Some of yesterday's Muslim clients (for example, the Taliban) are today's enemies. The new military alliance in Afghanistan is built around rival tribal warlords who live off contraband, drug trafficking and booty from local wars. However, the thread that unifies these changing alliances is the need to defend imperial spheres of domination. The apparent hypocrisy or double standard of the imperial elites is only in the eyes of a beholder who mistakenly believes the propaganda of empire and now feels betrayed by the switch in imperial clients.

US military advances in Afghanistan and Iraq have prepared the way for new wars. Elsewhere, severe structural contradictions and crises loom on the horizon.

Contradictions of Empire

The US imperial offensive faces two types of contradictions, which are conjunctural and structural. The Afghan War polarized the Muslim states between their pro-empire leaders and the mass of sympathizers for the Afghan people and Osama Bin Laden. This polarization has not yet produced any serious organizational challenge to client rulers, of which the key Saudi monarchy is most vulnerable. The military victory of the United States and its client "Northern Alliance" and the resultant Muslim coalition regime could dissipate amorphous Muslim mass opposition. However, the opposition of the EU and Arab states was activated as Washington extended its war to Iraq and destabilized European oil suppliers. However, these and other secondary conjunctural contradictions will not undermine Washington's imperial drive.

The more profound long-term structural contradictions of the new imperialism are found in military expansion during a time of deepening local and worldwide economic recession. Military Keynesianism — increased war spending — has not, and will not, reverse the recession, as few sectors of the economy are affected, and some that may receive a stimulus, the aerospace industry, for example, have been hard hit by recession in the civilian airline market.

While the military machinery of the imperial state promotes and defends the interests of US transnational corporations, it is not a cost-effective service provider. Its multi-billion-dollar overseas expenditures far exceed the immediate benefits to the TNCs and do not reverse declining rates of profit or open new markets, particularly in regions of maximum military engagement. Military intervention expands colonization without increasing capital returns. The net result is that imperial wars, in their current form, undermine non-speculative capitalist investment, even as they symbolically assure overseas investors.

As in Central America and the Balkans, in Afghanistan and Colombia the US is more interested in destroying adversaries and establishing client regimes than in large, long-term investments in "reconstruction." After high spending for military conquest, budget priorities shift to subsidizing US-based TNCs and to lowering taxes for the wealthy. Washington would prefer to leave it to Europe and Japan to clean up the "collateral damage" after US military victories. Post-war reconstruction does not intimidate possible adversaries, but B-52 carpet-bombing does. In Afghanistan, the military victor leaves the consolidation of a pro-imperial client regime unsettled. Just as the US financed and armed the fundamentalist victory over the secular nationalist Afghan regime in 1990 and then withdrew, leading to the ascendancy of the anti-western Taliban regime, the most recent victory and withdrawal there is likely to have similar results within the next decade. And the long-term nature of Iraq is also uncertain. Thus the gap between the strong war-making capacity of the imperial state and its weak capacity to revitalize the economies of conquered nations is a major contradiction.

An even more serious contradiction is found in the aggressive effort to impose neoliberal regimes and policies, especially when the export markets they were designed to service are collapsing and external flows of capital are drying up.

The recession in the United States, Japan and the EU has severely damaged the most loyal and subservient neoliberal client states, particularly in Latin America. The prices of the "specialized" exports which drive these neoliberal regimes have collapsed: exports of coffee, petrol, metals and sugar, and textiles, clothes and other manufactured goods, from the "free trade zones" have suffered from sharp drops in prices and glutted markets. The imperial powers have responded by pressing for greater "liberalism" in the South, while raising protective tariffs at home and increasing subsidies for exports. Tariffs in the imperial countries on imports from the third world are four times higher than those on imports from other imperial countries, according to the World Bank (2002). Support for agricultural TNCs in the imperial countries was $245 billion in 2000 (*Financial Times*, 21 November 2001: 13). As the *World Bank Report* (1999) points out, "the share of subsidized exports has even increased [over the past decade] for many products of export interest to developing countries."

The neoliberal doctrine of the "old imperialism" is giving way to the neomercantilist practices of the "new imperialism." State policies dictate and direct economic exchanges and limit the market to a subsidiary role, all to the benefit of the imperial economy.

The highly restrictive nature of neomercantilist policies polarizes an economy between local producers and the imperial state-backed monopolies. The highly visible role of the imperial state in imposing the neomercantilist system politicizes the growing army of unemployed and poorly paid workers, peasants and public employees. The decline and collapse of overseas markets means that less foreign exchange can be earned to pay foreign debts. Less exports sold means less capacity to import essential foodstuffs and capital goods to sustain production. In Latin America the export strategy upon which the whole imperial edifice is built is crumbling. Unable to import, Latin America will be forced to produce locally or do without. However, the definitive rupture with the imperial export strategy and subordination to empire will not come about because of internal contradictions — it requires political intervention.

Opportunities and Challenges for the Left

In the short run the Left faces the full thrust of Washington's imperial counteroffensive, with all that implies in increased bellicosity, threats and greater subservience from ruling client elites. Nevertheless, while this new military-led imperialist effort at "reconquest" is underway, it faces serious practical, ideological and political obstacles.

For one thing, the offensive takes place in the face of a major political resurgence of the Left in various strategic countries and a serious decline in neoliberal economies. In Colombia, Brazil, Argentina, Ecuador and Bolivia, powerful socio-political movements have emerged and consolidated influence over important popular constituencies, while incumbent client regimes have become deeply discredited, in many cases receiving only single-digit popularity ratings.

This situation presents both dangers and opportunities. Dangers come from the increasingly militarized and repressive response pushed by Washington and echoed by its Latin client regimes, as witnessed by the Ibero-American Conference declaration on terrorism on November 23, 2001 (*La Jornada*, 24 November 2001). Opportunities come from the fact that the resurgent Left has not suffered a major defeat during this period (comparable to 1972–76) and is in a strong position to make a leap from protest to power. Neoliberal regimes have failed to find overseas markets to sustain domestic production and to locate new flows of capital to compensate for the vast outflows in debt payments, profit remittances etc. The prolonged depression in Argentina is emblematic of the direction in which all of Latin America is heading.

The current crisis is systemic, in that it not only affects workers and unemployed — by increasing poverty, unemployment and inequalities — but also the very mechanisms of capital accumulation. What capital is accumulated in Latin America is stored in overseas accounts as "dead wealth." It is evident to any but the most wilfully blind academics — of which there are not just a few — that neoliberalism is dead and that the new neomercantilist imperial system offers no room for "market choices."

In this perspective, what is essential for converting these objective opportunities into substantial structural changes is political power. The social movements have mobilized millions, realized innumerable changes at the local level and created a new and promising level of social consciousness. In some cases they control or influence local governments and have secured concessions via mass pressure on the dominant classes. However, there are several issues to resolve before these movements can be said to prefigure a political alternative to state power.

First, politically, the movements espouse a series of programmatic demands and alternatives that are positive and important, but they lack a theoretical understanding of the nature of the evolving imperial system, its contradictions and the nature of the crisis.

Second, there is disunity, uneven development between urban and rural movements, and between the interior and the coast, and some of the movements are divided by rivalries based on personalities, tactics etc. If unified in a coherent, single movement, the existing movements would be significantly closer to challenging for state power.

Third, many of the movements engage in militant tactics and

articulate radical programs, but in practice engage in continual negotiation to secure very limited concessions, thus reducing their movements to pressure groups within the system rather than acting as protagonists to overthrow the current regime. The challenge is to develop a transition program adapted to the immediate demands of the people but which puts class demands at the centre of the struggle in the construction of a socialist alternative. The growing authoritarianism of the imperially directed client regimes requires the building of mass democratic and anti-imperialist movements.

The US imperial strategy of militarization to impose a neomercantilist empire requires a greater capacity for incorporating new allies and the need to prepare for diverse forms of struggle. The imperial strategists have selected Colombia as the testing ground for the new imperialism because it is there that they face their greatest politico-military challenge. All the reactionary forces in the hemisphere have been mobilized against the guerrilla armies and growing mass movements. All the peon presidents of the hemisphere have signed onto the anti-terrorist crusade, and the FARC/ELN have been designated as "terrorists" by the empire. Military success in Colombia will accelerate and encourage the military conquest and colonization of Latin America, just as the US-directed military coup in Brazil (1964) was followed by invasions (Dominican Republic, 1965) and subsequent military coups in Bolivia (1971), Uruguay (1972), Chile (1973) and Argentina (1976).

A victory or prolonged war by the guerrillas in Colombia would provide breathing room for the rest of the Left. Thus it is essential that maximum support and solidarity be extended to the Colombian struggle. Internationalism is not only a solidarity network against the new imperial military offensive in general, but it is one in support of the Colombian peasants and workers organized in their "people's army."

These are dangerous and hopeful times, with dangers that cut both ways, for the Empire and the Left.

3. Post-9/11
A Period of Empire Building

In the period after 9/11 the Bush administration has been engaged in a massive effort to impose a "New World Order," just as Bush's father had attempted to do in the aftermath of the 1991 Gulf War a decade earlier. To understand the Bush administration's efforts at empire building, it is essential to locate it historically, particularly in the context of the failed efforts of Bush the elder and the limited imperial advances of the Clinton presidency.

The second part of this chapter presents a theoretical and analytical framework for understanding the particularities of empire building in the new millennium, particularly the big push in the year following 9/11. This is followed by a discussion of the new themes, policies and strategic goals that were enunciated, and their application to specific regions. It requires an elaboration of the interrelationships among empire building, the particularities of the Bush regime and the changing nature of US capitalism. The concluding section focuses on the internal political and economic contradictions of the second effort at creating a New World Order, as well as the new international context, particularly conflicts with allies/competitors in the European Union, and the mass popular movements in Latin America, the Middle East and Europe.

Historical Context for Changes after 9/11

The key to understanding the changes in the period after 9/11 is to recognize the second effort to build a New World Order (NWO), one that the Bush (the elder) and Clinton regimes envisioned but were unable to impose. New World Order I, according to a high-level strategy paper, entitled "Defense Planning Guidance for the Fiscal years 1994–99," prepared for top officials of the Bush (the elder) administration, envisioned a world in which the US would be able to dominate its European and Japanese allies, isolate its adversaries and sustain its client regimes. The US would be the undisputed world power, capable of securing absolute control over strategic resources and a privileged place in the world market (*New York Times*, 8 March 1992: 14). Written in the first flush of military victory in the first Gulf War, the document projected the US-dominated military coalition as a basis for stable, long-term empire building. Predictably (Petras and Morley 1995), this NWO failed to materialize. The wartime alliance weakened, boycotts of adversaries were undermined and while the Empire advanced in the Balkans it was challenged in the Middle East, Latin America and the streets of Europe and the US. Iraq was accepted in pan-Islamic councils and OPEC, while most of Europe and practically all the Muslim countries opposed US military aggression. Iran and Libya developed diplomatic and economic ties to Europe, Middle Eastern countries, Africa and Japan. The European Union improved its competitive position by penetrating Eastern Europe and Russia, outbidding US firms in Latin America and the Middle East, while overseas, Chinese capital gained a big slice of the Chinese market. International protests beginning in Seattle and expanding throughout the world challenged the US and Europe-dominated World Trade Organization and plans to divide up the world economy. Even in the US the public rejected Bush the elder and his vision of a "New World Order," voting instead for Clinton, mistakenly thinking that he would turn to rebuilding (rather than destroying) the social safety net. In place of a US-centred NWO, public pressure and mass movements successfully pressured for international controls on corporate pollution, restrictions on the use of land mines, disarmament agreements, and limitations on corporate exploitation of third world labour. The Palestinian intifada, the advance of the Colombian guerrillas and crises in neoliberal client states further weakened the notion of a NWO. Internally, the crash of the speculative economy, particularly the IT sector in the early twenty-first century, weakened the attractiveness and centrality of the US as a haven for investors. While Clinton was able to expand the Empire into the Balkans via the war against Yugoslavia, to conquer Kosovo, dominate Macedonia and recreate a US-led war coalition, the gains took place in non-strategic regions with greater geo-military than geo-economic significance.

9/11 was the starting point for relaunching the second version of the NWO. The differences between NWO I and II are found in the "lessons" drawn by strategists from the failure of the first attempt and from the writings of Brzezinski (1997). Many of the same members of Bush the elder's team made their way into the second Bush administration. The major lesson drawn by the empire builders from the earlier failure was that one could not assume the loyalty of allies, that the earlier Gulf War had not gone far enough (to include the conquest of Baghdad, occupation of oil wells, direct colonization) and had been too "localized" and "time-bound."

In launching the new empire-building project, the second Bush administration took decisive steps to destroy all restraints on the exercise of US power, blaming international treaties and human rights legislation for the failure of NWO I. In systematic fashion, in the months prior to 9/11 and the launching of NWO II, the second Bush administration abrogated the Kyoto Protocol, the anti-ballistic missile (ABM) agreement, the International Court of Justice agreement and numerous other accords. The purpose of these unilateral actions was to create optimal conditions to favour US-based TNCs, engage in wars of conquest and expand military operations. There were several restraining domestic factors that had to be overcome in order to launch NWO II. The second Bush administration had a "minority presidency" gained through a questionable voter count, the domestic economy was mired in recession, the stock market was falling and the trade deficit was growing. Against this, the Bush administration could count on the precedent of Clinton's Balkan wars, rationalized as "humanitarian intervention," as a building block for new military adventures. Second, the influential Israeli lobby, solidly behind the ultra-right-wing Sharon regime, could be counted on to back any US military attack, particularly against Arab or Muslim regimes critical of Israel. Moreover, Sharon's use of "anti-terrorism" to justify massive state terrorism fit nicely with Washington's empire-building strategy.

The NWO II needed a trigger event that would overcome domestic restraints, shock allies into subordination and justify unilateral US military intervention, and 9/11 fit the bill. Through skillful mass-media imagery repeated endlessly throughout the world, a localized terrorist incident was transformed into an event of world significance, which was in turn used as the basis for launching a worldwide military crusade whose ultimate goal was a NWO II. On October 7, 2001, the new, more virulent empire-building project was launched. Afghanistan was bombed on the basis of tendentious arguments: that the terrorists of 9/11 were directed by Osama Bin Laden, and that al-Qaeda and Afghanistan, the country in which he resided, were ultimately responsible. Afghanistan's request for negotiations and offer to turn Bin Laden over to the US if convincing evidence were provided was rejected outright. The NWO II could not bother with merely reasonable offers when a higher end was being sought: a worldwide empire-building enterprise.

The mass-propaganda media played a major role in support of NWO

II — a deeply ideological effort. From the moment the Bush administration announced an open-ended "war" on a worldwide terrorist conspiracy that threatened each and every transport vehicle, public or private building, city, town or village, the mass media magnified and repeated the message in every locale. President Bush was transformed from a minority president into the father and protector of the nation and was entitled to restrict freedoms, spend endless sums on the military and intelligence, and engage in unlimited warfare.

The events of 9/11 effectively secured the ascendancy of the military-empire builders in foreign policy and the pre-eminence of crony capitalists in domestic policy.

Theoretical and Analytical Framework

Imperialism, Lenin wrote, is the final stage of capitalism, in which gigantic fusions between competing cartels of bankers and industrialists will set the stage for a final showdown between capital and labour on the world stage. The world political economy since 9/11 exhibits some of the fundamental characteristics described by the Russian revolutionary, many the result of large historical tendencies preceding the terrorist event. The methodological key is precisely to recognize that much of what emerged full-blown in the first year after 9/11 was present in a less virulent form during the preceding several decades. It is important to note these continuities when analyzing events since 9/11.

To start with, since the end of the Second World War, Washington has expanded its military, economic and political presence around the world via its TNCs, banks and military bases, interventions and wars. Imperial expansion has not been a linear process, rather it has witnessed a period of stop and go, aggressive pushes and forced temporary retreats. The decade preceding 9/11 combined an explosive combination of military conquests, wars, large-scale speculative expansion, pillage and a relative decline in political and diplomatic influence in key sectors of the world economy.

While Washington has been able to control Iraqi airspace and one-third of Iraq's territory via a Kurdish client regime, it had been unable to overthrow or isolate Saddam Hussein, and Iraq had recovered its position in international affairs — in OPEC, Islamic organizations, relations with many key Gulf States — and in open or barely covert trade relations with European, Middle Eastern and even US-owned multinationals. The same decline of US influence was evident in the cases of Iran, Libya, Sudan and Palestine — each nation either broke a US boycott or, in the case of

Palestine, was engaged in a major confrontation with Israel, the principal US ally in the region. Likewise, armed Islamic groups engaged in successful attacks on major US diplomatic and military targets in sub-Saharan Africa and the Middle East. The US, in turn, advanced its presence in the Balkans, conquering Kosovo and establishing client regimes in Macedonia and Serbian Yugoslavia. Clearly, Washington's empire was expanding in strategic military areas while losing ground in strategic economic regions.

Latin America remains a contested terrain. Almost all regimes are loyal clients of the US, facilitating and promoting large-scale, long-term pillage, but at the subnational level, class and national anti-imperialist and class-ethnic movements have been gaining strength, particularly in Colombia, Argentina, Bolivia and Venezuela. In the latter case, the nationalist foreign policy of President Chavez, particularly important as a key US oil supplier, has drawn special attention from Washington's destabilization experts.

Internally severe economic strains and a political legitimacy crisis weakened the foundations of the American global empire. The speculative bubble burst and the "new economy" went into a steep decline, carrying in its wake hundreds of billions of dollars in investor losses. The elections of 2000 were decided by electoral fraud and a partisan judicial decision, handing victory to a minority president without a mandate to rule. The illegitimacy of the presidency was a serious problem in managing and expanding the empire. Internal political and economic constraints on empire building, a weak presidential mandate and a severely weakened and recessive economy ran contrary to the empire-building ideology of the leading voices in the Bush administration — David Rumsfeld, Dick Cheney, Paul Wolfowitz, Condoleeza Rice etc. There was an obvious need for a dramatic "trigger event" which would allow the Bush regime to overcome these internal constraints and relaunch his father's vision of a New World Order dominated by the US. That event was 9/11, and the circumstances preceding it indicate foreknowledge among allies and top officials in the Bush administration that a major attack on US installations was in the works.

US responses to the events of 9/11 revived the vision of a New World Order and resulted in far-reaching domestic and foreign policy measures in pursuit of it. Three lessons were learned from the failed quest of Bush's father. First, empire building cannot be based on shared decision-making with European or Asian allies. Only unilateral decision-making will build a unique US empire. Second, a world empire requires continual wars, without limits of time and place, which lead to conquest and occupation and not merely the military defeat of an adversary who can arise from the ashes, as Saddam did after the first Gulf War. An ideology which mobilizes public backing for permanent war has to be elaborated to avoid an ebb of support and a return of public attention to domestic crises and the discredit of the regime, such as happened following the first Gulf War to Bush the elder, who suffered electoral defeat in the midst of the recession of 1991–92 (Furedi 1994).

There are two types of imperial appeals. One that mobilizes public identification with empire, based on race, or national superiority, and overseas colonial employment opportunities such as took place during the European colonial period of the nineteenth and early twentieth centuries. The second imperial appeal is designed to secure domestic support and is not based on national affirmation as much as national paranoia, cultivated and promoted by the state and magnified by the mass media. The Bush regime's anti-terrorist propaganda campaign focuses on a worldwide terrorist conspiracy always on the verge of attacking any individual at any location in the US or overseas at any time. This has served to unite the country behind the permanent worldwide empire-building project.

A whole series of institutions — Homeland Security, police state decrees, executive and congressional legislation (the Patriot Act), and vast increases in military, intelligence and police spending on surveillance and control — are based on the sense of mass insecurity and public willingness to support new authoritarian measures and overseas military intervention. Psychological terror is reinforced by widespread and arbitrary attacks on domestic Islamic institutions and Arab immigrants or Arab-American individuals — demonstrating to the frightened public that terrorists exist close to home.

The political changes since 9/11 bring to bear some of the main characteristics underlying US political culture and institutions: the reassertion of the imperial presidency of the Cold War era, a paranoid style of politics reminiscent of the McCarthy-Truman era, an expansive and arbitrary police-state apparatus similar to the era of J. Edgar Hoover, and an ideology of permanent warfare comparable to the worldwide anti-communist crusades of the past half century. What is unique is the combination of all these characteristics within the brief period of one year and its context — a period of deepening economic crisis and increasing loss of political allies.

Empire: Military Strategy and Economic Foundations

Empire begins with military and/or political conquest but ultimately rests on the economy. The current effort at building a world empire rests on fragile foundations and a voluntarist military concept in which initial military costs are more than compensated for by ultimate economic benefits. The ultra-voluntarism of the Bush regime is found in its unilateralist posture, its breaking of many international treaties and its demand for impunity for soldiers, spies and public functionaries committing war crimes in pursuit of empire. The military drive for world power has severely distorted the domestic and overseas economy of the US, provoking a huge budget deficit to match unsustainable external account deficits, and severely weakening the dollar. The terrorism doctrine only helps to generate flight from the dollar.

The deeper structural effects are a declining economy, a vast depletion of US pension funds and the impoverishment of tens of millions of present and future pensioners. Empire building is also accompanied by deepening inequalities. Expanding the capacity for war in a time of a shrinking economic base increases domestic malaise. Bush's worldwide "will to power" cannot be sustained in the context of enormous losses of financial resources by the majority of the middle class and the better-paid working class. The mass media have openly embraced the role of chief propagandist for the regime's various campaigns: propagating the paranoid "terrorism is everywhere" campaign, uncritically passing on the administration's imperial view of the world and defending all the authoritarian clients of the empire. At the same time the mass media have been forced to take a stand against corrupt crony capitalists linked to the Bush regime, undermining the administration's credibility and capacity to mobilize public support for new imperial undertakings.

Empire: Costs and Benefits

The question of who benefits and who loses from empire building is not easily answered, at least from the long-term perspective. At first glance, the Bush administration has benefited from the Afghan and Iraq wars and the anti-terrorism campaign. The regime's popularity increased, military bases were extended, repressive legislation was put in place, large military appropriations were secured and allies were forced into submission. However, over the medium run, many of these apparent benefits have a powerfully negative side. The budget went into the red from a previous surplus, and war and anti-terrorism funding did little to increase US competitiveness in world markets, resulting in another unsustainable trade deficit, or to prevent the fall of the dollar and a sharp decline in the inflow of foreign investment. The Bush administration's economic failure and its incapacity to improve the competitive position of domestic industries led to a sharp increase in protectionist measures and agricultural subsidies, which antagonized more-efficient European and third world competitors and called into question the commitment of the US to free trade, thus weakening the position of more competitive sectors of the US economy. The attempt by Congress to impose billion-dollar taxes on foreign-owned (European) subsidiaries and use the funds to favour US firms has led to threats from the European Union that investments from its TNCs might dry up, causing a collapse in the dollar. Finally, Washington's paranoid propaganda campaign has led to general insecurity among investors and the flight of overseas capital to safer havens outside the US. In addition, imposing strict controls over money laundering might very well undermine significant overseas financial transactions and even the US banking system. The costs of "doing business" in banking will rise, while a major source of superprofits will dry up.

In addition, the ties between the Bush administration and the leading CEOs in the Texas-based energy industry — a clear example of crony-capitalism — and the massive fraud and collapse of Enron and other energy giants have adversely affected investor confidence and millions of pensioners. The dual phenomena of corrupt crony-capitalism and permanent war policy have weakened the pillars of the US empire and the Bush administration.

In the middle term, the economic and political costs of empire building outweigh the short-term political advantages. The Bush administration has gambled on the "big play" to establish the US as the centre of a new world empire. Leading planners and strategists projected future expansion and conquest on early advances in Afghanistan and Central Asia, on positive outcomes in marginal areas of the world economy and on the basis of a narrowly focused military calculus, devoid of strategic knowledge of how the world economy functions and how dependent the US is on external economic centres.

The criteria of success of the empire builders are almost exclusively built around *changing the world agenda*. In the months preceding 9/11, in Europe and the rest of the world there were clear signs of a deteriorating US influence, a rising popular opposition to European/US capital and an increasing willingness of third world governments to break US boycotts of selected Middle Eastern countries (Iraq, Iran, Syria and Libya) and Cuba. Amid US public concern about medical and pharmaceutical costs, the crash of the IT speculative bubble and the huge loss of savings, come increased pressure for congressional action. A turn towards regulating corporate power, controlling drug prices and focusing government attention on social reform had been clearly in ascendancy under Clinton. The reaction of the Bush administration to 9/11 was specifically and overwhelmingly to bury the emerging anti-corporate social agenda in favour of a militaristic and security-based definition of the world political economy. Within a relentless propaganda campaign orchestrated and amplified at all levels of government via a homogeneous mass media, the Bush administration was able to shift public debate away from the failures of speculative capital and towards the threat of terrorism; away from the allocation of funds for health and drugs, and towards vast increases in military and security spending; away from domestic corporate reform and towards external wars; and away from investments in revitalizing the productive economy and towards state spending on a vast new network of military bases in the Balkans, Central Asia, the Philippines, the Middle East and Latin America.

The military definition of reality led to vast increases in sales and profits for the military industrial complex. The *Financial Times* headlined an article, "U.S. Defense Sector Cashes in on Bush's War on Terrorism" (18 July 2002: 16). Corporate reform was buried as national hysteria over imminent terrorist incidents was cultivated by members of the Bush administration and Democratic Party leaders such as Senator Joseph Leiberman. In the short term the military-terrorist definition of world politics favoured Washington for at least two reasons. First, the US was most prepared and interested in extending its global power via military and intelligence networks, military bases and repressive authoritarian client regimes. Second, the terror hysteria and mass propaganda campaign raised the Bush administration out of its minority status into a "massively popular presidency" and created the illusion of a leader fit to guide the North American people (and the rest of the world) in a global campaign against terrorists.

Manipulating the terror threat to the utmost, the Bush regime simultaneously declared war and promoted a series of anti-terrorist laws that undermined most of the democratic rights guaranteed by the Constitution. Repressive legislation and mass propaganda in turn led to the capitulation of many progressive intellectuals and celebrities and their embrace of the Afghan invasion and the administration's definitions of global terror.

A military definition of world politics was spread to all international forums and meetings and dominated agendas, temporarily subordinating all socio-economic issues and regional conflicts to the anti-terrorist campaign. By setting the agenda, Washington was able to further its military-political expansion and subordinate its allies in Europe and the third world to its project of global domination, euphemistically referred to as "world leadership."

The Bush administration used 9/11 to emphasize the particular terrorist threat to the US and, therefore, its right to act unilaterally in taking military action and breaking international treaties. In the months preceding 9/11 the Bush regime had already indicated its unilateralist posture in a desperate attempt to secure comparative advantages for declining US businesses (by reneging on the Kyoto agreement) and to increase military spending (by reneging on the ABM treaty) to promote its aerospace industry. With 9/11 the Bush administration combined greater state intervention at several levels: greater military/intelligence intervention; increased state control of US society via the Home Security Act; heightened state protectionism (for steel); and subsidies (for agriculture) to favour US capitalists against world competition. The military-mercantilist empire can only be constructed unilaterally because it adversely affects allies and competitors. Following 9/11, anti-terrorism became the political instrument to raise unilateral state action to its dominant role in defining Washington's empire-building project. Multi-level trade agreements were violated, the World Trade Organization was ignored and NATO was marginalized as Washington marched forward under the banner of the "war against terrorism."

The rules, agreements and treaties governing US relations with Europe, Russia and the third world were radically changed. With Europe the *fait accompli* replaced consultation. The International Court of Justice agreement signed by the EU would not apply to US soldiers. They would continue to have impunity against charges of crimes against humanity. This is only logical: whoever heard of an empire being built without genocide and military crimes against non-combatants? The US threatened to withdraw its troops from Bosnia and thus unleash its Bosnian Islamic clients, engulfing the EU in a Balkan war. Europe capitulated. In the Middle East, Bush's initial unconditional support for Sharon's genocidal war undermined any effort toward EU or Arab state mediation. There was no pretext of consultation, just impositions and friendly dismissals of visiting allied dignitaries.

With Russia the Bush administration simply tore up the ABM treaty on the basis that Russia had become a third-rate power and Putin was a ready client waiting to cut economic deals for his mafia allies in the oil industry ("Cheney Firm won $3.8 b in Contracts from Government," *The Observer*, 21 July 2002).

In the third world, Washington increasingly backed non-elected, authoritarian rulers and organized coups to expand its military, political and petrol empire. The Bush regime backed the Musharraf dictatorship in Pakistan, non-elected regimes in the Philippines, Indonesia and Argentina, a failed, right-wing military coup in Venezuela (whose first act was to dissolve all elected and judicial bodies) and was a prominent supporter of Colombian death squads. In other countries the Bush administration blatantly intervened in electoral processes in efforts to impose pliant candidates. In Bolivia, US Ambassador Rocha threatened to cut off US aid and close the US market if the electorate voted for peasant-Indian leader Eva Morales, a move that backfired, as Morales doubled his vote in the last two weeks of the campaign. In Palestine, Secretary of State Colin Powell called for the ouster of Yasser Arafat and the installation of a new client ruler. In all regions of the third world, Washington used the threat of terrorism to urge new, harshly repressive legislation and the establishment of US military bases and special "anti-terrorist" police-military apparatuses, most of which were used to repress popular movements. The "anti-terrorism" doctrine served to legitimate intervention throughout the world and abolish democratic rights. The lead figures of this wave of authoritarianism in Western Europe were English Prime Minister Tony Blair and President José Maria Aznar of Spain. Blair eliminated 800-year-old legal conventions, which barred double jeopardy and provided the right to a prompt trial, based on the presentation of evidence against the accused (hearsay and criminal-background information is nwo considered legal in trying a suspect).

The rise of authoritarianism in the Middle East and the third world is closely linked to the economic collapse of neoliberalism and the burgeoning political crises. Increasingly the popular movements have identified the IMF as an instrument of Western bankers and speculators and their local counterparts. The ability of the IMF and the other IFIs to "discipline" the majority of humanity (imposing measures that redistribute wealth upward and outward) has been weakened. Client regimes have in some cases, such as Argentina, been overthrown or been challenged (as in Brazil).

In the face of declining markets, deflated speculative activity and increased competition with the EU, Japan and Southeast Asia, Washington has attempted to use its national security doctrine to prop up failed neoliberal states (a doctrine of the new imperialism) and to gain enclaves within the strategic port cities of Western Europe. The US has established customs inspection offices in Canada, Holland and France and has plans to extend its operations to countries of Asia.

The Political Framework of Empire Building after 9/11

The particularities of the Bush regime and its empire-building project have given it a very marked militarist and leaderless quality. In the first place, overrepresentation of the energy sector and military-industrial groups have fueled a decided push to conquer strategic oil regions in Central Asia (Caspian Sea), Iraq, Iran and install a puppet regime in Venezuela. The tight links between the extractive capitalist sectors and the Bush regime are very visible in the presence of two central figures: Vice-President Cheney and Secretary of the Treasury Paul O'Neill. Extractive capitalists depend heavily on political and/or military intervention to secure privileged access in order to exploit the subsoil of nations, particularly in the third world.

Second, the Bush regime has been heavily immersed in klepto-corporate activity, whose structure and culture is based on deceptive propaganda, concentrated executive power, large-scale pillage of private investors and state protection (or at least tolerance). It is not a regime of successful entrepreneurs linked to bona fide capitalist innovators. Rather, the success of its leading members (including Bush, Cheney and others) and backers (Enron, Sun Oil, Halliburton etc.) is based on fraud, deception and stock manipulation. (At one point, Halliburton was fully owned by Cheney. He still maintains an interest in the company, held in trust, which is probably not unconnected to the $7 billion oil-field reconstruction contract given to Halliburton on May 7, 2003, less than two weeks after the "end" of "Operation Iraqi Freedom." Surrounded by practicing kleptocrats, who know best about market manipulation and cooking the books, it is not a regime capable of competing in markets and realizing earned profits. Its road to economic power is political influence, monopolization and control. In the international economy a kleptocratic capitalist elite finds it easier to secure market shares through military force and corrupt leaders, rather than product quality.

The corrupt and mediocre economic elite that surrounds and influences the Bush administration is incapable of imposing hegemonic rule; it must seek domination through force. The paradigmatic case is the US imposition of the Hamid Karzai regime in Afghanistan, based on the overt buying of delegates to the Jerga, the so-called "Council of Tribal Leaders."

A third characteristic of the Bush regime is its strongly regional character and close corporate and personal ties with Texas extractive capitalists. For example, Vice President Cheney's firm Halliburton has won billion-dollar contracts from the government. If Clinton's ties to IT swindlers led to the rise and collapse of the information–fibreoptics–

biotech bubble, Bush's ties to energy and petroleum felons and their CEO accomplices led to a collapse of stock prices, a massive flight of investor capital and a sharp decline of the dollar.

A fourth characteristic of the Bush administration is its lack of capitalist leadership. In the midst of dollar, investor and stock crises, Bush and his collaborators are incapable of structural initiatives to staunch the outflow of hundreds of billions of dollars. Empty rhetoric by the president, the bizarre optimism of Alan Greenspan (head of the U.S. Federal Reserve),and the seclusion of the vice president, who was facing congressional investigation for cooking the books, have only deepened the crisis. Coming from the small world of Texas insider trading, Bush is at a loss in the world of big-time swindlers under investigation. He lacks an external supporting cast to define an economic strategy that would confront the crisis of investment. Without external direction, Bush has few internal resources and little basic knowledge, political skill or organizational ability to put together a new team to avoid the fall. His only external resources are his war ministers, the war machine and the repressive apparatus. As the stock market weakens the real economy, and his economic cronies run for cover, Bush has relied heavily on saving his regime via war. The particularities of the Bush regime — its extractive capitalist background and crony culture, its immersion in a klepto-corporate milieu, its lack of a political economic strategy and reliance on the war apparatus to resolve the domestic crisis — makes it prone to see the world in a militarist and mercantilist way and to act unilaterally.

The Bush Doctrine

The policies undertaken under the Bush administration can be dubbed the Bush Doctrine, even if their formulation and implementation was done by others, namely Secretary of Defense Rumsfeld, Vice President Cheney and Rumsfeld protégé Paul Wolfowitz. The formulation of this doctrine, presented as the National Security Doctrine to Congress in September 2002, is attributed by some to Cheney and thus dubbed "the Cheney Doctrine." Essentially the doctrine envisions empire building as a military project, and, except for narrow economic concerns such as control over petroleum or promoting the military-industrial complex, no systematic consideration is given to the economic foundations of empire or to the economic consequences of global military commitments. There is little in the way of coordination between the military/anti-terrorist campaigns and the interests of multinational corporations. At its root the Bush Doctrine largely assumes that a global military framework under US domination will ensure a stable and favourable context for US economic expansion. This assumption is totally inadequate given growing economic competition, the high and prejudicial costs of military, anti-terrorist and "Homeland Defense" spending on the economy, and the deepening domestic economic crises.

The Bush Doctrine is essentially a highly voluntarist "will to power" project. It is "voluntarist" in several interrelated senses: it assumes that by projecting military power it can ensure domestic backing, force Euro-Asian compliance and support, and intimidate adversaries. The doctrine relies heavily on subjective responses, under the notion that objective reality can be redefined and instrumentalized to serve US empire building. It is in this context that the Bush Doctrine defines its key concept of *permanent war* — war not limited in time and space or qualified by any set of strategic economic priorities or domestic fiscal or financial constraints. Permanent war assumes unlimited economic resources, unconditional and enduring public support and perpetually compliant ally/competitors.

A second key concept of the Bush Doctrine is *unilateral action*. Washington will not consult, negotiate or share power. Creating facts will force eventual compliance among skeptical allies, who will then be brought on board to police and pay for maintaining conquered territories. Unilateralism is essentially a form of imposition: imperial conquest of adversaries and forced submission of allies. Unilateralism is clearly the hallmark of a military-based empire and its singular abrogation of disarmament and human rights treaties. It is designed to give a free hand to the military as the driving force. Prior to 9/11, unilateralism was used as an instrument to reject international environmental accords and limits to weapons use. Subsequent to 9/11 it has become the modus operandi in formulating and directing foreign policy. The invasion and conquest of Afghanistan was carried out following a unilateral US decision, the selection and decision to support the puppet Karzai regime was made in Washington, and the military attack on Iraq followed the same pattern. The organization and support of the coup against the constitutional government in Venezuela was exclusively in US hands. NATO has outlived its usefulness, as it implies some level of consultation with European allies before overseas engagement. The new international framework is total US control, and European and client-state provision of funds and policing.

A third key concept is the notion of *international impunity*. Military strategists know full well that imperial conquest and occupation inevitably involve crimes against civilians. The new military doctrine includes the bombing of life-sustaining infrastructure, torture and execution of political prisoners, targeting of civilians in regions of conflict and forceful maintenance of client regimes. Washington's definitive rejection of the jurisdiction of the International War Crimes Tribunal over its imperial armies is in essence a declaration of its "right" to use all means, including crimes against humanity, for empire building. The Afghan invasion is emblematic: the bombing of hospitals, neighbourhoods and weddings, the torture and interrogation of captured soldiers, and the denial of any responsibility for documented violations of Geneva accords speak clearly to the reason why the US has rejected the authority of any international court of justice. Impunity is especially important given the military nature of empire building.

A fourth component of the Bush Doctrine is intimately related to the dominant voluntarist mood: the idea that the US can engage in simultaneous and sequential wars. US military operations in the Philippines or Colombia, for example, are not at the same level as in Afghanistan and Iraq, yet they indicate a generalized war strategy without economic priorities, and with a sense of unlimited resources and public support. The doctrine of permanent war involves a vast increase in the state apparatus, a growth of state spending, and greater state intervention in the economy, crowding out productive private investment by competing with the private sector for financial resources. Whether intended or not, the Bush Doctrine is highly statist and thus potentially antagonistic to significant free market sectors of his coalition ("Land of the Unfree," *Financial Times Weekend*, 20–21 July 2002: 1). Statism was also pervasive in the economy, with huge, $185 billion subsidies to agriculture and up to 40 percent tariffs on imported steel to protect US steel producers. War, imperialism and statist economics to sustain them are the operational codes of the Bush Doctrine.

Anti-terrorist ideology legitimates the Bush Doctrine and is one of the doctrine's driving forces, a key element in the drive to empire via military conquest. From the perspective of military empire builders the beauty of the ideology is that it is open-ended. It allows maximum intervention in all regions against any opposition because it targets not only identifiable terrorist groups but also includes suspected countries from which terrorists allegedly operate, and any groups with whom they have interacted. Even more ominously, the term "terrorist" is used so loosely that any group engaged in opposing militarism, imperialism (so-called "globalization") or local authoritarian regimes could be labeled "terrorist" and targeted. Popular insurgencies like the Colombian FARC and ELN have already been labelled as "terrorist," allowing a massive inflow of US Special Forces and arms.

The Bush Doctrine has deeply ideologized US empire building, moving away from the ad hoc formulations of predecessors. The anti-terrorist ideology put forward by Bush has polarized the world. Washington tries to force the world to choose between empire and terrorism, between the militarist ultra-Right in Washington and the fundamentalist Right in the streets of the Middle East.

The Bush Doctrine has dictated a new political division of labour in which the US invades and conquers and Europeans and third world clients are expected to provide internal security (policing occupied territory) and subsidize economic reconstruction.

In the year after 9/11 a new belligerent imperial doctrine was formulated and applied, changing relations with allies and clients and moving toward conquest of territory as well as resources. Paradoxically the imperial leadership was increasingly parochial, lacking a broad economic vision of the needs of the capitalist class as a whole and devoid of respect for the fundamental rules of the market.

The Structure of Empire

While the Bush administration has given some attention to securing privileged positions in oil-rich countries in Central Asia, the driving force of empire building has been a new type of colonialism built around occupied countries and the construction of an extensive network of enclaves and military bases at strategic geo-military locations. While the new wave of military-base building began with Clinton, under that administration it was directed at specific geopolitical targets. For example, in the late 1990s this administration mounted military bases in Ecuador, San Salvador, Aruba and Colombia to complement the counter-insurgency war undertaken under Plan Colombia. The Bush administration has extended military bases throughout the world; new bases have been built in the Central Asian republics of Turkestan and Kazakhstan and in adjoining countries. The biggest self-contained military base in Europe has been established in occupied Kosovo, to complement bases in Macedonia. New bases have been established in northern Brazil and northern Argentina, augmenting the previous US base in Chapare, Bolivia. The so-called "anti-terrorist campaign" has converged with the anti-drug campaign and counter-insurgency operations to give a powerful thrust to worldwide base building and penetration of domestic repressive apparatuses, securing the free circulation of US intelligence and military operatives within one-time sovereign nations.

The application and replication of US anti-terrorist legislation and executive decrees by client regimes has facilitated US moves and made US legislation the *de facto* law of the land. US customs officials are now operating at the major ports of Europe and Asia, usurping functions typically performed by nationals of the countries affected. New military agreements have been signed in the Philippines, Eastern Europe and Latin America that provide for joint military operations under US command.

The peculiarities of the US empire today is found in the fact that this expansion of power is expensive and provides, at least for the moment, few economic benefits. The outflow of military spending benefits, in part, US construction companies, but overall the effect is to further unbalance overseas accounts. None of the major bases in the Balkans, Southeast Asia or Latin America is located proximate to profitable regions susceptible to exploitation. The only possible exceptions are the bases in Central Asia near the Caspian oil deposits.

The dissociation of US military expansion from profitable exploitation of economic resources is neither an accident nor a result of personal failure. It is largely the result of a leadership crisis embedded in the changing nature of US capitalism.

Political Leadership: Speculation and Crime in the Suites

Over the past twenty-five years, US capitalism has evolved from a regulated industrial form into a speculative-kleptocratic one. Beginning with the Carter presidency and accelerating thereafter, the state ceased to regulate the economy to benefit the capitalist class as a whole. Particularly under the Bush-the-father and Clinton presidencies, deregulation was accompanied by speculative fever and wholesale swindles — first by the $500 billion savings-and-loans collapse, then the bursting of the IT bubble and then one of the most far-reaching cases of corporate swindle and fraud in the history of the US. The whole political class, including leaders of both major political parties, was deeply involved in seeking funds and supporting the bankrupt savings-and-loan firms, promoting the IT bubble and receiving campaign contributions from leading CEOs involved in corporate fraud. Crime is a norm among the political and economic elite, and impunity is an important corollary.

Accumulation of private wealth, and protection by a political elite deeply enmeshed in promoting special capitalist interests, undermined the capacity and will of US political leaders to formulate a coherent global economic strategy to promote the corporate empire. By will and default, empire building fell into the hands of the military strategists, while corrupt politicians provided ideological cover. The inability of the US political leadership to respond to the massive flight of capital — out of stocks, away from the dollar and out of the country — was due to its being held captive by kleptocratic, crony capitalism and its dependence on financing by special interests. The Bush appeals to corporate responsibility or corporate conscience ring hollow to the great majority of investors, who have experienced the failures of corporate self-regulation. Criminal behaviour among CEOs and investment banking deception have seriously undermined the stock market and violated the fundamental rules of the marketplace. Equally important, they have produced a set of political leaders incapable of seeing beyond the crony capitalist circle and relying on the military-intelligence apparatus to define the style and content of empire building.

The results are dangerous to the world and have produced an unsustainable empire. The ultra-voluntarism expressed in unilateral projections of power isolates the US from its allies. Despite the claims of ultra-militarists such as Rumsfeld and Wolfowitz the US cannot rule the world alone. Military expansion cannot sustain client regimes, even if the civilian population is bloodied and battered. Equally important, the weakening domestic economic foundation of the empire is undermining political support and limiting the resources available for an escalating military and security budget. Finally, political opposition is growing against a corrupt and fraudulent corporate elite within the US, and mass popular opposition is growing outside in Latin America, the Middle East and Europe. Lack of internal corrective mechanisms — pending voluntary or punitive legislation notwithstanding — means that the economy is possibly moving in the direction of a major fall comparable to the collapse of 1929.

Theoretical Issues: Structure and Operation of the US Empire

The empire-building project of the Bush administration raises important theoretical issues. First and foremost, what are the relationships of the military-intelligence sectors of the imperial state to its economic components? Second, what are the relationships of the military sectors of the state to multinational corporations and the domestic economy? Third, what is the relationship between "crony capitalism" (sectors of the capitalist class with regional, personal and political ties to the Bush administration) and the state, and what is its impact on the economy and the capitalist class as a whole? Finally, what is the relationship between the state and the economy in a period of war and unilateral empire building?

The most striking aspect of empire building today is the autonomy of the Pentagon from most sectors of the capitalist class. The Pentagon has intervened in several unprofitable regions with high cost–low return ratios: Afghanistan, Kosovo, Macedonia, the Philippines, Pakistan etc. This military action has generated greater hostility in oil-producing areas, mainly the Middle East, which are currently lucrative areas for major US investors. Next, the Bush administration had given unconditional support to Israel against hundreds of millions of Muslims, favouring a belligerent militarily expansionist colonial power over and against vital US economic interests. Finally, the economic costs of military-based empire building are astronomical, and their economic benefits are restricted to a narrow circle of industries. The budget deficit has soared, security restrictions have raised the costs of trade via delays and bottlenecks, and the travel industry has been battered, particularly the airline industry, hotels and other services. Insecurity generated by the self-serving terror-mongering which serves to expand the budgets of the military and intelligence apparatus has undermined investor confidence in the United States. While the Bush administration speaks to and passes specifically pro-business tax legislation, the pursuit of its global military strategy tends to subordinate the economic aspects of empire building to the military.

While it would be wrong, theoretically, to speak of an absolute autonomy of the military in relationship to the capitalist class, its freedom of action certainly goes beyond the "relative autonomy" usually ascribed to a capitalist state.

The economically most important sectors of the capitalist class and the interests of the system as a whole have been subordinated to a particular set of influential, regionally based crony capitalists with long-standing political links to the Bush administration. Special favours, deep corruption and the privileged position of the Texas energy sector in the Bush administration define the nature of the regime. The collapse of Enron and subsequent revelations of widespread billion-dollar fraud and swindles resulting from cronyism have undermined investor confidence and put the entire equity market under a cloud. The "relative autonomy" of the crony sector from the rest of the capitalist class has severely undermined the position of the capitalist class as a whole.

The ascendancy of the military in the empire-building process has been accompanied by a general growth of statism, and by state intervention in the economy, society and personal lives and freedoms. The Bush administration is probably the most protectionist regime in recent history, establishing protective tariffs on textiles, lumber, agricultural products and other commodities, while increasing agricultural subsidies and imposing quotas on imports. Favouring the military and pursuing conquest by force of arms have weakened the US economy and, in particular, diverted public investments which would strengthen the competitive position of US enterprises. State intervention in civil society via police-state legislation such as the Patriot Act, the Homelands Security Act and TIPS undermines personal freedoms and weakens public opposition.

Imperialism under Bush is closer to mercantilism than neoliberalism. While "free market" rhetoric persists, it is increasingly overshadowed by the military-state rhetoric of "permanent war" and "anti-terrorism." As the economy is weakened and the capitalist class pressures the Bush regime to respond, the military-empire builders take the lead in seeing domination of strategic economic regions (Iraq and Iran) as the "solution." In the eyes of the military-empire builders, the war and colonization of Iraq will result in economic benefits to the capitalist class and strengthen their support for the permanent war strategy. It would also serve as a springboard for future wars and conquests in the Gulf region, namely against Iran. While war and economic crises have in the past frequently been interconnected, today the new wars will mostly benefit the crony sector attached to energy-petroleum interests and deepen the chasm between it and the rest of the capitalist class. War is thus an extension of cronyism through military means.

Military-empire building is decidedly colonial in style and content. The emerging empire is built upon the occupation of territory, imposition of rulers and management of colonized states and their economies. The US has established colonial relationships with former Yugoslav republics in Kosovo, Macedonia and Montenegro; and it controls Iraq. The Empire has established military garrisons throughout Central Asia and in Pakistan and the Philippines, and military installations and bases in Bolivia, Brazil, Colombia, El Salvador, Ecuador and Aruba. It has established "extraterritoriality" for its security forces and secured "anti-terrorist" legislation from its client states, obligating scores of countries on the five continents to follow US directives in pursing adversaries.

Imperial economic interests derive from regional (Texas) crony oil interests. The empire builders have been focused on conquering Iraq and probably Iran by military force, Central Asia and the Caspian Sea region via bribery and support for dictatorial regimes, and Venezuela via military coup. The empire builders are also aware of a possible future need for military intervention in Saudi Arabia, which is teetering on the brink of collapse (*The Observer*, 28 July 2002).

As only the US empire is at stake, and not the imperial system,

Washington's military intervention is based on unilateral state action. The weakening of US competitiveness has likewise led to unilateral decisions to impose increased tariffs while vigorously calling on the rest of the world to eliminate their subsidies and lower their barriers (*Financial Times*, 26 July 2002: 1). Retrocolonialism and its corollary of military-based empire building, unilaterally imposed protectionism, subsidizing economic policy and occupation of geostrategic territories form the framework for understanding the key features of the period after 9/11.

The Left Strikes Back: The Contradictions of Empire Building

Three sets of contradictions facing US empire builders have become exacerbated since 9/11: the internal contradictions between capitalist interests and the state; the contradictions between competing imperial interests (Europe and the US); and the contradictions between empire and powerful socio-political interests in Latin America.

In the period after 9/11, serious inter-regime conflicts and economic contradictions emerged. They can be listed concisely as: (1) the pre-eminence of the state (namely, the military-intelligence apparatus) over the interests of large multinational corporations (heightened security against business profits); (2) the privileging of territoriality over markets (occupying marginal countries instead of increasing market shares in prosperous countries); (3) promoting kleptocratic sectors of capitalism (Enron, WorldCom etc.) over domestic and foreign investors; and (4) increased spending on an expanding state apparatus at the expense of shoring up the fragile productive foundations of empire.

To these internal contradictions must be added intensifying external contradictions, particularly intensified conflicts with the European Union. One of the basic external contradictions results from an internal contradiction, namely, that overseas military power grows as the domestic economy declines, leading Washington to increase protectionism rather than reduce costly external projections of power. The result is heightened tension between European and other exporters and Washington. For example, the 30–40 percent US tariff on steel provoked the Europeans to threaten to retaliate with similar tariffs, and to take the matter to the World Trade Organization, which ruled against Washington. More generally, the powerful role of the state since 9/11 has conflicted with free market ideology, provoking a new round of protectionism.

US military definitions of empire have come into conflict with European market conceptions of empire building. This was particularly the case in the Middle East, where the United States' unconditional support for the Israeli war machine undermined European efforts to stabilize the region for investment and trade.

The second contradiction is the monopolistic and unilateralist conception of empire building that has jettisoned the "power sharing," consultative style favoured by Europe. Unilateral monopolization of empire isolates the US from essential economic and military support to sustain imperial conquests. In effect, monopoly power gives US empire builders a tactical advantage but undermines strategic consolidation, which is only possible with European inclusion and profit sharing.

Heightened contradictions between the US and Europe in trade, investment, colonial conquest and strategic approaches (military versus market) will not lead to war (US superiority makes that unlikely), but it could have more serious consequences: a crash of the US economy because of an overextended military empire combined with a drying up of external flows of capital.

The third and even more decisive external contradiction is that between empire building and the growth of powerful socio-political movements overseas, particularly in two strategic regions (but not confined to them): the Middle East and Latin America.

Since 9/11, Washington has proceeded to pursue aggressive policies beyond Afghanistan and Iraq, toward Syria and Iran, as well as towards secular and Muslim resistance movements in Saudi Arabia, Lebanon and elsewhere. Washington's massive military and unconditional political support for Sharon's reconquest of the occupied territories provoked a mass mobilization infused with anti-imperialist consciousness throughout the Arab world. Popular revolts threaten key US client states, particularly Saudi Arabia, racked by inter-regime conflicts and nationwide protests of its pro-US policies. Likewise, in Egypt and Jordan, mass unrest threatens regimes that closely identify with US retrocolonial policies. Bush's Middle Eastern "axis of evil" countries — the targets for the next imperial wars — are centres of anti-imperialist resistance.

However, it is Latin America where the socio-political and military polarization between US empire builders and popular movements is most acute. While most of the movements preceded 9/11, in the period after, US-sponsored militarization increased and the neoliberal economic strategy virtually collapsed, widening popular resistance and challenging client regimes defending the Empire. Moreover, the US military definition of political reality — putting anti-terrorism at the top of the agenda — has blocked any plans for an economic rescue package.

Popular challenges to imperial domination are located in a wide array of countries, including Colombia, Argentina, Bolivia, Ecuador, Venezuela, Peru, Paraguay and, to a lesser extent, Brazil and Uruguay. What is striking about the new wave of popular resistance is the degree to which political parties and leaders associated with pro-imperial policies have been discredited. In some cases, popular resistance is expressed in mass popular mobilizations (road blockages, demonstrations etc.); in others it is expressed in a combination of mass mobilizations and new electoral formations; in Colombia it includes mass protest and guerrilla warfare.

In Argentina, in the year after 9/11, four presidents were ousted and a fifth had less than ten percent support. The popular uprising of December 19/20, 2001, led to the overthrow of the discredited, pro-US president Fernando de la Rua and Wall Street-favourite Domingo Cavallo. With poverty levels exceeding 52 percent, and an unemployment rate of 25 percent, the Argentine economy was expected to decline by 15 percent in 2002, the fifth consecutive year of recession/depression. More than six million Argentines lost all their savings and hundreds of thousands crowded the streets in assemblies, protests, road blockages and general strikes. The political class, judiciary and private elite are totally discredited. And the most popularly repeated slogan is, "*Que se vayan todos*" ("All of them get out"). Central to this struggle is a repudiation of foreign debt payments and the identification of the IMF and the US as responsible for the economic collapse.

In Colombia the US-backed Plan Colombia and Bush's Andean Initiative are part of a large military and paramilitary campaign to exterminate or displace the peasant social base of the guerrillas. The latter includes between seventeen and twenty thousand members of the Revolutionary Armed Forces of Colombia and up to five thousand in the National Liberation Army. In the year following 9/11, Washington, through its client, the Andrés Pastrana regime, engineered the collapse of the peace negotiations, relaunched "total war" and promoted the election of paramilitary supporter Alvaro Uribe to the presidency. The results have been daily massacres of peasants, trade union activists, Indian leaders and human rights spokespersons. Confrontations between US-backed military and paramilitary forces and the popular civilian and armed groups occur in more than 70 percent of the country on a daily basis.

In Bolivia, Evo Morales, the leader of coca-growing farmers during nearly two decades of struggles against US-directed eradication, led his Movement to Socialism (MAS) Party into a runoff in the Bolivian Congress, where all the capitalist parties joined forces to block his bid for the presidency. The massive vote for two peasant Indian candidates exceeded the nearest neoliberal candidate by nearly five percentage points. This electoral advance was preceded by mass marches and road blockages that created an anti-imperialist class and ethnic consciousness that advanced Morales to the congressional runoff. Blatant intervention by US ambassador Rocha in the electoral campaign backfired. Rocha threatened Bolivian voters with the cut-off of US aid and markets if they exercised their sovereign right and voted for Morales. Morales' popularity jumped from 13 percent to 21 percent in the last two weeks before the election. The most significant aspect of the MAS campaign was that it explicitly repudiated the US-imposed coca eradication position, the regime's privatization of gas and oil resources, the US military base and US Drug Enforcement Agency (DEA) operations in Bolivia.

In Peru, massive public demonstrations encompassing the major cities of Arequipa and Cuzco and protesting the Alejandro Toledo regime's privatization program led to the wholesale resignation of his cabinet and, in particular, neoliberal economic minister Kuczinski. Toledo, a former employee of the World Bank, who donned the costume of highland Indian peasants for the electoral campaign, saw his popular ratings decline from more than 50 percent to less than 10 percent in a year. A US protégé who campaigned as a populist and acted as a US client, Alejandro Toledo faces severe difficulties in staying in power for the remainder of his term, given the intense hostility of a populace that feels betrayed. Toledo's avid support for the US anti-terrorist campaign relegated his purported concern with alleviating the poverty of 70 percent of Peruvians to the memory hole.

Ecuador has a pliant client regime led by President Gustavo Noboa, who has dollarized the economy and granted the US a major military base in Manta. Yet his rule is tenuous, rocked by general strikes, a hostile Congress and the third of the country ruled by a left-of-centre coalition of Indian-peasant parties. A mass movement of Indian-peasants, urban trade unionists and urban poor had previously joined with sectors of the military to overthrow Noboa's predecessor (Jamil Mahuad). This progressive junta was subsequently overthrown by the pro-US military, and Noboa was installed. While the regime houses US counter-insurgency forces along its borders, and its airspace is effectively colonized by US surveillance planes engaged in the Colombian civil war, the social foundations of the regime are eroding quickly, creating a volatile and unstable terrain for imperial advance.

In Paraguay, massive demonstrations and road blockages succeeded in forcing US client President Luis Gonzalez Macchi to withdraw a plan for the privatization of the state electrical network. The formation of a broad coalition of peasant organizations, leftist parties and trade unionists organized into the Democratic Convergence Front emerged to give leadership to the struggle. US plans to expand military and intelligence bases and operations at the eastern Paraguay-Brazil-Argentina border has become the focus of continuing confrontation.

In Venezuela a popular uprising inflicted a serious defeat for US empire builders backing a right-wing military coup. Under the direction of ultra-rightist Under-Secretary for Latin American Affairs Otto Reich, the US backed a military coup on April 11, 2002, supported by the Venezuelan economic elite, sectors of the military and almost the entire upper middle class. The coup leaders overthrew President Hugo Chavez and proceeded to disband all elected bodies and the judiciary and replace them with hardline, pro-US functionaries. The first measures of the dictatorial regime were of foremost interest to the empire builders: a breaking of relations with Cuba and withdrawal from OPEC. However, within forty-eight hours a massive march of hundreds of thousands of Venezuelans, mostly from the *ranchos*, the slums in the hills overlooking Caracas, convinced important sectors of the military to come out in favour of the restoration of Chavez. The coup collapsed as the mass of poor threatened to turn political restoration into social transformation. The defeat of the US-orchestrated coup demonstrated that the empire builders could be defeated and that mass organizations, even though loosely organized, were capable of restoring a president with a moderate nationalist foreign policy. As in Argentina, the Venezuelan populace demonstrated that client regimes of the Bush administration are vulnerable and capable of being ousted, at least temporarily. The march of empire building is not a linear process inevitably destined to succeed.

In Brazil the leading candidate in the presidential campaign was Lula da Silva, a politician from the center-left Workers Party (PT). While the PT dropped all of its anti-imperialist and anti-liberal demands, it was still perceived as an adversary by Wall Street bankers and the Bush administration . The empire builders' opposition stems from Lula's mass popular base of supporters, who in most cases are to the left of the party leadership. Prior to his victory, Wall Street feared that Lula would respond to post-electoral pressure for social reforms, economic regulation and opposition to US military expansion. Wall Street responded by speculating against the Brazilian *real* and by capital flight, a scare tactic to undermine or turn Lula further to the right. Washington's chosen candidate to be President Cardoso's successor was José Serra. Despite the backing of the state apparatus, Serra lagged well behind in the electoral campaign and in the second runoff vote received less than half of the votes received by Lula. As it turned out, Lula won the election, but not before providing Wall Street and Washington an iron-clad guarantee that he would continue the market-friendly neoliberal policies of his predecessor, Fernando Enrique Cardoso (Petras and Veltmeyer 2003).

In Mexico, Washington's client, President Vincente Fox, has been unable to push through a massive privatization campaign because of Congressional opposition. Foreign Minister Jorge Castañeda has surpassed all previous government ministers in his servility to US empire builders. His anti-Cuban policies have discredited him both in Congress and among the wider public. Although both Fox and Castañeda will probably continue in office, their effectiveness as pliant clients of Washington is severely limited. The Zapatistas continue their efforts in Chiapas, and peasant and trade union struggles continue in some cases to achieve great successes, such as by blocking Fox's airport plans.

Washington's empire builders have support among the regimes in Central America, in the Caribbean (except Cuba) and in Chile, none of which have much strategic importance in terms of continental markets, population or strategic resources. In the Dominican Republic and Haiti significant extra-parliamentary popular movements oppose the US and neoliberal reforms.

It is abundantly clear that since 9/11 Washington has increased its military presence in Latin America. At the same time its client regimes have been severely weakened and their liberal policies have failed. The military-empire builders have returned to the strategies of the empire-building days of the Cold War era: military coups (Venezuela), state terror (Colombia), economic blackmail (Bolivia) and threats of direct intervention.

Nevertheless, the period after 9/11 saw the collapse of the neoliberal model and the emergence of powerful socio-political movements with a demonstrated capacity to defeat US client regimes. With few exceptions, the Latin American Left has struck back at the empire, the number of its supporters has grown geometrically, and it has demonstrated its effectiveness in blocking key legislation and isolating client presidents, reducing them to single-digit support.

Despite Washington's bellicose posturing and deepening military penetration, it has lost the hearts and minds of the great majority of Latin Americans. As we have seen, each US intervention and attempt to impose the imperial agenda has provoked massive popular resistance in the streets and at the ballot box. The most striking example was President Bush's demand that Cuba surrender the socialist content of its revolution. More than eight million Cubans marched and then voted overwhelmingly in favour of making socialism an irrevocable part of its constitution.

Conclusion

Since 9/11 the empire builders in charge of the White House have given themselves a free hand to act militarily and have largely rejected international constraints. They have repudiated international treaties from Kyoto to the International Court. Their unilateral politics have led to greater diplomatic isolation and weakened their capacity to build "coalitions." Equally important, their actions have brought together and activated millions of people opposed to globalization, war and human rights violations. Washington's clearly imperialist agenda has led to the re-emergence of anti-imperialist politics.

Washington's empire builders have abandoned all pretext of fighting for democracy. They have relied on non-elected, authoritarian rulers to carry out their policies: Pervez Musharraf, who won 99 percent of the vote in rigged elections in Pakistan; Gloria Macapagal Arroyo in the Philippines, who took power by deposing the incumbents; Hamid Karzai in Afghanistan, elected through the purchase of votes; Central Asian dictators in the ex-Soviet republics, who are key allies; the coup's leader-for-a-day Pedro Carmona in Venezuela, was a Washington protégé; and Eduardo Duhalde in Argentina, who was selected by Peronist bosses and approved by the US Embassy. These authoritarian rulers and subjects of empire faced rising opposition and increasing conflict. The struggle for democracy converges with the fight against the empire builders and their authoritarian clients.

A military-security definition of reality does not eliminate class and national conflicts; rather, it intensifies them. While the military-security empire builders (Donald Rumsfeld, Dick Cheney, John Reich, Paul Wolfowitz, Wesley Clark) consolidate the position of the Far Right in the Bush regime, they further polarize the European public and most of the third world against their imperial pretensions. While the empire builders flaunt their weapons systems, the economic foundations of the Empire show severe fissures and cracks. The "security blanket" precludes the emergence of self-corrective mechanisms from within the regime. In the post-9/11 period, it is empire that counts, and it is from growing anti-imperial movements abroad that change will come. If and when the economy cracks, forces within the United States may gain sufficient support to transform the Empire into a popular republic.

4. Argentina

Between Disintegration and Revolution

Throughout the early and mid-1990s the international financial institutions (the International Monetary Fund and the World Bank), the regional financial institution (the Inter-American Development Bank) and the G-7 countries (North America and Western Europe) praised Argentina's liberalization program as an economic model for the third world. Then-president Carlos Menem and his economic minister Domingo Cavallo promised the Argentine people that they would soon become part of the "First World."

Today Argentina is in total disintegration. Not only is the economy in recession/depression, but its banking system has collapsed, its unemployment rate has skyrocketed and more than half the population lives below the poverty line. The first part of this chapter examines the neoliberal policies advocated by the IFIs and the G-7 and implemented by the post–Menem regimes of Fernando de la Rua and Eduardo Duhalde from the 1990s to 2002. We argue that these policies and the socio-economic forces that implemented them led directly to the disintegration of the country. In order to measure the depth and scope of national disintegration, we focus on three sets of indicators: (1) the collapse of the economy at the levels of industry, finance and services; (2) the conditions of mass impoverishment — employment, income, health and nutrition — and (3) the breakdown of political authority and level of social conflict.

In the second part we turn to an examination of the causal links between the government's neoliberal policies, structures of state power and subordination to outside forces and the disintegration of Argentina. The last part of the chapter focuses on the consequences of Argentina's disintegration in relation to (1) its former patrons in the IFIs and G-7, (2) demands made by its erstwhile external benefactors and their implications, and (3) the alternatives to disintegration and subordination embodied in two distinct programs, Plan Phoenix and Plan Prometheus.

Our study and presentation of Argentina's political economy was guided by the following ideas:

- the Argentine economy is in a process of irrevocable and continuous regression, leading to the disintegration of national sovereignty, mass impoverishment and economic depression,
- the principal cause of this regression can be located in the neoliberal structures of power and policies that facilitated pillage of the economy, massive corruption and rising foreign debt with no commensurate growth in productive forces,
- failed neoliberal policies, economic pillage and spiraling foreign debt made Argentina unattractive to foreign investors and official lenders, who proceeded to demand greater sacrifices while effectively refusing new financing to refloat the regime and economy, and
- failed neoliberal states such as Argentina confront three alternatives: (1) to convert citizens of the country into neo-imperial colonial subjects; (2) to embark on a neo-structuralist project; or (3) to undertake a process of revolutionary transformation.

These ideas, derived from prior study and extensive field research, guide our inquiry into the causes of failed neoliberal states and the kind of purposeful action that can avoid, reform or revolutionize nations that have become ensnared in the neo-imperial trap.

Economic Collapse and Mass Impoverishment

No country has fallen more quickly and deeply into mass poverty or experienced as prolonged an economic collapse as has Argentina. Although most Latin American countries have applied neoliberal policies, none had done so as thoroughly and rapidly as Argentina had. Moreover, no Latin American country was as industrially advanced or had as diversified an economy as Argentina (Romero and Romero 2000; Schvarzer 2000). Argentina had the highest standard of living in the region, the most qualified and skilled labour force and the political leadership most determined to follow the precepts of the IFIs and the G-7.

Argentina is a test case of the efficacy or failures of the neoliberal approach under optimal conditions: a willing government, a well-developed infrastructure, a skilled labour force, long-term links to world markets and a significant middle class with consumption propensities compatible with Euro-American cultural patterns.

The results of more than twenty-seven years of neoliberalism provide us with an adequate time frame to evaluate its impact on an economy and society and avoid simply circumstantial or conjunctural causes.

The number of Argentines living below the poverty line has grown geometrically. In 1992 it was less than 15 percent, in 2000 it was 30 percent, but by June 2002 the Duhalde regime acknowledged that more than 18.2 million Argentines, 51.4 percent, were living below the poverty line (*Clarin*, 10 June 2002). Of these, 7.8 million were indigents, according to Siempro (Sistema de Información, Monitoreo y Evaluación de Programas Sociales [System of Information, Monitoring and Evaluation of Social Programs], an official institution under the jurisdiction of the president. Children and adolescents living in poverty make up almost half of the poor. Immiseration has been growing at an accelerating rate. Between January and May 2002 the number of poor grew by 3.8 million, or 762,000 a month, 25,000 a day. The rate of indigent poor was growing even faster than the overall poverty rate. For example, in 1998, 28.9 percent of the poor were indigent, in June 2002 they accounted for 42.6 percent. From October 2001 to October 2002, according to official sources (*Clarin*, 11 May 2003: 8), the poverty rate increased from 38.3 to 57.5 percent, while the rate of indigence more than doubled, increasing from 13.6 to 27.9 percent. The extreme poverty is manifested in the high rates of malnutrition among children, for example, among more than 58 percent of the children in Matanzas, a working-class suburb of Buenos Aires. In the interior there are numerous reports of children fainting in school for lack of food, and more than 60 percent of the children in Misiones suffer from malnutrition — a result of government cutbacks in school meal programs to meet G-7 and IMF demands.

Not including the top 10 percent of the population and foreign capitalists, the working sectors of the population and pensioners have experienced an average 67 percent decline in monthly income. This decline has been profound and sudden and it continues. Speaking from here onwards in US dollars, in 1997, the United Nations Development Programme (UNDP) calculated Argentina's per capita annual income as $8,950, but by March 2002 it was only $3,197 (*La Nación,* 17 March 2002: 3). This decline affects all geographical regions of the country. If we use as rough indicators of class the different regions of the province of Buenos Aires, we can approximate the social impact of the crisis (see Table 4.1). The income in the capital city of Buenos Aires, which we can take as largely middle class, saw average incomes fall from $909 a month in December 2001 to $364 by March 2002; in the working-class suburbs (*conurbano*) of the city of Buenos Aires, income fell from $506 to $202; in the province of Buenos Aires, income fell from $626 to $251. The largest decline is among workers in the informal sector and among pensioners. In the capital, income of the "informals" dropped from $643 to $257; in the working class suburbs, from $334 to $134; and, in the province, from $395 to $158. Among pensioners the decline was similarly devastating: from $437 to $175 in the capital, from $320 to $128 in the working-class suburbs and from $361 to $144 in the province (*La Nación,* 17 March 2002: 3).

The situation is far worse in the other provinces, where pay scales are lower, unemployment is higher and there are frequent three-to-six-month delays in payment of salaries and pensions.

For the working and middle class, the loss of formal employment brings a sharp decline in income. With unemployment doubling between 1999 and May 2002, the number of destitute and poor from the former working class and middle class has grown geometrically. Employed wage earners in the private sector of the capital who earned $904 in December 2001 were under-employed and earning $257 in the informal sector three months later. With a 30 percent rise in prices during the same period, the real purchasing power in December 2001 dollars was reduced even further.

The decline of income among the different occupational categories indicates the absolute and relative decline of the middle class, a clear process of proletarianization: bank employees in the capital have seen their income decline by nearly 60 percent, from $1,081 to $432 per month, and public employees in the capital have experienced a drop from $1,144 to $458 per month. The income as of April 2002 of the former middle class did not cover their basic necessities of rent, food, transport, school and

Table 4.1 Average Income Structure after the Devaluation (US$)

Type of income	Capital of BuenosAires Dec. 2001	Capital of BuenosAires Mar. 2002	Suburbs Dec. 2001	Suburbs Mar. 2002	Greater Buenos Aires Dec. 2001	Greater Buenos Aires Mar. 2002
Average overall income	909	364	506	202	626	251
Self-employed	881	353	392	157	522	209
Bank workers	1,081	432	735	294	848	339
Informal workers	643	257	334	134	395	158
Public employees	1,144	458	624	250	810	324
Private employees	904	362	550	220	648	259
Pensioners	437	175	320	128	361	144

Source: *La Nación,* 17 March 2002: 3.

health expenses, and hence the necessity for multiple employment — which is near to impossible — for all household members. The downward mobility of the middle class is clear if we compare their current salary with that of employed workers before the devaluation. Private salaries among suburban workers were $550 before the devaluation, but middle-class incomes after the devaluation were only 75 percent of former working-class salaries.

If we take the figure of $400 as the cut-off for the poverty line, and $250 as the cut-off line for indigence, we find that every occupational category of the working class in the suburbs or greater Buenos Aires is below the poverty line and several categories are indigent. In the capital, 60 percent of the occupational groups are below the poverty line (the self-employed and the informal sector and private sector workers).

Pensioners who depend mainly on their pensions are indigent in all geographical sectors, as are all unemployed workers (25–30 percent of the labour force) living in the suburbs and greater Buenos Aires. Even if we assume that some unemployed workers are working in the informal sector, almost all are near or below the line of indigence. The massive growth of unemployment to between 25 and 30 percent nationally, to 40 to 60 percent in the working-class suburbs and to even higher in some of the former one-industry towns of the interior, the downward mobility and the impoverishment of the working and middle classes are reminiscent of the worst years of the US Depression of the 1930s and of Weimar Germany in the 1920s.

Accompanying and interrelated with the impoverishment of the mass of the middle and working class is the concentration of wealth in the ruling and upper middle class and among foreign capitalists and bankers. In 1974 the top decile received 28 percent of national income, in 1992 slightly more than 34 percent and in 2001 more than 37 percent; the poorest decile received 2.2 percent in both 1974 and 1992 and 1.3 percent in 2001, before the devaluation and sharp increase of unemployment (*Clarin*, 31 March 2002: 10). In 1974 the top decile of income earners received twelve times the income of the poorest. If we take into account the common understatement of income by the wealthy, the government statistical office estimates that current inequalities are much greater, that the top decile earns forty times that of the poorest decile.

Together, the upper classes — the ruling elite and the upper middle class — apparently received 53 percent of declared income prior to the devaluation, although the real proportion was closer to 65 percent. Given the fact that the upper classes were able to withdraw their funds ($30–40 billion) from the banks and send their money outside the country and avoid confiscation (as of December 2001), the percentage of wealth in the hands of the upper classes is probably close to 80 percent. Neoliberalism has had the profound dual structural effect of impoverishing the working and middle class and enriching the upper classes. In the early 1990s, unequal growth of national incomes based on the entry of speculative funds, foreign borrowing and privatization of public firms artificially and temporarily raised average income. However, when these short-term injections of capital ended, incomes and employment plummeted for 80 percent of the waged and self-employed labour force, while mobility of capital, high liquidity and nonwage sources of income for the very rich protected their wealth and led to a vast increase in inequalities.

While impoverishment and income inequalities increased with the recession/depression beginning in 1998, the precipitous fall in income and living standards for the middle class (40 percent of the population in Buenos Aires) took place with the onset of the depression of 2001–02, followed by the confiscation/freeze of bank accounts in December 2001, and the subsequent devaluation and inflation. The estimate of financial experts is that, at the beginning of 2001, Argentines had $86.5 billion in mostly foreign-owned banks in largely dollar accounts (Llorens and Cafiero 2002). During 2001 and especially beginning in April to November, the upper classes withdrew $40 billion from the banks and sent it out of the country. In December the government froze accounts and subsequently converted them to pesos (as of June 1, 2002, from 3.3 to 3.5 pesos to the dollar). In effect, the accounts were reduced from $45 billion to approximately $13 billion and are declining since there is no indexing. The regime's attempt to convert the remainder into state bonds redeemable in ten years at 2 percent interest devalued the savings even further, given the 30 percent rate of inflation for the first quarter of 2002. This attempt by the regime to swindle the remaining savings was prevented by massive demonstrations of the impoverished middle class who stormed the banks and whose pot-banging (*cacerolazos*) created a storm that blew all the way into Congress.

The social disintegration and polarization is rooted in the collapse of the Argentine economy, and the deep and chronic industrial depression. During the first three months of 2002, industrial activity declined by more than 18 percent (*Clarin,* 18 April 2002: 11). Industrial regression accelerated from 2 percent in April 2001 and 4 percent in July, to 10 percent in September, 12 percent in November and 18 percent in March 2002. Automobile production was down 55 percent in March 2002 compared to the same period the year before, while textiles and manufacturing were down 48 percent. Over the same period, industry declined by ten percent. The number of plant closures accelerated throughout the 1999–2002 period, reaching unprecedented levels in the last trimester of 2001 and the first half of 2002. In early 2002 almost three-quarters of industrialists predicted that the downturn would worsen. Unused industrial capacity was running at more than 50 percent in most sectors of the economy, including metal, textiles and auto parts.

The financial system is nearly bankrupt, in part because of large-scale financial transfers to home offices by foreign-owned subsidiaries. The foreign debt grew from $58.7 billion in 1990 to $139.9 billion in 1998, while capital flight and interest payments over the same period grew to $115 billion and $81.7 billion, respectively (Basualdo and Lozano 2000: 60–66). In other words, external borrowing largely financed capital flight and part of the mushrooming debt payments, leaving a net deficit in capital flows. This eroded the economy's capacity to sustain growth and subsequently led to the recession and further budget cuts, which in turn turned the recession into a depression and a partial debt default. The massive withdrawal of funds, aided and abetted by foreign banks, led to the confiscation of the savings of millions of Argentines and a virtual collapse of the financial system. Throughout 1999–2001, IMF loans merely served to pay back private banks and the IFIs, while exacerbating the debt problem, deepening the recession and lowering living standards. In order to get short-term loans, Argentina was paying 16 percent over US Treasury notes as late as August 2001 (*Financial Times,* 23 August 2001: 12). Once the fall took place, the IFIs, World Bank and G-7 were all unwilling to lend new money, unless the central government repealed its "Economic Subversive Law" (designed to prosecute illicit banking practices), abolished the provincial currencies which kept local economies afloat and fired several hundreds of thousands of health, education and other public employees.

The key concern of the IFIs with repealing the Economic Subversive Law was that it was an instrument to prosecute the G-7 banks involved in the illegal transfer of more than $50 billion in the year 2001–02. (In June 2002, under IMF pressure, the law was repealed). While the IMF blamed the bank withdrawals of panicked Argentine savers for the financial crisis, substantial data demonstrates that private, principally foreign-owned banks had already consummated a massive transfer of funds out of the country and were unwilling to recapitalize the banks (Llorens and Cafiero 2002). Furthermore, the IMF and World Bank pressured the Argentine government to assume the private banks' obligations to their depositors and issue ten-year, state-guaranteed bonds in lieu of direct payments to holders of savings accounts. In the absence of funds and an unwillingness of the head office to recapitalize their Argentine subsidiaries, private banks claimed to be on the verge of bankruptcy. With a threatened run on the banks by depositors anxious to withdraw their savings, the only measure that would prevent a massive collapse was a freeze on withdrawals. At least, this was the position taken by the government of the day.

To sum up, not only has the neoliberal experiment impoverished most of the people, ruined the country's industries, driven more than a quarter of firms into or close to bankruptcy, and robbed the middle class of their savings, but it has also undermined the very foundations of the capitalist economy. In addition to creating monumental inequalities, the neoliberal economy led to the pillage of the economy, with the transfer of tens of billions of dollars out of the economy and into overseas investments, saving accounts, real estate and treasury notes. For capitalists with fixed capital and limited working capital, the neoliberal policies had disastrous consequences because of exorbitant interest rates and unfair competition from the unrestricted entry of cheap imports, and the collapse of the domestic economy because of high unemployment rates and the plunge in middle-class living standards. Neoliberalism is like "the sow which eats her own kind."

Causes of the Collapse

The immediate cause of the collapse of Argentine capitalism was the role foreign owned banks and the IFIs, led by the IMF, played in emptying the country's financial system. The longer-term causes are rooted in the regressive structural changes (privatization, structural adjustment programs, open markets) and the quasi-criminal "deregulation" of the economy that led not only to the collapse of domestic production but also to the wholesale pillage of the economy and millions of saving accounts.

Economic experts and other apologists for the financial elite argue that the bank crisis was the result of savers withdrawing their deposits and removing them from the banking system. While withdrawals by savers was a cause of the crisis, it was not the main or determining cause. During the period leading up to the crisis (February–November 2001), the financial assets (loans and other credits) of the financial system declined by \$44.8 billion, of which \$37.3 billion came from the private sector (83.4 percent), and of which \$26.5 billion (59.1 percent) came from the ten biggest private banks. In other words, in the months leading up to the crisis, the ten leading banks moved approximately $27 billion out of the Argentine financial system. This is evident from an analysis of the assets and liabilities of the banks — "*other* credits by financial intermediaries" (assets) and "*other* obligations by financial intermediaries" (liabilities). The existence of these categories reveals that the Argentine financial system operated on two levels: a formal system of deposits and loans, and an "informal sector" where mega-accounts operated, largely to launder funds and carry out speculative activity in the financial sector. In February 2001 the "other" categories amounted to $56.9 billion in assets and $60 billion in obligations (Llorens and Cafiero 2002). By November the total of "others" declined to $25 billion in assets and $35 billion in obligations. A closer analysis reveals that of the $25 billion decline in assets, more than 74 percent took place among the ten biggest banks. The IMF loans to Argentina covered the growing drain of resources out of the financial system by the financial elites, while imposing harsher cuts in public spending and investment. The triple phenomena of deepening economic depression, financial flight and growing indebtedness was caused by the alliance of the IFIs, foreign and local big financiers and foreign-owned banks. Small and medium-sized Argentine depositors were *victims* of a covert financial swindle, not the perpetrators, as the economic experts charged. Their desperate but belated effort to withdraw their savings was a reaction to the financial swindle executed by financial elites. Most small and medium savers, however, were not successful. The bank's liabilities after the flight of big accounts and the drying up of overseas credits far exceeded their assets; with the economic crisis, many of their outstanding loans were delinquent and there was no way that headquarters would inject new funds to cover the demands of depositors. The government intervened to save the banks by effectively freezing all deposits and preventing depositors from recovering their savings. The gross class character of the government's financial rescue plan infuriated the dispossessed middle and lower class. The subsequent devaluation of the peso in effect robbed them of two-thirds the face value of their frozen savings and depressed their income, while the upper-middle and ruling classes who got their money out of the financial system were able to lower their costs of living, production and consumption by a commensurate 65 percent.

The financial collapse and economic depression are rooted in neoliberal economic policies and the context in which they were inserted. Even more fundamental are the nature and structure of the ruling and governing classes who imposed the neoliberal model that has destroyed the Argentine economy. Unlike much of the rest of Latin America, Argentina was a highly industrialized country with one of the highest percentages of workers employed in the manufacturing sector in the world during the mid-1970s. Even by the late 1980s, Argentina was still proportionately the most industrialized country in the region. With a highly skilled labour force that was relatively better paid than the rest of Latin America, and a welfare system for unionized workers comparable to those in Europe, Argentina had a substantial domestic market. It possessed some of the richest and most extensive cultivatable land in the world, a very competitive agro-export sector, as well as plentiful energy sources (oil, natural gas, hydro power). In short, Argentina possessed an attractive market for exporters, profitable resources for investors and substantial banking deposits for overseas bankers. Rapid liberalization of the economy had a shattering effect on this heavily industrialized country. Argentine industry was pressured by cheap consumer imports from low-wage areas (Asia) and imports from high tech, large-scale and heavily subsidized Euro-American manufactures. The liberal argument that the competition would make Argentine enterprises more efficient was false — few Argentine companies had the scale and financing to compete with the top US and European multinationals, and even the lowest-paid Argentine workers could not compete with dollar-a-day Chinese workers. The rapid lowering of barriers precluded any preparation for competition, and the lack of reciprocity in lowering subsidies and barriers in the United States and Europe prevented Argentine companies that were competitive from capturing overseas markets.

The experience of the United States and the countries of the European Union with liberalization policies has been a gradual, selective process, at least in contrast to the Argentine experience. Free convertibility in Europe did not take place until the economies there were on their way to sustained expansion, which for some did not take place until well into the 1960s. Trade barriers, including quotas, tariffs and non-traditional constraints (health barriers, unfair trade and anti-dumping rules) are still frequently used to protect non-competitive sectors. Massive state subsidies and fiscal deficits are used to promote exports and stimulate domestic growth.

In Argentina the trade barriers came crashing down. The peso was tied to the dollar, limiting monetary policies to stimulate the economy. Subsidies were cut, and debt payments took priority over productive investments. Loans were secured by privatizing strategies affecting lucrative sectors of the economy, undermining public earnings, increasing costs of production and thus lessening competitiveness. Privatization led to severe cutbacks in transport linking the provincial economies, undermining their industrial and commercial transactions. In mineral- and raw material-export economies such as Chile, liberalization opened the economy up to foreign investment in established export sectors that were competitive and complementary to the industrial capitalist economy, but in Argentina's much more developed and diversified economy, industry was adversely affected. The flood of imports and the decline of national industries led to bankruptcies and unemployment, the conversion of manufacturers into importers and merchants, and, in the provinces, an inflation of the public sector as the employer of last resort. Large sums of investment money moved from risky, productive activity into high interest-bearing financial instruments (Basualdo 2001).

The Menem regime gave the appearance of an "affluent regime," based on heavy borrowing and windfall income from the sell-off of public properties. Most capital inflows increased upper-class consumption and facilitated wholesale corruption of the entire political class and its entourage of public officials, judges, customs officers, police and military officials (Sbattella 2001: 75–90). Foreign bankers were willing to lend because interest rates were from ten to twenty points above European and US rates, ad there was easy liquidity given free convertibility, and the *de facto* dollarization of the economy ensured monetary stability. Thus each step of the liberalization process weakened the fundamentals of the economy: the domestic economy shrank, entrepreneurs fled into apparently lucrative speculative activity, debt payments skyrocketed, loans-for-privatization deals were finite and reaching their limits, and external flight of capital accelerated as the upper classes sensed the whole liberal edifice would eventually collapse and there would be neither a productive system nor monetary resources to revive it.

Crucial to the collapse of the economic bubble economy was the behaviour of the Argentine grand bourgeoisie (Azpiazu and Schorr 2002: 73–90). Powerfully ensconced in the Menem regime, they were the initial beneficiaries of the privatization process and the loans from overseas lenders (Basualdo 2001), and were also the group that dictated economic policy. The Menem regime's point of reference for developing the liberal agenda was first and foremost the dominant Argentine classes, who had investments overseas, were tightly linked to overseas banks via joint investments in privatized banks and via foreign loans and demanded a peso easily convertible into dollars. Liberalization taken to the maximum allowed this "transnational" Argentine bourgeoisie to buy public banks and enterprises on the cheap and sell them to foreign capital (Basualdo and

Azpiazu 2002). Deregulation of the banks allowed massive transfers of funds out of the country and the laundering of illicit gains. Cheap imports, easy loans and fast exits of funds were the Argentine elite's definition of liberalization.

For obvious reasons the G-7 countries and the IFIs were wildly enthusiastic: they gained control over banks and deposits, and over lucrative telecommunication, airline, oil and other money-earning public enterprises, and encouraged the regime to move full speed ahead with reckless abandon.

As the domestic economy, particularly in the provinces, collapsed, the provincial governments ran huge debts — partly to finance corrupt political machines to sustain the national government and partly to avoid popular revolts. Unlike in South Korea, China and Japan, large-scale corruption did not grease the wheels of national production: bribes greased the hands that sold off lucrative public enterprises to foreign investors, who stripped assets and reduced local production in favour of large-scale speculative activity. There was an inverse relation: as corruption grew, industry declined, tax receipts were negligible and competitiveness became an empty slogan.

Foreign ownership, which liberal advocates described as a dynamic force for sustained growth, also turned out otherwise. The Argentine experience describes a vicious parabola: an initial increase in foreign investment encouraged the Menem regime to exuberant (or delirious) deregulation and privatization, which led to a large-scale influx of capital — portfolio and direct — followed by a sharp decline as lucrative sectors were taken over, workers were fired, local markets shrank and massive outflows occurred. The result was one short spurt of growth in the early to mid-1990s, followed by decline and collapse. This sequence had been entirely predictable as foreign investors initially took advantage of easy buyouts with almost guaranteed profits (in monopoly markets) and exorbitant rates of interest, and then silently but quickly withdrew funds, leaving the economy with few assets and a highly uncertain future. The IFIs led and followed the parabola, conditioning public loans on greater liberalization during the initial period, in support of foreign investors, and then, as the economy ran down and liabilities and social discontent mounted, imposing even harsher conditions for further financing.

The process of regime-IFI negotiations changed over time. In the beginning, when many resources, markets and opportunities were available to foreign investors, the IFIs gave the regime a blank cheque, lending billions of dollars and giving the green light to private bankers and overseas investors to exploit the "emerging market" for extraordinary profits. The result was a major takeover of lucrative banks, telecommunications and petroleum by Spanish banks and multinationals and US investors. Meanwhile, foreign investors moved in on the agro-industrial sector, retail trade (mega malls), real estate and hotels, in association with a small nuclei of the Argentine economic elite and sectors of the kleptocratic political class headed by the extended Menem family.

The first major adverse effect was a slashing of employees in a process of preparing public enterprises for privatization. The state fired hundreds of thousands of workers in the telephone, railroad and waterworks sectors, assuming the economic costs and taking responsibility for repressing the ensuing protest. Many cities in the interior, such as the petroleum city of Neuquen, were turned from prosperous cities into ghost towns, with unemployment rates rising to 30 to 40 percent. Promises of "alternative employment" were never kept, as provincial and local officials linked to the central government either stole funds outright or used them to finance their political machines, through expansion of unproductive "administrative" jobs.

The second negative result was the reduction of services and transport, isolating regions from regional, national or even international markets and suppliers. The balance sheets of the privatized companies were based on enterprise profits, not the returns and revenues of the multiplicity of industries and farms which depended on the power, energy, telecommunications and transport networks. Thus, while the balance sheets of private, foreign-owned enterprises showed up in the black, the outlying economies were in the red and becoming increasingly dependent on central government subsidies. Moreover, the public costs of maintaining infrastructure to sustain the privatized enterprises increased, while state revenue declined, thanks to large tax exemptions and subsidies. The net effect was increased public spending and intervention to promote privatization — while revenues declined — and a need for social budget cuts, and increased overseas borrowing at increasing rates of interest, as foreign debt doubled and interest payments increased 2.5 times between 1992 and 1998. Privatization deprived Argentina of low-cost inputs for industry, increased transport costs and overvalued the peso, thus pricing Argentine products with high value added out of the international and even regional markets. Far from increasing the competitiveness of Argentine industry, liberalization led it down the road to bankruptcy and the de-capitalization of basic research and development (R&D). Support for industry and innovation was severely depleted as public funding for university and research centres declined and private funds increasingly turned to the bloated and high-earning financial sector.

The Menem government's unilateral lowering of tariff barriers weakened local enterprises without rewarding efficient producers, especially because the regime failed to secure reciprocal agreements with the US and EU to lower their trade barriers. The net result was that Argentina was playing by two sets of rules: following the rigid precepts of liberalism in relation to its economy while accepting the flexible "liberal/protectionist" rules of its major trading partners.

The continuation and deepening of liberalization policies throughout the 1990s — the time bomb ready to explode — was based on the structures of state power. Menem led a highly authoritarian regime which bypassed Congress or bribed legislators, packed the courts to secure compliant majorities, centralized power in non-elected officials and organized and generally financed a powerful party-state machine that inhibited or isolated organized opposition in the poorest neighbourhoods — until the collapse of the late 1990s. In addition, selective state-party thuggery organized by the intelligence agencies silenced media-based critics through threats and occasional assassinations.

The centralization of legislative and executive powers in the presidency — in his very person — and the dictatorial methods Menem used to legislate (most industries and banks were privatized via presidential decrees) facilitated rapid and extensive liberalization. The concentration and centralization of Argentine capital was both a cause and consequence of liberalization and grew in tandem with the centralization of executive power. The political reference points and strategic outlook of the Menem regime were profoundly influenced by structural links to the big economic groups that emerged during the dictatorship and thereafter (Azpiazu et al. 2001). While the internal composition of the big groups varied, their outward politics were consistently liberal and tied to broadening and deepening ties to European and US financial networks. For President Menem and his economic czar Cavallo, these big economic groups and their international circuits and partners were the economic reality: the purpose of the state was to cater to their interests, consolidate their structures and expand their opportunities. Neoliberalization meant the elaboration of policies facilitating the big economic groups' buyout of public enterprises, the easy transfer of capital abroad, facile access to foreign loans and socialization by the state of private losses.

The state under Menem was involved in funding the consolidation of private economic empires, rather than financing productive investments by rising small and medium entrepreneurs. Its liberalization of trade allowed the big economic groups to turn to finance, real estate and commerce rather than to investments in upgrading productivity in manufacturing. Neoliberalism meant that the regime specialized in selling off public resources, not increasing production or productivity. The big Argentine economic groups in turn bought public enterprises not to convert them into efficient productive or service units, but to resell them at a profit to foreign capital. The large influx of EU and US capital changed the configuration of the Argentine state from a liberal to a neocolonial liberal state, which, lacking domestic revenues, depended increasingly on overseas loans and export income generated by foreign-owned enterprises.

The transition from a mixed economy to a liberal and then neocolonial liberal economy accompanied the rise and fall of the "vicious parabola" of the Argentine economy, a sequence that could be described as like a Greek tragedy, where the hubris of the liberal protagonists foreshadowed the ultimate collapse of a deeply flawed relationship. The analogy, however, is itself deeply flawed, because the protagonists — the Menems, the bankers, the IFIs — are not the ones who in the end suffered downfall, the Argentine nation and 80 percent of its people are the tragic victims.

Consequences: Disintegration, Abandonment and Destitution

As the Argentine economy went from recession to a full-scale depression, as industrial production declined from 6 percent in the last quarter of 2001 to 15 percent in the first quarter of 2002, and as the financial system headed for a crash and it became apparent that Argentina would default on most of its foreign debt, the IFIs, the overseas banks and the G-7 countries refused new loans except under the most onerous of conditions (*Financial Times*, 14 May 2002: 5). In December 2000 the banks granted a $40-billion, IMF-led package, and in August 2001 the IMF granted the tottering De la Rua regime an $8-billion standby credit, $5 billion of which went to the Argentine central bank and out of the country as the upper middle class moved billions between January and November. Several billion dollars were destined for debt restructuring, in effect paying domestic and overseas bondholders. Neither allocation did anything to stimulate the local economy, lower interest rates or prevent private withdrawals of bank deposits. In effect, the IMF loan to Argentina increased its debt from $130 billion to nearly $140 billion in 2001 without tackling the fundamental structural problems, thus setting in motion the final collapse of December 2001.

The reason the loans failed to "save" the Argentine economy was because they were not meant to; they merely provided funds to be recycled through the economy to "save" the upper class and the big bond holders. Big lenders recognized the perilous conditions: the interest-rate spread between Argentine government debt paper and US treasury notes rose to 16.7 percent by late August 2001. By November, speculators were not buying Argentine paper at any price, as the government inevitably headed for default.

As the Argentine economy collapsed, its overseas lenders and subsidiary banks pressured the regime to freeze deposits, threatening to pull down the financial system and withdraw from Argentina. The government complied. It devalued the peso, reducing the bank's obligation to its dollar depositors. The banks delegated the IMF to play the lead role in negotiations to recover their loans, even as the economy was starved for new funding and state and private investments.

Lacking profitable public resources, companies or banks to generate earnings thanks to his earlier privatization policies, the so-called "economic genius" of the Argentine miracle, Domingo Cavallo, received no lifeline from his friends on Wall Street. What Cavallo mistakenly assumed to be his personal genius and confidence among world bankers turned into a mirage — the banks were not interested in floating an economy they had bought and pillaged and were now in the process of discarding as they moved on to more lucrative sites. Cavallo's secret formula is familiar to any financial swindler: he rolled overdue high-interest government bonds into bonds with even higher interest rates, an unsustainable process destined to collapse.

The response of the IMF to the eventual collapse was embodied in its mission to Argentina in April 2002. Led by Anoop Singh, the mission intervened, interviewed and publicly dictated policy for each and every aspect of Argentine domestic economic and social policy (*Página 12*, 14 April 2002: 6–7). In the midst of the recession, he demanded that Argentina cut spending, eliminate provincial currencies and debts, liquidate debtor enterprises and facilitate creditor takeovers, and abolish banking legislation which provided sanctions on foreign banks engaged in illegal movements of currency. In other words, Singh demanded a state austerity policy geared to securing a government surplus to repay overseas bankers, while providing facilities for further outward transfers of funds and easier takeovers of indebted enterprises by foreign banks.

In political-economic terms, this was picking the meat off the skeleton. With Argentina in a major depression, the last thing it needed was to balance its budget and reduce public spending, especially with six out of ten workers unemployed in the poor suburbs and three out of ten nationally.

However, Horst Kohler, president of the IMF, thought that Argentina should be squeezed further. "Argentina," he stated in April 2002, "must take the bitter medicine to get out of the crisis." The "bitter medicine" was more cuts in public spending, elimination of more public services and greater unemployment. As Kohler himself admitted, at least 450,000 public employees would have to be fired, on top of the 30 percent unemployed. This would raise the number of unemployed to between 35 and 40 percent, a catastrophic situation. He then proceeded to blame the victim, saying, "The problems that Argentina is suffering from are of domestic origin" (*Clarin,* 18 April 2002: 8), as if ten years of IMF-conditioned loans, overseas missions, adjustment programs and liberal ideology had played no role in bringing about the crisis.

US Secretary of the Treasury Paul O'Neill weighed in on the side of the IMF's "final squeeze," endorsing its bailout of the bankers and the takeover of the remaining sectors of the economy. But he demanded, in typically euphemistic language, "a political solution" (*Clarin*, 21 April 2002: 6). He called for a strong authoritarian regime capable of ramming the mass job firings, budget cuts and abolition of local currencies policy down the throats of the impoverished Argentines. O'Neill questioned "the leadership capacity" of the Duhalde government. In an interview, (*Página 12*, 21 April 2002: 2), O'Neill said Argentina's problems boiled down to a single question: Will the Argentine government do what it has to do, namely, implement the IMF policies? What O'Neill and others in the IFIs and G-7 mean by "political will" is precisely the will to override the interests and survival of 33 million Argentines, and elected congressional officials, governors and mayors, and force upon them further bankruptcies and unemployment, pushing beyond the 53 percent level of impoverishment to satisfy overseas bankers and investors.

The EU took an equally hard line on Argentina. According to the then French economic minister Laurent Fabius, "The responses that the Argentine government has given us [related to the IMF austerity prescriptions] are not satisfactory" (quoted in *Página 12*, 21 April 2002: 3). Probably the most offensive remarks came from Anne Krueger, second in command at the IMF, a US appointee and a former Stanford professor. In an interview in the *Financial Times* (20 April 2001) she claimed that "the Argentine authorities are not sufficiently realistic." Realism, according to Krueger, means that in the midst of a depression, one should cut public spending, lower living standards and increase unemployment. The "realism" referred to is the world of finance capital and its voracious appetite to squeeze even more interest payments from bankrupt provinces, businesses and public treasuries, to withdraw even more savings from Argentina with impunity.

The US embassy staff in Argentina went even further. Political attaché Michael Matera claimed the crisis was caused not only by Argentina's political leaders but by the Argentine people. "The viewpoint of international economists is incompatible with the national mentality of the Argentines. Argentinians have a collective incapacity to change; they are immature and paranoid" (*Página 12*, 21 April 2002: 3).

There is some evidence that a prime reason for the European-US-IMF hard line is Argentina's unilateral default on its $140 billion debt. According to one Argentine congressman, an IMF functionary told him, "What we will never forgive is your Congress people celebrating and applauding after [ex-president-for-a-week] Adolfo Rodriguez Saa declared the default." From this vantage point the hard line is meant to warn any other Latin nation that contemplates debt default of the harsh consequences.

The Duhalde regime, which is structurally tied to Argentine transnational financial capital, the agro-export sector and foreign capital, can only find a solution via an agreement with the IMF, which presumably would loosen the purse strings of private lenders and lead to a renegotiation of impending debt payments. The Duhalde regime's unwillingness to develop an alternative plan, as dissident Argentine economists demand, is based on major, longstanding structural links between the regime and the ruling class. Given the total discredit of that ruling class, the disastrous results of its policies for 80 percent of the Argentine population, the disintegration of the nation and massive active opposition, Duhalde's political authority is virtually nil and his decision-making power is narrowly circumscribed.

The historical background for the finance-pillage-abandon sequence of G-7 and IFI policies and the shift towards a hard-line position is based on two considerations. Over the previous fourteen years European and US capital got everything they wanted from the Menem and De la Rua regimes. However, the easy and lucrative pickings of the past are no longer available, only intensive, as opposed to extensive, exploitation can provide returns at this point in history.

The previous history of IMF priority setting and Argentine government compliance has conditioned lenders to assume regime obedience rather than a need for negotiation and reciprocity. Overseas lenders have always been aware of the venal character of the Argentine ruling and political class, but they were willing to lend funds, even if later pilfered, as long as they could, in turn, pillage the economy. However, with pillage completed, the choice now is between returns to the banks or mismanagement of funds to sustain corrupt provincial electoral machines. The lenders are demanding that the political class cut off the provincial bosses and their bloated public sector, to meet external obligations. If this means adding to the opposition and undermining political support, then the bankers insist, by all means take extraordinary measures, show political will, turn the regime into an authoritarian dictatorship. How this leadership would rule, even with dictatorial power, given the eventual impoverishment of three-quarters of the population, is a question which Krueger, O'Neill, Kohler and Wolfenson do not ask and do not have an answer to.

Nevertheless, the IFIs and the G-7 know that, structurally, Duhalde has no alternative except refinancing by an IMF-led group of bankers. They know he is a captive and lifelong representative of foreign capital and its domestic partners and therefore easy prey to pressure. The perceived vulnerability of the regime encourages a "hard-line" approach.

A third factor conditioning the IMF and G-7's hard-line response is the increasing radicalization of the Argentine population and the massive, almost daily protests, demonstrations and popular uprisings. The "risk factor" in Argentina is extremely high in the eyes of investment bankers. The fear is that, if Duhalde falls or is overthrown, a populist nationalist regime might be formed and renege on any agreements. Paradoxically, the demands of the IMF and G-7, if met, would likely ignite a major uprising. The higher the IMF and G-7 raise the bar to secure funding, the harder the fall of the regime after jumping it. Implicit in hard-line economic strategy, especially among the political and economic elite in Washington and Madrid, is the idea that the Argentine military would intervene to overthrow an popular adversarial regime. However, a military coup in the present context would take place in a political vacuum bereft of social support.

The style and substance of Argentina's relations with the G-7 speaks to a new imperialism: pillage of the economy, growth of vast inequalities, economic stagnation followed by profound and enduring depression and massive impoverishment of the population as a consequence of the greatest concentration of wealth in Argentine history (Petras and Veltmeyer 2001a). The new imperialism works directly through the inter-state system and subsidiary financial institutions such as the IMF to dictate policy. The April 2002 mission of the IMF, with its public pronouncements on every aspect of the Argentine economy, and the blatant dictates of the US embassy and the G-7 economic ministers strongly resonate with the colonial relationships of the past. The subservience of the Argentine regime and its willingness to implement policies which profoundly lower living standards, to meet imperial demands, speaks loudly and clearly of a new type of colonial empire. This new colonialism, imposed on a formerly industrialized country with relatively high third world living standards, has not only provoked greater economic inequalities but also extreme political and social polarization, which is highly skewed against the imperial-colonial powers and the entire Argentine political class.

Popular Uprisings

In a trip to Tucuman Province in April 2002 we visited the vast *villas de miseria,* or slums, and spoke to some of the multitude of poor and destitute: they told us that between 2001 and 2002, in just one year, the number of children suffering from malnutrition had increased six fold. The combination of mass firings, inflation and the cut-off of food rations has made the poor destitute, unable to meet even their basic food needs.

One week later, while meeting with a union delegate from the bank workers' union in Buenos Aires, we were informed that the banks were planning massive firings.[1] One month later, a newspaper close to the financial elite, *La Nación* (19 May 2002), published a report that the banks were planning to fire two-thirds of their employees, 80,000 of the 120,000, and reduce the pay of their remaining staff.

By early July the streets were noisy with demonstrators, crime was rampant, university professors with three positions (*cátedras*) were making $200 a month, highways were blocked and the pot-banging, impoverished retirees and former middle class were meeting to demand the ouster of not only the regime but also the entire political class.

The deepening political polarization in Argentina has taken a variety of social and political forms: a national uprising overthrowing the De la Rua regime in December 2001; permanent rebellion in the provinces; constant mass mobilizations of the unemployed (*piqueteros*); and impoverished middle- and working-class neighbourhood assemblies (*caceroleros*).

On December 19 and 20, 2001, hundreds of thousands of Argentines took to the streets to protest the government's declaration of a state of siege and the banning of public demonstrations; the confiscation of $40 billion in savings; the deepening recession; and the 23 percent unemployment rate (*El Pikete*, 2, no. 6).[2] The uprising which finally forced President De la Rua to resign and exit the presidential palace via a helicopter was the culmination of a series of mass road blockages by the unemployed *piqueteros*; pot-banging neighbourhood marches and assemblies; provincial mobilizations; and attacks on governors, mayors and federal officials. While each particular mass action had its own specific social base, forms of direct action and priorities, all converged in rejecting repayment of the foreign debt, IMF austerity programs and confiscation of savings.

The mass unemployed workers movement, discussed in more detail in Chapter 9, was the detonator for the uprising of December 19/20, even if the organized unemployed were not a decisive force on the day of the ouster of the president. The Unemployed Workers Movement (MTD) has spread geographically throughout Argentina and escalated its struggle as the recession turned into a depression and millions of former unionized factory workers were fired and became long-term unemployed. The MTD is organized territorially, by barrio, municipality, across municipalities, in some cases divided among competing national organizations. The main tactics are to barricade major highways, blocking the transportation of goods, services and labour from industries, banks and other sectors (see Table 4.2). Their demands invariably include state-financed jobs and food. They are usually autonomous from the main trade unions and political parties, though there are important exceptions. The MTD usually meets in assemblies in neighbourhoods to decide on tactics, demands and the distribution of jobs secured by successful struggles. By early 2002 more than 200,000 unemployed workers were organized, though many more workers and underemployed had participated in street blockages and marches. The MTDs draw support from rank-and-file trade unionists, regional trade union leaders, particularly from the public employees unions (ATE) and the dissident labour confederation (CTA), and the Marxist parties. The MTD clearly spearheaded the organization of opposition to the neoliberal regime in the absence of any sustained opposition from the political parties and the official trade unions.

From June 2001 to June 2002 the number of road blockages escalated, merging with other forms of struggle, including massive marches of the *cacerolazos* (middle-class pot bangers), citywide uprisings (*puebladas*), assaults of supermarkets in search of food, and the national uprising of December 19/20, 2002.

Several theoretical points emerge from an analysis of the MTD. First, the idea that the unemployed, outside the factories, cannot be organized because they are too dispersed, fragmented and without social leverage is

Table 4.2 Road Blockages by Month (1997–2001)

Year	Number of Blockages Per Month
1997	11
1998	4
1999	21
2000	42
2001 (Jan.–May)	64

Source: *Clarin*, 24 June 2001: 6–7.

false. The MTD demonstrates that in their common social situation the leadership from below, rooted in former unionized workers working through popular assemblies in horizontal structures, can succeed in organizing in the midst of a depression, despite the hostility and indifference of the entire trade-union and political-party leadership. The locus of collective social action has shifted from the factory to the street, especially as unemployment in the working-class barrios has reached from 40 to 60 percent, underemployment from 20 to 30 percent, and hunger affects more than one-third of working-class school children.

The activist mass has become largely "feminized," as women are in most cases the head of the household and have taken the lead in organizing the barricades and logistical support systems (roadside soup kitchens). Women from working-class families bring to the MTD the experience of two decades of neighbourhood organizing, first via the local reform schemes of the various regimes, and over seven years through the autonomous, militant MTD. The road blockages have evolved from sporadic, quasi-spontaneous actions into systematic, organized activities coordinated among thousands of unemployed. There were 51 road blockages in 1998, 252 in 1999, 514 in 2000 and nearly a thousand in 2001. In 2002 the road blockages were often combined with generalized uprisings, particularly in the provinces of the interior, but also in the greater Buenos Aires region. In January 2002, for example, road blockages accompanied popular mobilizations in Cordoba, Santa Fe, Chaco, Misiones, Santiago del Estero, Salta and Formosa (*Quebracho*, 5, no. 31: 4). The combined struggles included both the demands of the MTD and those of other protesting sectors, such as back pay for public employees, housing for the homeless, an end to the confiscation of savings, and food distribution. In some cases municipal buildings were sacked, supermarkets were raided and governors' mansions and state legislatures were occupied.

The sacking of retail stores can be differentiated according to the organizers and objectives: (1) those organized by the ward bosses of the Peronist (Justice) party, particularly before December 19/20, 2001, to destabilize the presidency of De la Rua, a leader of the Radical Party; (2) those that were "spontaneously" organized by the destitute and famished poor; and (3) those organized or threatened by the MTD as a pressure to negotiate with the supermarkets to secure voluntary donations (*El Pikete*, 2, no. 6: 2).

The degree of organization and the work of the MTD varies greatly throughout the country. The MTD in Matanza, led by Luis D'Elia, has 25,000 affiliates, organized by barrio in the municipality of Matanza, a city of more than one million residents. In Mosconi, Cutral-Co and Tartagal, former one-industry, petroleum-producing towns, the MTD is led and organized by well-paid, formerly unionized oil workers. In Mosconi an impressive set of small workshops and micro-enterprises has been established, in place of the make-work state work plans, that includes bakeries, metal works, construction and other lines of work.

It is clear that the *piqueteros* are not all what they appear to be — unemployed workers fighting for social justice. Particularly the Peronist party, in power, has used job subsidies to try to divide the MTD, handing out job application forms via their barrio ward bosses and organizing thugs to disrupt local meetings. In addition, local Peronist bosses have hired unemployed to assault and intimidate assemblies in popular barrios, though they seldom attempt to threaten the MTD.

In some municipalities the MTD has been gradually expanding but has had problems organizing small-scale production. In Solano, for example, membership has doubled to more than twelve hundred members in one year.[3] Some projects such as a local bakery, construction, metal works and garment shops have succeeded, but home gardens have failed due to frequent flooding and lack of farm experience. The MTD also faces the problem of maintaining work discipline, especially among some sectors of the young unemployed who are militant in the barricades but have never experienced time-clock punctuality and promptness in fulfilling job obligations, which causes dissension and conflict within the collectives (*Brecha,* 12 April, 2002: ix).

The MTD is a potent force, although it is increasingly divided into conflicting and competing socio-political organizations. The MTD in Matanza, led by D'Elia and those influenced by the CCC (class-based coordinators), collaborate and negotiate with the Duhalde regime. Tactically they have sharply diluted the impact of road blockages in their search of what they call a poli-class alliance. This particular organization of the MTD works closely with the dissident CTA labour confederation, subordinating confrontation to negotiation. Both organizations did not participate in the mass uprising of December 19, and D'Elia opposed participation on the 20th. This form of MTD is clearly reformist.

The radical MTDs are dispersed throughout the country and in the greater Buenos Aires region. They include Anibal Veron, Mosconi, Almirante Brown, Teresa Rodriguez, Solano and many others, including regional affiliates of the CCC who have retained a militant confrontational style of social action, total blockage of highways and autonomy from all trade-union confederations.

However, the radical MTDs are themselves internally divided along political lines, with the Trotskyist Workers Pole (*Polo Obrero*), the Communist Land and Liberation (*Tierra y Liberación*) and other formations competing for hegemony (*Página*, 16 January 2002). The result is that the radical MTD at best have only tactical alliances, while more often than not they are in conflict, even to the point of conducting separate negotiations with the regime.

Despite the formidable growth and power of the MTDs, they have not realized their full potential. They have been successful in securing temporary survival assistance but have not been able to develop into a force for a systemic transformation. This is due in part to the barriers imposed by the collaborationist trade-union bureaucracy between the employed and unemployed workers, and in part to competition and conflict among the MTDs. The MTDs do not have a recognized and accepted national leadership capable of organizing a national plan of struggle which could coalesce with the popular assemblies, popular uprisings and dissident trade unions, particularly that of public sector employees. When a mass popular uprising did take place in the capital, the MTDs neither led it nor provided the principal actors, though their previous years of escalating direct action created a favourable climate.

The Popular Uprising of December 19/20, 2002

The usually ubiquitous red flags and banners of the Marxist Left, dissident trade unions and *piqueteros* were almost completely absent when tens of thousands of Argentinians marched to the Plaza de Mayo facing the presidential palace, the Casa Rosada, on the hot summer afternoon of December 19, 2001. This was the beginning of a two-day uprising that ended the despised regime of De la Rua and his economic czar Cavallo and cost the lives of between thirty and forty protesters and resulted in thousands of injuries and arrests.

The populace which filled the Plaza de Mayo included the Madres de Plaza de Mayo (a human rights group), young people, pensioners, progressive activists protesting the state of siege declared by the regime (banning public assemblies), and most significantly tens of thousands of downwardly mobile and impoverished pot-banging, middle-class protesters. The centrepiece of the protest march was the "*corralito*," the regime decree confiscating or freezing all savings, time deposits and chequing accounts of millions of Argentines, mostly from the middle class. The state of siege (*estado de sitio*) was the last straw. It was one thing to confiscate lifelong savings, it was another to tell the victims to stay home and keep their mouths shut.

What began as neighbourhood pot-banging protests quickly took to the main avenues and mushroomed into a massive, loud but peaceful protest. The middle class saw the writing on the wall without savings or access to their chequing accounts, many being without jobs or on the verge of losing their jobs, unable to pay home mortgages, school and health fees. They saw themselves heading down toward the working class and beyond into poverty. For many it was their first initiation into mass street politics. They had believed fervently in Menem's promises of joining the first world; they had spent and borrowed, visited the sparkling chic boutiques in the new malls, and been annoyed by or had ignored the street blockages of the unemployed. Only the public employees, the white-collar middle class, facing redundancies and, in the provinces, long delays in salary payments, expressed any solidarity with the burgeoning mass movements. When the recession set in 1999 and deepened in 2000, unemployment began to affect middle-class businesses and the clientele of psychologists, and services fell off.

By 2001 the recession was turning into a depression, foreign financing was drying up and, with default on the horizon, sectors of the upper and upper middle class began to withdraw funds, followed only belatedly by the middle and lower middle class. By late November, when the economy was collapsing, the middle class made a run to withdraw their funds, only to be shut off when both major parties, the court system and the regime blocked their moves. Forced to rely on their own voices, they congregated aggressively in front of the banks, particularly the foreign banks — the Bank of Boston, Citibank, Galicia, Scotiabank — trying to force entrance, angrily protesting their deception and expressing their political awakening. For more than two decades the banks had pillaged the country, its resources and its public treasury, as earnings from exorbitant interest rates filled their coffers, while the middle class had supported the bipartisan regime (Radicals/Peronists) that oversaw the pillage. Then it was the turn of the middle class. Moving from complacent conformity to raucous shouting in the streets, the middle class wanted access to their money. The banks and the regime became the targets of their wrath.[4]

Neighbours went to meetings to discuss their plight and express their anger and solidarity. From informal neighbourhood gatherings, they began to extend their horizons beyond the barrios to the main avenues, where they had witnessed the poor, the *piqueteros*, march. They took to the streets and some took out their anger on bank teller machines, and windows of banks were shattered. The streets were filling, the clatter of pots grew louder and more pot-banging neighbors came down from the balconies of their apartments to the streets. They converged on December 19 in front of the Casa Rosada, ignored by the president, confronted by mounted police and engaged in an illegal demonstration. Figures on attendance varied upward from 100,000 to 200,000, but the significance was that the middle class was in front of the palace calling for the president's resignation, and in fact, for the ouster of the whole political class ("*Que se vayan todos!*"). The police attacked with clubs, tear gas and live ammunition. Several protestors were killed, hundreds were wounded and a peaceful protest march turned into a pitched battle, as older protesters fled and younger people fought back. Message workers on their motorbikes provided logistical and intelligence reports. Downtown Buenos Aires was a gas-filled, bloody battlefield of burning tires, rock-throwing street fighters and trigger-happy cops, reminiscent of the Palestinian intifada.

Neither completely spontaneous nor minimally organized, days and weeks of anger followed the bank confiscation, the indignity of a deaf ear to public voices, and the grotesque salaries and perks of the legislators ($12,000 per month plus bribes and payoffs); it was all a huge provocation rupturing lifelong conformity and belief in the electoral system and the notion of representative government.

In the barrios, assemblies filled the neighbourhood parks, where public distrust became evident: the assemblies rejected leaders, fixed agendas and party labels (even of the Left); everything was to be discussed and voted on, but frequently little was implemented.[5]

The absence of the Left on the first day of the uprising (December 19) can be attributed to several factors, both ideological and organizational.[6] Most of the Left operated from a rigid class analysis, from which it deduced political behaviour. The Left was generally "workerist" — what didn't come out of the factories was suspect. It rigidly adhered to the following logic: factory worker unionization, revolutionary party, general strike, revolution. In the meantime the unionized workers became a minority, most workers were unemployed or underemployed and many were organized in the MTD. Belatedly the Left began to organize, mobilize and fragment the MTD.

The Left also missed the rapid downward mobility of the middle class, its impoverishment and proletarianization. Having lost all their savings, deeply alienated from their traditional conservative moorings, the middle class had nothing to lose. It was open to a radical democratic style of street politics and direct forms of assembly-style democracy.

The Left only moved into the uprising on the second day, December 20, and then only the activists and militants, as the leaders remained in headquarters strategizing. On December 20, important contingents of public-sector trade unionists, *piqueteros*, Marxist activists and tens of thousands of independent, radicalized middle-class people poured into the streets. Thousands of young people, from lower middle class students to young unemployed *piqueteros* joined the march and the eventual battles with the police in front of the presidential palace in Buenos Aires and in other major cities. The downwardly mobile middle-class demonstration was the detonator of the assault on power. In fourteen days, four governments came and went.

The uprising was successful on several important counts: the Saa regime declared that Argentina would not meet its debt obligations; the populace was able to force the resignation of four presidents; and the uprising delegitimized the political class and the judicial system, exposing their venality and anti-national, anti-popular character.

The December 19/20 mass uprising was historically unique for several reasons. It was the first time in Argentine history that a popular uprising had overthrown an elected or dictatorial leader. It was the first time in history that the majority of Argentines had confronted and rejected the entire political class. The uprising and the solidarity that ensued led to the creation of new and creative forms of direct popular representation in the form of barrio assemblies, and new tactics of struggle, pot-banging demonstrations which were capable of blocking state decisions adversely affecting the people (such as the Duhalde regime's attempt to convert the confiscated savings into fixed bonds redeemable in ten years).

Following the selection of Duhalde as president by a cabal of Peronist party bosses and governors, and a few demagogic promises, the two official trade unions, the CGT (Confederación General de Trabajo) and CGT (Moyano), backed his regime. The vast majority of the people were opposed from the beginning and increasingly so over time. Six months into the regime his support had withered to less then 10 percent and he faced a new wave of street blockages and general strikes.

The popular assemblies increasingly relied on work commissions to implement policy changes as the Marxist sects began to penetrate, debate and argue over tactics, programs and party turf, alienating many and recruiting few (*Argentina Arde,* February, March and April 2002). There was a temporary retrogression from the high point of December 2001.

The pot-banging movement demonstrated its capacity to veto presidential nominations and decrees. However, its lack of a clear political focus and its diffuse organizational structure weakened its capacity to consolidate a powerful national movement. The warfare within the Left undermined the attractiveness of the assemblies to many participants. Despite emerging weaknesses, the political experience and sense of power has sustained an increasingly radical and growing current of opinion among the impoverished middle class. Public opinion polls on presidential candidates in late May 2002 favoured a Marxist, Luis Zamora, over any and all of those from the major parties.

Revolt in the Provinces

On April 17, shipyard workers from Ensenada, in the province of Buenos Aires, stormed the governor's mansion demanding their back pay from the previous month. They were joined by public employees from their trade union (ATE) and teachers from their union (Suteba) (*Clarin*, 18 April 2002: 18). On the same day thousands of striking teachers in Cordoba marched on the state legislature, while thousands of trade unionists and *piqueteros* demonstrated in support of the unemployed occupying the labour offices, who were demanding public works jobs. Throughout Chubat Province thousands of unemployed workers and trade unionists demonstrated in all the major cities for jobs and against budget cuts, while, in Catamarca, municipal workers were in their second day of a province-wide strike demanding back pay for March (*Clarin*, 19 April 2002: 22). In San Juan, public employees stormed the state legislature, battling the police and demanding their delayed salaries. On April 18, public employees and the unemployed in the provinces of Chubut and Jujuy confronted the police while forcing their way into the provincial legislature. The demonstrators included bank workers, teachers and public employees demanding back pay, and unemployed workers demanding jobs. In Jujuy, in addition to attacking and partially destroying the legislature, demonstrators sacked a supermarket and attacked the headquarters of the ruling parties and the houses of two pro-regime politicians.

The provinces are burning, and the government is arming. The regime's secretary of security asked the state police (the *gendarmería*) to design a provincial police-training program to repress social conflict, and solicited international technical support (including weapons and advisers).

The rebellion in the provinces is deeply rooted in the liberal policies of the past quarter of a century that deindustrialized the provincial economies. Today there are few packing houses in Argentina's third city, Rosario. Where the fathers were employed as meat cutters, the sons are unemployed. Their only experience of cutting beef was a raid on an overturned truck carrying cattle to market, the only meat in their diet for many months, if not years (*Clarin,* 29 March 2002: 34).

Deindustrialization is a result of privatization, the lowering of Argentine trade barriers, the mass entry of cheap imports and the maintenance of trade barriers for beef and farm products in Europe and the United States. The increase in costs of transportation and power, and the lack of regime investment in upgrading industries and promotion of new enterprises, has also contributed to the demise of industry.

The massive layoffs and high unemployment rates affecting Buenos Aires from the late 1990s to the present began a decade earlier in Rosario, Tucuman and other cities of the interior. The free market undermined the domestic producers in the provinces, while the short-term beneficiaries in Buenos Aires enjoyed cheap imported consumer goods. The food, textile and consumer goods industries declined and the agro-export sector suffered from the subsidies and protection of European and US producers. Moreover, the export enclaves in the provinces (oil, mining, agriculture) were capital-intensive. They absorbed few workers. Privatization wiped out tens of thousands of jobs, particularly in the petroleum industry, as new foreign owners closed down operations in the provinces, turning the few enclaves in provinces such as Neuquen into centres of unemployment and social explosion. The regime promise to create alternative employment for the workers displaced from the privatized enterprises never materialized.

Individual income declined as business bankruptcies multiplied. Interprovincial trade declined as the result of transportation cutbacks by privatized airlines and railroads, while road transportation costs rose because of higher tolls by private owners.

The budget revenues of the provincial governments declined precipitously, while their fixed costs rose with the social crisis. To bridge the widening deficit and avoid social explosions, the provincial governments increasingly turned to federal funding and to printing local currencies. The provincial public sector expanded into non-productive services while the productive sector declined. The public sector became the employer of first and last resort. The dominant political parties and provincial party bosses stole tens of million of pesos from the local and federal government, siphoned earnings from provincial enterprises and financed extensive electoral party machines, thus perpetuating themselves in power via jobs for some, while running down the economy and impoverishing the many excluded from the spoils of office.

The leading IFIs (World Bank, IMF and Inter-American Development Bank [IDB]) did not complain, because the corrupt provincial political bosses backed President Menem and his liberal agenda, and enforced and implemented the privatization process in their own provinces. Living on federal handouts, which reinforced social and regional inequalities, was a form of counter-insurgency. When popular rebellions intensified, the corrupt provincial governors and legislators would secure a loan or aid package from the federal government to pay back salaries or create make-work jobs.

When the recession and then the depression hit the country, particularly Buenos Aires and the federal government, funds to the provinces declined. Local governors printed their own currencies, redeemable and recognized only within their jurisdiction, limiting interprovincial transactions, transportation, mobility and travel. With the end of the supply of public assets to privatize in order to secure new financing from the IFIs, the federal government was forced to accept drastic cuts in aid to the provincial governments. With debt default, the IFIs demanded imposition by the federal government of tight fiscal restraints on the near-bankrupt provincial governments, and elimination of local currencies, thus provoking massive firings, bankruptcies and immense growth in poverty.

The provinces rebelled. As the *Financial Times* (22 May 2002: 6) noted, "With poverty levels rising daily and cash strapped provincial governments unable to pay workers and offer handouts to the poor, there are fears of a new wave of violence." One week later, a massive one-day general strike was in force. Class political conflict intensified throughout 2002. The end result of the logic of privatization and liberalization of markets was a generalized political rebellion, spreading from province to province and moving to the centre of Buenos Aires and the seats of political and financial power.

The provincial rebellions are much akin to popular uprisings, as they incorporate a wide variety of social strata in the same mass mobilizations: public employees, school teachers, unemployed workers, unpaid industrial workers. The hard and fast lines between bureaucratically led trade unions and the unemployed workers movement in Buenos Aires is blurred in the provinces. In the latter, more often than not, the ATE and teachers union engage in joint actions with workers, supporting the demands for back pay for the employed and state-funded jobs for the unemployed. The social distance between the leaders and followers of provincial trade unions is smaller. Many families include both public employees and unemployed. The class struggle is mainly against the state, the neoliberal state, though the demands for an alternative are nebulous. Many rebellions have been ended by the return of the "patronage state," paying a back salary here, creating a few jobs there. By 2002, however, the ability of the patronage state to temporarily end rebellions was extremely limited, precisely as incomes declined and unemployment reached from 30 to 40 percent in the cities and 60 to 70 percent in the villas.

The result was the *puebladas* — whole cities rose in rebellion, seizing public buildings, blocking highways and holding legislators hostage. The cycle of radical action followed by an election of conservative politicians is changing. The period of popular mobilizations is extending and the levels of action are intensifying, while electoral politicians, without patronage, are totally discredited. The collective actions in the streets are more representative of the interests and attitudes of the people than the sitting governors and legislators. The *puebladas* create a short-term dual power in governance, which, however, has not found the way to institutionalize itself.

The deepening crisis has homogenized vast sectors of the population: professionals have seen their income decline by two-thirds, public employees have not been paid in months (salaries reduced by 70 percent) and savings have been confiscated. The *puebladas* are a clear expression of the growing homogenization of social classes, and their common social situation. The joint action and solidarity among employees, professionals and the unemployed embodies this decline in socio-economic distinctions.

While provincial social rebellions are more frequent, intense and inclusive, and even though they may occur at the same moment, they are not coordinated and have neither an agreed-upon interprovincial leadership nor an alternative economic program. The tactics are offensive; the demands are defensive. In only a few instances has the working class taken the initiative to create alternative patterns of ownership and social relations.

Worker Takeovers: Brukmann and Zanon

The powerful *piquetero* movement of the unemployed, the widespread neighbourhood based assemblies, the uprising of December 19/20, 2001, and the general strike of May 29, 2002, point to massive opposition to neoliberal regimes, policies and leaders. Equally important, these collective mass activities demand profound changes in domestic and foreign economic policies and relations with foreign banks, the IFIs, Washington and the G-7. There has not been a clear definition of a radical political-economic alternative at the national level. However, at the local level, two examples indicate the revolutionary alternative, a transformation in property and social relations: worker occupation and operation of several factories. The best known took place in Neuquen at the Zanon ceramic plant, and the other occurred in Buenos Aires at the Brukmann garment factory. Both worker-run factories point to an alternative to plant closings, subsistence public make-work and soup kitchens.

During the first half of the year 2002, plant closings multiplied and the firing of workers accelerated. In January, 1,000 workers a day; in February, 2,000 a day; in March more than 65,000 were out in the street. Several factories threatened with closings were occupied by workers to prevent further firings and the sell-off of machinery. The owners, aided by collaborationist trade-union bureaucrats, proceeded to obtain court orders of eviction, and police were sent to the premises to dislodge the workers. The workers' occupations followed a specific sequence. First, workers in the factories voted to replace factory delegates beholden to union bureaucrats with elected militant representatives who responded to factory-based assemblies. They then proceeded to vote out of power employer collaborators in the local union. With new leadership, and decisions taken by general assemblies in the factories, the workers voted to resist plant closures by occupying and operating the factory. The worker-operated factories and the new unions secured support from popular assemblies in the city, from local trade-union activists, university students and, above all, from the MTD. Faced with threats of dislodgement, the worker assemblies called on their allies in the neighbourhood organizations and MTD to confront the police. Faced with mass resistance from a wide array of determined organizations, the police withdrew.

The worker-operated factories have secured technical advice from universities and administrative personnel from the factory. But the main organizational innovation has been the establishment of commissions to deal with supplies and sales, health and solidarity, and other areas as challenges emerge. In the Zanon ceramic factory, the ex-owners pressured suppliers to cut off the sale of inputs, reducing production from 80 to 25 percent of capacity between February and March 2002.[7] Since then the worker commission has moved to re-establish supply networks.

The workers in Zanon and Brukmann do not see the occupation of isolated factories as the solution, given the general crisis and high level of unemployment. They support a generalized offensive by workers to occupy factories and demand public ownership under workers' control—socialism. The experiences in Brukmann and Zanon have received national attention and have become points of reference for other workers facing plant closings. But the first step toward any social transformation resides in establishing assembly-based, democratically elected factory representatives and union leaders who respond to factory assemblies. In all the struggles to prevent plant closings the national trade-union confederations and their local representatives have been major obstacles to factory occupations. The examples of Zanon and Brukmann indicate that the ouster of current bureaucratic elites is the first step in a successful confrontation with factory owners and the state. The factory occupations are seen by the new democratic leadership as the first step toward a national transformation. Thus their support for the demands of the MTD for genuine employment at livable union salaries, in productive, socially necessary employment (building schools, hospitals, low-cost housing, making articles of popular consumption). The worker-operated factories are based on class organization in the workplace by and for workers; the success of their class struggle perspective sharply contrasts with the collaborationist approach of the national bureaucrats who failed to stem the mass layoffs and have explicit or implicit accords with the regime in hopes of securing make-work for the unemployed or simply protecting their salaries and perquisites.

While the scope of the worker factory takeover movement is limited and lacks the numbers involved in the other forms of mass mobilizations it is certainly the most significant in pointing to a powerful alternative social system, and a democratic alternative to the corrupt, elite-driven electoral system which has led Argentina down the road to disintegration.

Programmatic Alternatives: Plan Phoenix or Plan Prometheus

In light of the complete and total collapse of the Argentine neoliberal model, several alternative models of development have emerged. One of them, Plan Phoenix (PP), put forth by more than one hundred economists and political scientists, is the most widely circulated and influential in intellectual circles.[8] The other, which we can call Plan

Prometheus, is articulated within the emerging revolutionary democratic organizations.

PP is both a critical diagnosis of neoliberal policies and a prescription for change and development. The critical diagnosis covers a wide range of economic policy, from tax policies, public spending, the Free Trade Agreement of the Americas (FTAA) and Mercosur, to privatization and technology policy.[9] While most analysts are critical of neoliberal policies, some are more so than others. Azpiazu and Basualdo (2001: 180–93), for example, are more critical of the structures of economic power than Katz and Stumpo (2001: 150–63), who are fairly orthodox liberals. PP's main virtues are found in its criticism of the total deregulation of the economy, the indiscriminant opening to the world market, the unilateral and radical reduction of tariff barriers (without reciprocity), the loss of control over monetary policy via the *de facto* dollarization, the dismantling of the state as an instrument of economic policy, the great concentration of economic power, and the lack of transparency in the privatization of public enterprise. PP's rejection of the argument by globalization ideologues that the nation-state is no longer a viable tool for policy-making is part of a new project to revitalize the role of the state in pursuit of an industrial policy that prioritizes the internal market and international competitiveness.[10]

In the areas of reforms, PP focuses on securing reductions in debt payments via a moratorium or reduced payments — the document is contradictory. In any case, its moderate proposals have been bypassed by subsequent events, because three months after PP was published, the government defaulted. PP favours increased taxes on the rich, the financial groups and other "nonproductive" sectors, and elimination of subsidies to privileged classes. The revenues raised would be channeled towards employment-generating investments in socially useful areas (schools, low-income housing, child care centres), as well as worker training programs. The basic premise of the PP document is that a coalition of political parties, productive private sectors, and civil society would be the political bases for a new regulatory regime. The state would direct financial capital to fund productive capitalism, foreign capital to reinvest profits in the national economy and productive capital to invest in socially useful activities. PP seeks to devise an economic policy that will reorient capital towards the domestic market, regional (re-)industrialization and processing of raw materials to add more value to exports in the international market. The priority of PP is to develop a national development plan to reactivate the economy, fix social priorities, selectively protect local producers, seek sources of domestic funding and then negotiate with the IFIs, including the

IMF. The focus would be on internal transformation and the role of the national state, not on external agreements with the IFIs.

PP proposes to reprogram debt payments to secure a grace period via negotiation with the IFIs and to secure credits from the G-7 to develop a welfare state based on a state-regulated private economy. Citing examples from Western Europe in the 1960s and early 1970s, PP believes that a welfare state and capitalism are compatible. The social coalition to carry out their policies resembles the national popular alliance of the 1940s and 1950s.

PP contains an informed critique of several sectors of the economy with an entirely out-of-date conception of socio-political economic realities, particularly the behaviour, interests and orientation of the social classes, political parties, foreign banks and IFIs. PP is basically a neo-structuralist plan that accepts the privatization process, the distribution of property and existing social relations of production. The existing owners of banks, factories, telecommunications, real estate, land and minerals are not at all called into question. The basic reform is to insert the state to regulate their behaviour, reduce the excesses of the market, increase taxes and convince them to increase their contribution towards industrial investments, domestic consumption and social welfare.

There are several problems with the regulatory policies. The dominant capitalist and financial classes have evaded and resisted any attempts to reorient them, because they are tied to international circuits. Previous attempts at regulation led to massive capital flight — as seen when PP was published, although the two events were not directly connected. Regulation presumes that a viable economy is in place, which Argentina's is not at this time. PP was published in the midst of a depression. While the economy regresses by 15 percent per year and incomes fall by more than 60 percent, to propose regulation in the context of rising rates of bankruptcy makes no sense. The issue of state intervention involves massive direct public investments in a public sector, which can only come about via the resocialization and nationalization of strategic economic sectors.

Social welfare measures and public investments cannot be financed through additional taxes when many investors have sent their earnings abroad and incomes and profits are dropping. When the Duhalde regime attempted to retain earnings from the agro-export sector, the latter organized a production boycott, causing the regime to back off.

The proposals put forth by PP greatly underestimate the scope and depth of the Argentine crisis — the disintegration of the economy and society. Proposing policy palliatives at a time when the whole private productive-financial-distributive system is breaking down is a totally inadequate way to restart the economy.

PP assumptions that the IFIs and the private banks will cooperate in reducing profits (via taxation) and lower their overseas remittances to the home office, flies in the face of the practical realities. The private banks withdrew massive amounts of earnings and depositor savings and resisted refinancing their subsidiaries throughout 2000–2002, behaviour hardly compatible with paying higher taxes, reinvesting profits in Argentina and expanding welfare. On the latter point, the restructuring proposed by the foreign banks includes saddling the state with their deposit liabilities, firing up to two-thirds of their workforce, reducing the number of subsidiaries and, in some cases, closing and withdrawing from the country, as was the case with Scotiabank and several others.

The refusal of the IFIs to fund or extend credit to Argentina because the country is not making more liberal concessions and cutbacks is hardly a sign that they would negotiate new credits and refinancing to a regime that adds taxes to foreign bank transactions, limits profit remittances and encourages banks to lend to Argentine productive sectors, producing for the domestic market, as the PP proposes.

PP underestimates the links between the IFIs and foreign capital in the context of the 1990s. Their extrapolation of the European welfare state of the 1960s, when labour was strong, communism was an alternative, capitalism was expanding and finance capital was subordinated to industrial capital, is a gross misunderstanding of the present global and national context. Capital is linked to international markets and profoundly hostile to the welfare state everywhere. Trade-union bureaucracies have little influence, and national popular political parties are no longer in existence.

The PP extrapolation fails to realize that, today, European and US capitalism cannot be "regulated" — it disinvests, moves and organizes resistance; it destabilizes to avoid regulation, welfare and progressive taxes. *The issue is to nationalize capital in order to regulate it, to change the character of property relations to reallocate investments, invest in the local economy, and finance social welfare and infrastructure.*

Yet the major failing of the PP document is its total dependence on the state to stimulate, collaborate and encourage "private agents": subsidizing the private sector (to create jobs), working with foreign capital to reinvest profits, regulating the behaviour of privatized firms to correct excess charges and poor service etc. The critique of ALCA runs along the same lines. ALCA is criticized because of US tariff barriers and subsidies, rather than the structural inequalities between the productive sectors of the giant TNCs in the North and Argentina's industrial sectors. The PP criticism, even if it were accepted by the US (extremely unlikely, as the Bush administration increased subsidies to agriculture), might increase some agricultural exports but would continue to prejudice local industrial and IT producers. Equally problematic is the kind of state PP proposes. The problem is not only incompetence, nepotism and corruption — certainly serious problems — but the political composition of the state and the entire political class.

Following the collapse of the Argentine economy, the entire political class has been discredited, including all the parties that PP proposes as components of its "new social coalition." The PP-proposed coalition of productive forces lacks realism. Employers are firing workers, reducing hours, lowering pay, hiring temporary workers, closing factories, moving to new sites (in and out of the country) and transferring their capital to other sectors or out of the country. Workers are occupying factories, and the unemployed are blocking highways, seizing municipal buildings and even rising to overthrow presidents. This reality makes the proposed social coalition enviable. The level and intensity of social conflict, and fierce competition over scarce resources, have broken all links between capital and labour. The "national producers" have shown no propensity to finance welfare programs except their own survival and flight.

The poli-class bases for a mixed welfare economy have not materialized over the past twenty years of electoral politics. On the contrary, every victorious electoral coalition over the past two decades (Alfonsin, Menem, the Alianza) has been based on a national-popular coalition, and when in power has implemented harsh neoliberal policies, following the direction indicated by leading entrepreneurial and financial groups.

The small and medium-sized producers (the PYMES) of the interior and in Buenos Aires can play a role but certainly not in terms of exports, financing and large-scale, long-term job creation in the present context (Schvarzer 2000: 56–65). The highest rates of bankruptcy are precisely in this sector, and they are paying the lowest salaries and provide the least social coverage for workers. The PYMES are hardly model employers from the workers' standpoint.

The danger of PP is that it fails to understand or even mention the problems of confrontation with US imperialism. Debt default is a reality today and the US Treasury and the G-7 have issued an ultimatum: pay up, cut back, fire workers and end provincial deficits or suffer a credit and finance blockade. There is no strategy or understanding in the PP document of how to deal with a global political confrontation. Oblivious to European and US economic (and military) aggression, the authors act as if it is a question of making reforms at the national level and negotiating at the international. But it is precisely the reforms at the national level — even incremental changes — that are not acceptable to the US and Europe, for fear of the effect that successful reforms will have on adjoining countries.

The PP document is dissociated from the powerful social movements and political uprisings that have occurred. These are not even mentioned in passing. The organized unemployed, the popular assemblies, the factory takeover movements and the provincial rebellions, all of which have the most direct stake in the welfare, development and employment goals of PP, are ignored. Instead, PP looks to the discredited trade-union bureaucrats of the confederations, the political parties and leaders who have been the main cause of the disaster to re-enact a new national-popular coalition with foreign capital and credit from the IFIs.

Following the political and social logic of PP means that any regime that emerges will be pressured by its own private economic agents to discard the welfare provisions and national regulations to secure minimum cooperation for production. Internal hegemony would revert to the private agents, and the welfare programs would be subordinated to maximizing short-term profits.

If, on the other hand, the "social forces" of the coalition gain ascendancy, the "private economic agents" would likely ally with foreign capital and the G-7 to destabilize the regime and provoke intensified social conflict, leading to political instability favourable to the Right.

Given the non-viability of the regulatory reform program of PP in the Argentine and global context of today, the choice is between reversion to bankrupt neoliberal policy or revolutionary change that incorporates the welfare reforms of PP into a realistic socialized economic structure supported by its principal beneficiaries.

Plan Prometheus: The Revolutionary Alternative

First and foremost is the need for a new social coalition of the 80 percent of Argentines suffering a severe decline in living standards, including the 57 percent below the poverty line. Employed and unemployed workers alone amount to close to 50 percent and the impoverished middle class includes another 20–30 percent. This is a broad-based coalition that is not linked to overseas banks, which are sworn enemies since confiscating their savings. Thus a socialist state is given the basis to renationalize the banking and financial system and is provided with a political base to resist pressures from G-7 bankers. The nationalization of foreign trade would provide the state with a mechanism for reorienting foreign exchange to finance public investment and national industrialization. The renationalization of petroleum would provide income and revenues to stimulate job training, and infrastructure and social projects generating employment. Progressive tax collection can be enforced by threats to expropriate the property of tax evaders and tax delinquents.

The state reforms proposed by the PP document should be articulated with new, assembly forms of popular representation and the incorporation of new social movements (*piqueteros*) in local and municipal governments. Popular assemblies should exercise direct control of allocations and expenditures, an advanced form of participatory budgeting. Ownership of strategic sectors of the economy is essential to sustain redistributive policies, as recent decades attest. With privatization the inequalities widened, and decisions concerning macroeconomic policy were monopolized by powerful economic groups.

The economic crisis has cut per capita income by two-thirds. Given scarce resources and a disintegrating productive base, only public takeover under workers' control can expand the material base and generate greater equality. Greater equity depends on social control of the income to be distributed. Social ownership is at the center of Plan Prometheus. It combines the tax and expenditures of Plan Phoenix, but within a vastly expanded social property sector, democratically controlled by direct producers and administered by a meritocratic public administration. It is Promethean because it involves the total reconstruction of a disintegrating economy with a shattered social fabric in the face of powerful US and European imperial adversaries. Having control over the basic economic sectors, however, means the return and reinvestment of earnings in Argentina. Debt default means savings of more than 50 percent of export earnings. Diversification of production and reactivation of the economy mean that optimal use can be made of existing unused capacity — more than 50 percent of the total. Mercosur, China, Arab countries, sectors of the EU and Russia offer alternative markets to any IFI-organized boycott. Public investments in innovation, technology, and research and development can engage Argentina's highly trained but currently underutilized labour force. Reactivation of internal markets and selective protection of provincial producers can expand markets. Public investments in infrastructure can employ the unemployed and facilitate interprovincial and inter-Mercosur trade.

Plan Prometheus incorporates the criticisms made of Plan Phoenix but extends them by insisting that modifying the behaviour of political actors is insufficient. It is necessary to transform the structure in which they are positioned. Plan Prometheus incorporates some of the specific welfare reforms of PP but locates them in a more realistic political-economic property framework that avoids the constraints and threats of private/foreign non-cooperation. Prometheus replaces the PP-proposed national-popular social coalition with a more realistic popular coalition rooted in existing social movements.

Epilogue: Perspectives

The election of Nestor Kirchner in May 2003 marked a new dividing line in Argentine politics, one that will probably have a significant impact on the working class and popular struggles in the immediate future. Kirchner's inaugural remarks, cabinet appointments, military purge and promises to clear the corrupt right-wing Supreme Court judges and meet with human rights groups augers well for the future of the country. His appointments reflect a moderate pragmatic approach mixing personal supporters from his home state of Santa Cruz, a heterodox social liberal economic minister and several supporters of the outgoing Duhalde regime. His opposition to IMF demands for immediate debt payments and promise to postpone or condition payments on the economic recovery of the country are rational responses to a country in which 60 percent of the population live below the poverty line and more than 20 percent are unemployed. His "retirement" of fifty right-wing generals and admirals, and their replacement with officers stationed in his home province of Santa Cruz, is a security measure to weaken the coup capacity of the US and its allies among the Argentine elite. Kirchner has given priority to financing a $3-billion public works project to reduce unemployment.

These are progressive measures that appeal to the vast majority of Argentines. However, there are several contradictory elements in Kirchner's agenda. First and foremost is the issue of political power: his economic strategy of state-regulated and -directed capitalism depends on the cooperation, investment and production of the banking, agro-export and foreign-controlled firms — none of whom have indicated great liking for the above measures. If, as seems likely, they continue their speculative activities, send earnings abroad and fail to invest, Kirchner will face the choice of increasing the role of the state and re-nationalizing lucrative firms, or capitulating and backing off from his commitments. The second contradiction is between, on the one hand, his promise to maintain a tight fiscal policy and provide compensation for private firms who lost out because of the devaluation and, on the other, the need to increase state spending to finance employment-generating projects. Kirchner proposed to finance new investment via tighter tax collection and punishing evaders, but, if past history is any example, he will have a tough time enforcing the measure. Moreover, most of the Argentine ruling class consider punishment of tax evaders as a "hostile act" and may condition their offers of future investment on a lenient policy towards tax evasion.

Additionally, the right-wing Peronists, including supporters Menem and the Bush regime, and the bankers, are a significant force in Congress and in the Supreme Court, and among governors of several provinces. They were to be up for election in 2003. If Kirchner hopes to pursue his pragmatic policy, he needs to mobilize and organize the popular classes, requiring a break with the Peronist party, which is unlikely to happen. As a consequence, he will resort to the use of presidential decrees, or compromise away most of his reform to the institutional power structure.

At the time of his inauguration, he had the *de facto* support of the three trade-union confederations, the great mass of the impoverished middle class, important sectors of public employees and their unions as well as the majority of small and medium-sized enterprises. At the same time he was being pressured by the IMF and local and international finance capital to allow creditors to take over mortgages of tens of thousands of properties owned by lower middle class Argentines, the latter being the very same classes which look to him for new initiatives to move the country to greater development.

The advent of Kirchner is a major challenge to the new unemployed workers movements and militant trade unionists. They had mostly agreed to suspend militant confrontations for three months to give the regime time to define and implement its social and economic policies. Given Kirchner's broad support, this is a realistic and practical approach that leaves open the possibility of reviving direct action if he fails to deliver.

Conclusion

Argentine politics have gone full circle from a populist uprising forcing the resignation of a president and several would-be presidents to the return of a quasi-elected president (Kirchner's opponent, Menem, resigned before the runoff). Argentines have gone from street fighting to the ballot box, from despising traditional politicians to expectations that the newly elected president will begin to reverse the decline in living standards and reactivate the economy. The turn of the cycle was not some automatic "pendulum movement" but was based on the inability of the Left, Marxists, socialists, anarchists, "horizontalists" and many others to organize and channel the widespread angry discontent that circulated throughout the country following the collapse of the financial system and mass impoverishment. If ever "objective circumstances" favoured a radical transformation, the period between December 2001 and July 2002 (see Chapter 9) was that period. It featured mass movements in the streets, a middle class proletarianized in living standards if not in outlook, a ruling class badly discredited but neither dislodged nor decisively defeated, and a movement by unemployed factory workers to occupy abandoned factories — 160 factory takeovers among the 2,500 closed firms in 2001–2002.

Beyond tactical mistakes, several theoretical issues came to the forefront. First, a massive popular rebellion is not a revolution. To conclude, as many leftists and anarchists did, that a "pre-revolutionary situation" was present (between December 2001 and February 2002) and to act as if tending to "reformist issues" and coalition building with progressive trade unions was no longer necessary, led to an isolation of the advanced detachment of the movement and to a loss of touch with the great majority of discontented unemployed workers and the middle class. A second theoretical point was that no organization had the necessary support to assume a leadership role (even as each pretended to be self-sufficient) and define a political project towards taking state power over time. In the absence of unified and cohesive leadership, intellectual dilettantes and local leaders carved up the movements in the name of autonomist fetishism or vainglorious vanguardism — they all "put the pail over their heads" and believed their own "spontaneist" or revolutionary slogans — which certainly did not resonate with the masses.

A third point is that social movements, even (or especially) ones that lack a political vocation for power and reject *political* struggle, end up as pressure groups within a political system dominated by traditional politicians and parties. An anti-political slogan "*que se vayan todos*" ("all politicians get out") intimidated any promising Left candidates and ultimately led to the domination of electoral politics by the traditional Right parties.

The final and crucial point was that when the mass of the populace rebelled and turned their back on traditional parties, they were not up for an insurrection or organized for a "barricade" style of politics. Instead they sought a unified, credible mass political formation capable of offering the electorate a way out of the crisis. While perhaps a minority of activists felt the time was ripe to strike for power, they were fragmented, divided and lacked any experienced leadership capable of organizing a serious bid for power. Clearly, the "insurrectionary" illusions of the "new radicalism" faded after the heady days of December 19/20, 2001, and early January 2002. The task of organizing the three to four million unemployed (see Chapter 9) was on the agenda; the employed workers in the private sector were still controlled by trade union bosses. These challenges were never met. Radicalized activists in the hundreds of thousands did not extend to millions. Yet, there was a way to organize a unified mass electoral alternative to begin the process of change since the ruling class was divided into five competing factions. That was also lost — to anarchists who rejected elections, to movement leaders who rejected politics as by nature corrupt and to Marxist sects who each presented their singular gurus to consolidate their two percent of the vote.

The missed opportunity for transformation does not tell all of the story. As our case studies of Zanon, the Rio Turbo miners, and young telephone workers demonstrate, substantial victories were achieved: Zanon demonstrated that worker-managed factories can succeed, temporary workers can change their labour contracts and popular assemblies can work with trade unionists and unemployed groups. The December uprising *is* a point of reference for millions in Argentina. The heroic days of mass solidarity and changes in regime is a reminder of what popular power can and will do, even if it is mostly spontaneous. It is a reminder, too, that if President Kirchner fails, the cycle may turn again towards mass politics.

5. Right/Left Polarization

The Ballot Box and the Street

The news media, academics and conventional politicians have focused on the growth of the electoral power of the Right and Far Right. The most recent first-round elections in France, where the combined vote for the extreme Right totalled 20 percent, is cited as an indication of a turn to the ultra right. Within a few days, more than a half-million demonstrators took to the streets of Paris and other cities against Le Pen.

We argue that there is no general shift to the right, but rather a sharpening polarization between the Right and the Left, with the former expressing itself at the ballot box and the latter in the streets. This polarization reflects diverse and complex situations and takes a variety of forms and expressions. The very conception of a Right/Left polarization needs to be clarified, given the confusion that surrounds what "Left" and "Right" mean.

We specify the terms of our discussion, proceed to analyze and describe the polarization and conclude by focusing on theoretical and political implications.

The Right and Left Today

Academics, journalists and political publicists have created a great deal of confusion in their careless labelling of political regimes. For example, French political leader Jean-Marie Le Pen is correctly tagged as "Far Right" for his racist, xenophobic rhetoric. Yet the George W. Bush administration, engaged in wars (Afghanistan, Colombia, Iraq) and coups (Venezuela) is mistakenly referred to as "conservative," instead of correctly identified as "Far Right." Likewise, England's Tony Blair, France's Lionel Jospin and the previous Bill Clinton administration are labelled "Centre-Left," even though they slashed welfare programs and promoted financial speculation, overseas conquest in the Balkans and, in the case of Jospin, privatized more public sector enterprises than any of its conservative predecessors. Clearly the most appropriate label is "conservative" or "Centre-Right."

In practice, many of the Centre-Right politicians are not conservatives in the generic sense of supporting existing constitutional norms: Blair and Clinton greatly exceeded constitutional restraints by usurping war powers in the Balkans, while Jospin privatized Air France, France Telecom and the defence industries without parliamentary consent. The transition from the "Centre-Right" to the Right and Far Right has its roots precisely in the negative effects generated by their socio-economic policies on their popular voting constituencies.

Today the significant and dynamic force of the genuine Left is found in the streets; it finds expression in massive mobilizations and not in the electoral process. In Italy, 300,000 demonstrated against capital and two million against Silvio Berlusconi; in Spain, 400,000, mostly anti-capitalist demonstrators, protested the EU summit and the Spanish presidency of José Maria Aznar.

What was considered the "Centre-Left" has moved to the centre-right or right; what was considered the Right has become the Far Right. Today the Centre-Left is weakening or non-existent; the electoral debates are between the Centre-Right, the Right and the Far Right. Unlike the Left, the parties of the Right operate through the institutions of power and have little capacity or interest in street mobilizations except during electoral campaigns.

The policies that define all varieties of the Right include privatization of public enterprises, cutbacks in public sector services, deregulation of the economy, the weakening of labour unions, implementation of laws that undermine job security and social welfare, and support for past and future imperial wars.

The differences between the various right-wing parties include varying degrees of protectionism (Bush and Le Pen are strongest, Blair and Aznar are more liberal) and policies on immigration (most of the European Right are restrictive; Le Pen and Joerg Haider are for expulsion) and the Middle East (the US and Le Pen support Ariel Sharon unconditionally, the rest of the Europeans are mildly critical).

In Latin America the Right and Far Right include almost all the regimes that support US wars and interventions, accept the Free Trade Agreement of the Americas (FTAA) and follow the prescriptions of Euro-American financial institutions such as the IMF. In reality, this includes all regimes except Cuba and Venezuela.

In Latin America the electoral Left, namely the Centre-Left, has moved to the centre-right and beyond, or is a minor force. The major expression of the real Left is found in the major socio-political movements and organized popular uprisings, such as those which have toppled two presidents in Ecuador, four in Argentina and one in Bolivia. The Left has many different expressions, demands and forms of action, but there is a common thread. It relies on mass street mobilizations — "direct action" — and rejects US imperialism (Plan Colombia, the FTAA etc.), debt payments, structural adjustment policies and other IMF prescriptions. In most cases, it supports agrarian reform, nationalization of banks, vastly increasing the economic role of the state via public investments in social services, protection and promotion of the domestic market, new direct forms of popular representation, greater social equality via progressive tax legislation, expropriation of monopolies and confiscation of illegal fortunes.

There still remains an electoral Left, particularly in Europe (France and Italy mostly) and in Latin America (Argentina, Brazil, Mexico, Ecuador), but it has not had a significant impact in its institutional role. Only when the activists and leaders of the electoral Left become part of the larger direct action movement do they have any impact.

In summary, the old electoral divisions between the Centre-Left and Right have become irrelevant: most of the Communist and Social Democratic parties have adopted centre-right and right-wing policies, favouring capital and imperial wars, and abandoning welfare-state social legislation. The Left/Right divisions, however, are more relevant than ever if we take as our protagonists the growing Left mass movements and the electoral-institutional forces of the Right.

The Right Turn: The March through the Institutions

The electoral successes of the ultra-right-wing political parties in France (Le Pen), Austria (Haider) and Israel (Sharon) are directly related to the right-wing shift of former "centre-left" coalitions. The putative "centre-left" regimes have demonstrably been in favour of reducing state expenditures, threatening the social security system affecting the elderly, reducing trade barriers undermining small-scale farmers, and selective immigration, while introducing "labour flexibility" (lowering the cost and increasing the ease of firing older workers), thus increasing worker insecurity, emphasizing police measures instead of job expansion to fight youth crime etc. The result of the right turn is that significant sectors of the populace feel cheated and abandoned by the traditional left- and right-wing parties. Moreover, the former "Centre-Left" has extended the privatization of public enterprises, thus becoming firmly entrenched in popular consciousness as a big-business coalition indistinguishable from the conventional Right.

On the right, the blurring of differences with the Centre-Left on socio-economic interests has had a dual effect of pushing the Right closer to the Far-Right on issues of police repression (law and order), immigration (greater restrictions) and increased public identity with big business. In this context, the Ultra-Right's xenophobic and chauvinistic appeals are legitimated by the Right, while its protectionist and neo-liberal policies appeal to small businesspeople, farmers and shopkeepers threatened by the liberal policies of the former Centre-Left.

Equally important in the international sphere, the extremely militarist and imperialist policies emanating from Washington have strengthened the Far Right. The Bush administration's support of the extreme rightist Israeli leader Sharon, and the massacre of Afghans, Palestinians and Iraqis reinforces and legitimates the far-right-wing anti-Arab, anti-Muslim and anti-immigrant posture. Moreover, Washington's embrace of unilateralism, a "US empire first" position, and its domestic chauvinistic campaign fuelled by antiterrorist rhetoric fit perfectly with the positions adopted by Le Pen, Haider and the rest of the European Ultra-Right.

A powerful argument can be made that the major advance and impetus for the Far Right is the election and rule of the Bush-Cheney-Rumsfeld regime. The European Ultra-Right's program seeks to imitate the US administration. However, they have a public relations problem, since they also carry the ideological baggage of overt anti-Semitism and publicly expressed racism.

While the mass media speak and write of the "conservative" Bush administration, in reality it is everything but conservative in the style and substance of its policies. The Bush administration has reneged on and unilaterally rejected a series of basic international agreements: the Kyoto Protocol on global warming, the anti-ballistic missile (ABM) agreement with Russia, the treaty on biological and chemical warfare. The Bush administration has rejected the formation of an international tribunal that would have jurisdiction over crimes against humanity. It has imposed tariff barriers and quotas to protect uncompetitive timber, textile, sugar, automobile, steel and other industries, violating GATT and World Trade Organization (WTO) rules. The Bush regime does not conserve the economic status quo; rather, its policies represent a radical rupture and a move toward ultra-right-wing politics. In foreign relations the Bush administration has deepened and extended Clinton's policies of military conquest by instituting a permanent war strategy. Its wars against Afghanistan and Iraq, preparation for new wars elsewhere, proliferation of military bases in Central Asia, the Philippines, Latin America and the Balkans, and organization of the failed Venezuelan military coup mark a new virulent stage of imperial expansion.

In style as well as substance (in the form of unilateral military expansion), top US policy-makers defend the destruction of Afghanistan, reject European influence and openly embrace intervention in other countries. Bush calls Sharon a "man of peace" while the latter's armed forces slaughter, jail, torture and displace hundreds of thousands of Palestinians. US federal police raid hundreds of Muslim homes, offices and businesses and hold incommunicado and indefinitely close to two thousand Muslims.

The record of the Bush administration's wars on Muslims is far more right-wing than the rhetoric of Le Pen and Haider, and certainly far exceeds the policies of conventional European rightists such as Berlusconi and Aznar. Le Pen talks of protecting French industries from "globalization," while Bush has instituted a vast array of barriers. Le Pen threatens mostly Arab immigrants, whereas Bush has jailed and harassed hundreds of thousands of Arab immigrants and supplied strategic arms, diplomatic support and economic aid to an Israel that is displacing Palestinians. Le Pen proposed to project French imperial power in the world; Bush's empire building has exceeded Le Pen's dreams several fold. Le Pen proposes to increase police powers to reduce crime and terrorist activities; Bush, via the Patriot Act and a $27 billion budget, has, already in place, legislation facilitating military tribunals and other police measures which violate the US Constitution. Le Pen supports Sharon's anti-Palestinian war of words; Bush supports Sharon with arms and money.

The main difference is Le Pen's use of anti-Semitic rhetoric, which Bush eschews. If, as most commentators, politicians and media pundits correctly believe, Le Pen represents the Ultra-Right, then certainly the Bush administration represents the ultra-Ultra-Right. On issues of war, economy, politics, empire, Arab immigrants and international treaties, which are used to define Le Pen as an ultra-rightist, Bush is a much more forceful, direct and consequential practitioner. Moreover, the electoral support of Bush and his ascent to power is very much in line with or exceeds Le Pen's approach. Bush received only 24 percent of the electorate's votes (only half of the 50 percent who voted), a minority of the popular vote, and resorted to illegal procedures in Florida to gain power; Le Pen and the Ultra-Right have secured approximately 18 percent support and have not resorted to illegal methods to grab power.

The significance of the ascent of the Ultra-Right is not based on its electoral support but on its policies instituted once in power. Once in office, the ultra-right-wing minority Bush administration seized on war and mass manipulation of the terror scare to define its political agenda worldwide and to secure a domestic majority.

Equally significant, conventional right-wing regimes such as those of Chirac, Aznar and Berlusconi and former centre-leftists turned conservative such as Blair, Jospin, Schroeder et al. collaborated with the ultra-right war policies of Washington or offered feeble and inconsequential opposition. Only when US protectionist measures on steel infringed on European and Japanese business interests did they respond with threats of sanctions. Among European conservative regimes, only England's Tony Blair has followed Washington's far right-wing imperial agenda by supporting Bush's war plans in the Persian Gulf.

If the Ultra-Right in Europe is gaining greater prominence, it is not only or principally because of domestic issues, but because it has a role model and competitor in the Bush administration. We mention the growth of the Ultra-Right as a supposition and not a fact, because comparative electoral figures in Le Pen's vote hardly sustain the thesis of a powerful upsurge of the Ultra-Right. Le Pen's vote in the second round of the 2002 presidential elections replicated his vote seven years earlier. The combined vote of the Left (Trotskyists, Communists, Left Socialists and Greens) in the first round was nearly the same as Le Pen's. The significance of the vote for the Ultra-Right is not in its domestic matrix, but in its imitation of the Bush administration's international and national politics. While respectable far rightists in the Bush and Blair administrations forcefully criticize Le Pen and the Far Right in Europe for their rhetorical excesses, they deliberately overlook much larger similarities in global outlook. The success of the Bush administration in gaining popular backing for its attack on Muslim groups and its anti-terrorism campaign has seized the imagination of European ultra-right politicians. Equally significant, Washington's economic threats, unilateralist posture and trade protectionism threaten European sovereignty and expansion. The feeble response of the European Right (both the former Centre-Left and traditional conservatives) to Washington's global bullying provides fertile ground for the Ultra-Right's "France First" policies, a mirror image of Washington's practice.

If the "right turn" has advanced furthest and taken its most extreme expression in the US, it is nonetheless the case that a similar rightward shift has gained momentum in European electoral politics. If we discount the traditional "centre-left" and "centre-right" labels of the past, the actual practices of the European regimes in the past decades describe almost unrelenting anti-labour and pro–big business strategies. Shifts to the right, however, vary in speed and scope and depend on each country's particularities, especially the strength of its mass movements and trade unions. No European country, whether governed by ex–Social Democrats, Christian Democrats, Conservatives or other traditional parties has increased social welfare for the working class. On the contrary, all regimes have weakened legislation protecting jobs, worker security and trade union rights, and social, health and education benefits have been slashed to varying degrees. With the possible exception of France, for which the regime bears little responsibility, the working day has not been reduced; indeed, the multiplication of precarious and poorly paid employment has resulted in multiple jobs and longer hours. European regimes have participated in and supported US-led wars, bombings and invasions in Iraq and Yugoslavia — with permanent bases in Macedonia, Kosovo, Albania and Afghanistan — and, prior to the US war on Iraq, air control over all of Iraq. The coalition-led "Operation Iraqi Freedom" did split the NATO political and military alliance, with France, Belgium and Germany on one side, and the UK, Spain and Italy on the other. However, the depth and ultimate results of this split are unclear. What is clear is that all of the European regimes have adopted the military-neoliberal agenda promoted by their banks and multinationals — and have financed overseas expansion into Eastern Europe, Russia, the Middle East and Latin America, many times in competition and/or collaboration with the United States. The convergence of major European political parties on the neoliberal-military agenda means that there is a political vacuum on the electoral Left — no party represents those adversely affected by neoliberal policies, military expansionism and subsidies to big business and banks. The European multi-party system has been converted into the US one party–two factions system. In this context of electoral party unanimity, and popular adversity and discontent, two polar opposite forces have emerged and gained mass support: the electoral Ultra-Right and the extra-parliamentary Left.

Opposition to the coup in Venezuela did not initially come from elected representatives, Congress or the armed forces. It came from the hundreds of thousands of poor, both organized and unorganized, who took to the streets of Caracas and other major cities to restore Chavez to power. This show of popular power encouraged "loyalist military opposition" to the politics of the neoliberal parties. Their base of support is older people fearful of rising crime, derived from social decay and neoliberal policies, by unemployed youth, particularly young immigrants. They also draw support from small businesses and farmers threatened by imports and competition by big business. In this regard, the Ultra-Right combines a protectionist policy towards foreign producers and a liberal policy towards domestic monopolies. The ultra-rightists also appeal to veterans of colonial wars, Christian traditionalists and long-standing ideological supporters of fascist or quasi-fascist sects or movements. The most potent appeal, however, is to nationalist sentiment, by providing affirmation of national sovereignty against the undemocratic, big business-controlled EU, and US cultural influence and political domination. The Ultra-Right is hostile to trade unions on both ideological grounds (they are run by "communists") and economic grounds (they hinder productivity). They appeal to workers to join in "protecting their jobs from foreigners," rather than from the TNCs who fire them. Finally, the Ultra-Right echoes the anti-terrorist line to reinforce its strong police-state appeal, combining it with anti-immigrant and anti-leftist policies to attract conventional rightists.

This mixture of anti-establishment rhetoric and a pro-establishment liberal programs overlaps with conventional "old right" appeals to God, country and big business. The vitriolic rhetoric of the Far Right heightens the sense of political, religious and racial polarization between Right and Left while trying to obscure increasing class divisions emerging from neoliberal policies.

The Far Right has advanced electorally and chosen the terrain of institutional politics. It has not demonstrated significant power in the streets. Its millions of supporters vote for the Far Right because its policies are directed toward strengthening the state in the pursuit of neo-liberal policies at home and abroad. The attacks of the Far Right are on parties, not the police or army; on personalities and not on private property and relations; and on particular aspects of liberal policies, not on liberalism itself. The "exclusionist" approach to non-Europeans and overt embrace of greater police repression ("law and order" or "zero tolerance" policies) have drawn on the restrictive immigration legislation approved by the new and old Right in power, the anti-terrorist campaign orchestrated by Washington and the harsh police powers promoted by the "zero tolerance" ex-mayor of New York City, Rudolph Guiliani, who was so successful in reducing the crime rate that he was invited to Mexico City (for $1.3 million) as a consultant. The institutional and electoral approach of the Far Right has given them a certain "constitutional legitimacy" — they play by the same rules as the conventional neoliberal Right — and, given their programatic convergence on basic issues, a reason to work within the system.

Institutional polarization and intense inter-party competition over who best represents European capitalist interests (small versus large capital, international versus domestic producers) overshadows the Far Right and conventional Right's common hostility to the growing extra-parliamentary Left.

The Left Turn: The Streets Are Ours

The convergence of ex–Social Democrats and ex-Communists with liberal and conservative parties in support of international capital, imperial wars and anti-labour legislation has provoked hundreds of thousands of workers, public employees and particularly young people to turn to "street politics." From Seattle to Ottawa, from Melbourne to Genoa and Barcelona, tens of thousands have organized first against globalization and more recently against capitalism. The demonstrations have reached tens of millions of people and led to the proliferation of a vast network of supporters, organizers and international coordinating groups. Regional movements against the Free Trade Agreement of the Americas (FTAA) have grown in scope and intensity. The electoral arena has been bypassed because of heavy institutional blockage — the bourgeois parties' monopoly of the mass media, the constraints embedded in voting procedures — and because elected legislative bodies are impotent in the face of the centralization of power in central banks and other non-elected, executive institutions. The corruption, co-optation and impotence of elected representative institutions have forced workers, peasants, the unemployed, dissidents and the left opposition to turn to extra-parliamentary forms of struggle which have proven to be more effective in raising issues and securing change.

The mass demonstrations in Seattle, London, Genoa, Melbourne and Barcelona have been more effective in politicizing and activating a new generation of youth than all the "Left and Centre-Left" electoral campaigns combined. The demonstrations by the anti-globalization, anti-capital forces have been more effective in calling attention to the injustices of the new imperial order and international financial organizations (the IMF, World Bank, Inter-American Development Bank [IDB] etc.) than any and all congressional critics. Public debates on foreign debt, privatization and neoliberalism in the mass international forums are far more effective in creating international solidarity with the poor and exploited in the third world than are the deafening silence in the halls of the US Congress and the lonely critics in European parliaments. Extra-parliamentary mobilizations against the IMF, the TNCs and the WTO have put these organizations on the defensive: every place they hold their meetings they are surrounded by hundreds of thousands of activists and protected by barbed wire and thousands of police accompanied by helicopters and armoured vehicles.

The class polarization pits youth, workers, farmers, employees and professionals against the financial and industrial ruling classes. As the former Social Democratic and Communist parties move to the centre-right and embrace the right-wing neoliberal agenda, the extra-parliamentary movements occupy the space on the left and proceed to engage the Far Right and the neoliberal policies of the new and old Right.

In France the mass workers' movements of 1995–96 precipitated the defeat of the right-wing government, and the same mass pressure was successful in forcing the neoliberal (socialist) Jospin regime to introduce the thirty-five-hour week, before proceeding to privatize Air France, the defence industries and telecommunications and "flexibilize" working conditions, favouring employers.

It was not the toothless resolutions of the European Parliament criticizing the international banks that forced the WTO to meet on a God-forsaken island in the Persian Gulf. It was the threat of a bigger and more militant "Genoa."

The polarization between right-wing electoral regimes — including the former "Centre-Left" and the conventional Right — and the extra-parliamentary Left finds expression in Asia as well as Latin America. In the third world the Euro-US right turn — the rise to power of the Ultra Right in Washington and its accommodation by Europe — has deepened and radicalized the Left-Right polarization.

Deepening Polarization in Latin America

There are many signs of the move to the extreme right in Latin America. In Mexico, the Vicente Fox regime has broken with previous practices and openly embraced US interventionist positions and the proposed Plan Pueblo-Panama, turning the Mexican economy into a huge *maquiladora* (assembly plant economy); provoked a near break in relations with Cuba; and through its foreign minister, Jorge Castañeda, abandoned any pretext of an independent foreign policy. In domestic policy it promotes the gradual privatization of the lucrative petroleum industry and a tax on staple items of popular consumption. The Fox regime is a clear example of the form and content of the move to the far right: total subordination to the US project of unilateral empire building, unrestricted acceptance of US control over strategic resources of the economy and uncritical embrace of

US-sponsored free trade agreements. As the Fox regime moves further to the right, the level of popular opposition has increased. Massive May Day marches throughout Mexico, involving the major and minor trade unions, and peasant and Indian organizations, repudiated Fox's hostility toward Cuba and his craven servility to the Bush administration. The congressional opposition of the centre-left (PRD) and right (PRI) parties criticizes Fox and tries to modify his policies. However, the defeat of Fox's agenda will have to come from the mass of Mexicans outside of the halls of Congress, from the May Day demonstrators in the streets.

Venezuela has experienced the highest degree of socio-political polarization in its recent history. The pro-imperial Right, directed, financed and supported by the Bush administration and backed by the bourgeoisie, backed a failed military coup that was defeated by the mass of the urban and rural poor and sectors of the army. Even the institutional powers were divided: a minority sided with the US-bourgeois coup, but a majority supported the popular masses' successful restoration of liberal democracy. The Far Right in Washington found expression in the Far Right in Venezuela. This was clearly evident in the April 2002 failed coup. The first measures of business leader Pedro Carmona, the head of the coup, were totally in line with Washington's agenda: cutting off petroleum exports to Cuba, rejection of OPEC oil quotas, the embrace of Bush's foreign policy, and dissolution of all elected institutions, almost all with Chavez majorities. The coming to power of the Ultra-Right in Venezuela took the form of a puppet authoritarian regime at the beck and call of Washington and prepared to massively purge all public institutions of representatives of the Bolivarian movement (supporters of President Hugo Chavez's presidency).

Notwithstanding media accounts that stressed the dominant role of the military, the real turning point in the restoration of Chavez and democracy was the hundreds of thousands who reoccupied Caracas and threatened to storm the presidential palace. The bulk of the military was faced with a choice of siding with coup-makers and provoking a bloody civil war (with an uncertain outcome) or intervening so as to prevent the populace from seizing the reins of government and radicalizing the political process. The military intervened, as much to block further popular radicalization as to restore Chavez and liberal democracy. The complexity of the Venezuelan situation, where Chavez, representing a hybrid of nationalist foreign policy and neoliberal domestic policy confronts a domestic bourgeois and corrupt union bosses totally subordinated to Washington, is superimposed on a real class polarization. Long-standing privileges, racism, corruption and pillage by the upper class confronts a mass of the angry poor and downwardly mobile lower middle class suffering from unemployment and underemployment rates of up to 60 percent and poverty that has reached into 80 percent of households: residents of Miami condos and Wall Street speculators versus the poor living in *ranchos* in the hills overlooking Caracas; hunger in a land of plenty.

Chavez has neither organized nor met the basic demands of the mass of poor people who support him. He has, however, politicized and given form to their hostility against the rich and powerful, inculcated racial pride in being of African ancestry and affirmed Venezuela's national identity with his independent foreign policy. Popular participation and independence infuriates Washington and the local ruling classes, encouraging them to prepare the terrain for another coup. Another coup — in one form or another — will likely materialize sometime in 2003 or 2004. The forces pushing for it — primarily in the US — were gaining strength at the time of this writing (May 2003).

The coming to power of the Far Right in the US means a green light for coup-makers and open public support for greater repression to sustain continued foreign pillage of the economies. Colombia is a third example of the upsurge of the Ultra-Right in electoral politics. President Alvaro Uribe is the voice of Washington in its policy of total war against the popular insurgency. In the context of this war, declared as a war against drug trafficking and terrorism, the Bush administration is preparing a new, additional, multi-year and multi-million-dollar military aid program specifically directed against the peasant-based guerrillas. In Colombia the Washington-backed Andrés Pastrana regime broke peace negotiations initiated by the Uribe government and launched a failed military assault against the guerrillas, resulting in an escalation of the conflict and heightened military-paramilitary killings of civilian non-combatants.

Plan Colombia, Clinton's initial military aid package to stem the advance of the popular insurgency in Colombia, has been extended by the Bush administration through Plan Andina, the militarization of Ecuador and Peru; new military bases in San Salvador, Manta (Ecuador) and north central Peru; and direct involvement of US military officials, Special Forces and contracted mercenaries.

US militarization of Colombian politics has fomented a polarization of civil war proportions between the oligarchy and military, on one side, and the guerrillas and peasantry, on the other. Politics has moved completely outside the realm of Congress: it is the military high command versus the extra-parliamentary popular insurgency.

Argentine politics also highlight extreme social and political polarization between a non-elected (President Eduardo Duhalde was not elected by the voters) "electoral regime" and the vast majority of the electorate. The popular uprising of December 19/20, 2001 (see Chapter 9), was a spontaneous outpouring of anger, hostility and rejection of the political class — the major parties, provincial, municipal and congressional leaders and particularly the president, who fled the Casa Rosada (the presidential palace) by helicopter to avoid the hundreds of thousands of formerly middle class and unemployed demonstrators.

The social polarization could not be more stark: the banks (mostly foreign owned), backed by the government, confiscated all the savings of the middle class, more than $45 billion, while between $30 billion and $40 billion belonging to the elite fled the country just prior to the seizure of bank accounts. The financial class (with its yearly returns of more than 30 percent per year), via the self-selected Duhalde regime and backed by the IMF and World Bank, proposed that the government issue ten-year bonds at two percent interest as payback to the depositors whose savings the banks claimed they could not cover since the funds were shifted to home offices.

The move to the right and the far right in the US and Europe within the political class and among the governing parties has had a powerful impact in Latin America. In the first instance, it led to a pillaging of the economies in the region, provoking a deepening economic crisis. Second, it deepened socio-political polarization by concentrating wealth and encouraging massive multi-billion-dollar banking fraud at the cost of depositors and taxpayers. Third, the new Right in Europe and the US seeks to further pillage near-destitute populations and depressed economies through new demands undermining recovery and facilitating greater transfers of wealth upward and outward. Fourth, given the total isolation of client regimes and unanimous rejection of the new measures, Washington is turning toward an open embrace of military intervention and authoritarian, dictatorial regimes — with or without civilian electoral facades.

Nothing captures the ascendancy of the Far Right in Washington as much as the extreme economic measures and socio-political polarization in Latin America. Throughout Latin America the political class has failed to prevent the collapse of living standards, the impoverishment of the middle class, and the growing number of unemployed and underemployed, who now represent between 50 and 80 percent of the labour force. On the contrary, the right (formerly centre-left) parties have been accomplices in the process, approving regressive legislation that slashes public services and privatizes profitable public enterprises to meet debt obligations. The left electoral parties have been vocal but impotent critics, sidelined by the growth of executive powers and the dominant role of the Euro-US bankers and functionaries in the IMF, World Bank and IDF. In many cases the left parties have moved across the spectrum to the centre and even the right in order to accommodate the imperial power. The result is that the socio-political polarization in Latin America is between the extra-parliamentary movements and a US-Euro imperialism linked to domestic political elites and ruling classes.

Brazil is a good example. In the 1990s the Brazilian Social Democratic Party of Fernando Henrique Cardoso moved to the right, embraced neoliberal policies and allied itself with the Far Right, the landlord party (PFL) and the right-wing (PMDB), embraced Wall Street and received support from Washington. In the 2002 election the so-called "Workers Party" moved from the centre-left to the right, embraced the neoliberal agenda, attacked the landless workers movement, expressed support for Washington and allied itself with the far-right Liberal party.

The only organizations that remain to express and defend popular interests and demands are social movements such as the rural landless workers movement (MST). The "street" and not the ballot box is the road toward creating authentic forms of democratic representation against corrupt, impotent and complicit official political institutions. Only mass social movements have been successful in overthrowing presidents who are complicit with imperial institutions in impoverishing populations and pillaging economies. The list of presidents ousted by mass movements is long and growing: four in one month in Argentina, two in Ecuador and one each in Venezuela, Brazil and Bolivia. The social power of mass movements has settled more than 300,000 landless families on farms in Brazil, defended the livelihood of thousands of coca farmers in Bolivia and Colombia, and defeated a US-orchestrated coup and restored democracy in Venezuela. There is a striking contrast between the power, integrity and effectiveness of the mass, leftist socio-political movements and the impotence, opportunism and marginality of the left electoral parties.

Right-wing extremism in the US and Europe has weakened the centre-left electoral option in Latin America, undermining its basis for "democracy" among the trade unions and what remains of the middle class, and setting the stage for a classic confrontation between dictatorial reaction and revolution.

Polarization in the Middle East

The move to the far right in the United States has encouraged and promoted the extreme Right throughout the world. There are innumerable examples, from US backing of Israel's invasion and destruction of Palestinian territories; to Washington-ally General Pervez Musharraf's consolidation of his military dictatorship in Pakistan; to closer ties with the anti-Muslim, Hindu extremist, free-market Bharadiya Janatra Party (BJP) regime in India. In Central Asia the rulers of the former Soviet republics open their doors to US military bases, in effect becoming subordinate clients of the US empire. In India the BJP regime, lined up with Washington's anti-terrorist campaign is allied with Hindu fascists in Gujarat who organized anti-Muslim programs that killed or maimed thousands and displaced more than 150,000. In Pakistan, General Musharraf has allowed US Special Forces to intervene and attack tribal communities in Pakistan, while organizing a fraudulent referendum to extend his rule (he "won" 98 percent of the vote) — all reported without irony or criticism by the Western imperial press. In the Philippines the Gloria Macapagal-Arroyo regime has violated all constitutional restraints and allowed the United States to re-establish military bases and directly involve senior US military officials in military operations against Muslim separatists. The move to the far right in Central Asia, Pakistan, India and the Philippines (as measured by increased recolonization of territory, imperial military penetration and harsh repression of minorities and dissidents) is directly linked to the rise of the Ultra-Right to power in the US and mutual interests in consolidating local power in the service of US imperial domination.

The Bush-Sharon alliance is the best example of the convergence of the Far Right in power. The Israeli military invasion of Palestinian towns and the scorched earth policy that left hundreds of thousands homeless and tens of thousands dead, wounded or imprisoned in concentration camps was militarily supported by Washington and received the overwhelming backing of the US Congress and Senate: in the Senate the support was 94–2, in the House 352–21. In the midst of the slaughter of Jenin, President Bush praised Sharon as a "man of peace" and denounced the Palestinian resistance as "terrorists." Powerful Jewish congressional leaders, led by Senator Joe Lieberman, made the connection, linking Israel's war on the Palestinian people to Washington's worldwide military offensive. Israel's ultra-right-wing policy of demolishing Palestinian economic, social and political institutions is designed, as Israeli writer Uri Avnery has written ("A Second Nakba," *Ma'ariv Daily*, 19 May 2001), to expel them from the territories, a position that is publicly supported by US House Majority Leader Richard Armey, who called for the forceful removal of all Palestinians from the occupied territories. This fascist-like "Final Solution" comes from the politician third in the line of presidential succession, after Bush and Vice-President Cheney. US and Israeli extremism has totally polarized Palestinian and Arab opinion in favour of armed resistance and put enormous pressure on US political clients in Egypt and Saudi Arabia and on Yasser Arafat. Except for three Arab sheikdoms in the Gulf, the Israel–US axis is totally isolated and its war against Iraq almost unanimously condemned.

The dynamics of the US embrace of extremism in the Middle East is closely tied to powerful Jewish lobbies in the United States. The American Israel Public Affairs Committee (AIPAC), which employs 140 people, is described by the *Financial Times* as "one of the top five lobbying groups in Washington" (2 May 2002: 4). In propagating Israeli state policies and securing political and military support, AIPAC works closely with the thirty-seven Jewish members of Congress, the American Jewish Committee, the presidents of major Jewish organizations and influential, ultra-right fundamentalist Christian politicians, particularly congressional leader Thomas Delay and House Majority Leader Richard ("I'm content to have Israel grab the entire West Bank") Armey. Within the Bush administration, the ultra-right, unconditional supporters of Sharon include both Jews (Richard Perle and Paul Wolfwitz in the Pentagon) and non-Jews (Vice-President Cheney and Defense Secretary Rumsfeld).

This powerful constellation of ideological and ethnic/religious forces has marginalized the US petroleum companies allied with Arab petroleum producers in shaping US policies in the Middle East. The result is an extremely unbalanced pro-Israel policy based strictly on narrow military considerations and Israel's role in providing surrogate counter-insurgency operatives, reportedly operating in Colombia, Venezuela, Peru, Ecuador and elsewhere.

The US-Israeli war against the Palestinians has made the issue of anti-colonialism and anti-imperialism the central point of confrontation in the Middle East, marginalizing parliamentary critics in the region and in Europe. Sharon and his US backers have raised the stakes: unconditional surrender to military force or armed resistance. The Ultra-Right has undermined the position of the centre. Sharon's support has increased dramatically in Israel to more than 75 percent among Jews; among US Jews, close to 100,000 marched in support, while AIPAC and allied Jewish organizations raised hundreds of millions in emergency Israel bond sales and secured near unanimous support in the US Congress and mass media. On the other hand, millions of Europeans and tens of millions of Arabs and Muslims have taken sides in favour of the Palestinian resistance. As Sharon and his Labour allies affirm their right to massacre Palestinians, they adopt Bush's slogan of "you are for us or against us," rejecting all criticism from the United Nations, the Red Cross and other organizations. The US backed Sharon's rejection of a UN commission seeking to investigate the slaughter in Jenin. Israel's arrogance in the face of the condemnation of world public opinion is a tribute to its confidence in Washington's backing and in the capacity of the Jewish lobbies and politicians to influence both houses of the US Congress.

Europe and the US: Polarization or Convergence?

The polarization between imperialism and socio-political movements is a growing factor in European politics. The anti-globalization movement (see Chapter 10) has radicalized in recent years, adopting an anti-capitalist, anti-imperialist and anti-Israeli position in the face of the US worldwide military offensive, and the Israeli invasion of the Palestinian nation. From London to Prague to Genoa and Barcelona, the demonstrations have grown in size and radicalized programatically. The socio-political movements have grown in direct relationship to the right turn of the former Social Democratic parties. The British Labour Party is now the party of the City of London, the party that opposes lowering British working hours and raising wages to the level of the rest of Europe. The Socialist Jospin and his Green and Communist satellite partners have privatized more public firms than the conventional right-wing parties. Aznar, the Spanish ruler, has backed Bush's far-right worldwide military agenda, followed Washington in supporting the failed military coup in Venezuela and is in the forefront in supporting the IMF's efforts to impose new draconian measures upon the Argentine working class to rescue Spanish bankers and Spanish petroleum and telecommunication monopolies. In line with Bush and Blair, Aznar has severely curtailed democratic freedoms through a series of anti-terrorist measures which have led to the outlawing of dissident parties and restricted peaceful civil protests. During the march against the EU summit meeting in Barcelona in March 2002, Aznar mobilized more than twenty thousand police and members of the armed forces, and helicopters and warships to intimidate protestors. The move failed as more than 400,000 demonstrators filled the streets.

In Italy, Germany and France, electoral politics move to the right, and social movements occupy a privileged place as the major opposition. In France, in the first round, Jospin's coalition was resoundly defeated, abstention surged to nearly 30 percent and the ultra-rightist Le Pen secured nearly 20 percent of the vote. In the runoff, however, nearly a million street demonstrators mobilized against the fascist right and diminished his support. Unfortunately, the extra-parliamentary Left was unable to persuade voters to reject the right-wing winner Chirac.

In Italy more than two million workers demonstrated against Berlusconi's anti-labour legislation in the biggest protest since the end of the Second World War, successfully blocking the legislation — something the electoral Centre-Left and Left was incapable of doing. As pressure from US imperialism intensifies, and popular discontent from below increases, the European ruling class alternates between criticizing the United States and capitulating and backing US policy.

European socio-political movements have forced European governments to accept the Kyoto Protocol, to criticize Sharon's massacre of the Palestinians, to support the International Tribunal on Crimes Against Humanity, the international anti-biological and chemical warfare agreement and the ABM treaty on missiles, in opposition to Washington's unilateral rejections. On the other hand, the European ruling class has by and large backed the US military global offensive. The EU, for example, supports the IMF-US position on Argentina and Europe, and it has followed the US trade policy of protectionism at home and liberalization abroad. The latter has led to a series of major trade disputes, as rival imperialists compete for global markets. US tariffs on EU steel and subsidies for US exporters have provoked retaliation from Europe. The US-proposed free trade area in Latin America is an attempt to monopolize markets at the expense of Europe, and US unilateral decisions on the environment are designed to lower US industrial costs to improve its competitive position. US military interventions and their accompanying atrocities require Washington to reject international judicial authority.

The dynamic of the current drive for US world supremacy does not include wealth- and market-sharing with its European imperial partners. To paraphrase Bush: You are either under us or with the enemy. The ultra-imperialism of the Ultra-Right in power has created a certain limited polarization between the EU and the US, with Washington stronger militarily and the EU stronger economically. Up to the Iraq war, after expressing doubts, reservations and even criticism on all major issues, Europe capitulated to Washington. The Iraq war did expose and open up a division within Europe, but with the rise of the Right in England, Italy,

Spain and France, the EU will continue to follow Washington's militarist-interventionist policies except where they might prejudice European strategic interests, such as a situation in Iraq that would choke off the oil stream and undermine their economies. Trade disputes are not likely to break into a trade war, mainly because Europe does not have the will to confront the United States. Nevertheless, given the growing power of the anti-capitalist movements in Europe and the militancy of the French, Italian and, to a lesser degree, German trade unions, the European Right cannot embrace the US agenda without prejudicing their own TNCs and provoking mass opposition. The key to deepening the polarization between Europe and the US depends on the extra-parliamentary movements, not the capitalist calculus of the right-wing regimes.

Conclusion

The worldwide polarization is between the Right/Far Right holding state power and the Left located in the streets and in mass socio-political movements. This is the defining political reality of the early twenty-first century. The rise to power of the Ultra-Right in Washington, with its doctrine of permanent wars and total domination, has deepened the polarization in Latin America, Asia and Europe. The right turn of the Centre-Left and its accommodation on the right has resulted in the left socio-political movements becoming the only alternative to US empire-building.

The power of the Right/Ultra-Right is found in its control of the state, including the means of repression and the basic economic institutions. These power bases provide continuity of action and control over the mass media. The power of the Left is found in its capacity for mass mobilization and its occasional ability to oust political leaders, paralyze economic activity and confront summit meetings of the imperial powers. The weakness of the Ultra-Right/Right is found in their structural position as the root cause of world pillage, exploitation and ecological destruction that adversely affects several billion people while benefiting a small minority. The weakness of the Left is the discontinuity of its actions and its lack of a clear strategy for taking state power. Powerful as an opposition, the left socio-political movements lack the Right's vocation for state power and rulership.

As time progresses, the intensity of the conflicts inherent in this major polarization deepens. As the Ultra Right in Washington intervenes militarily throughout the world, it presses its clients to impose draconian cuts in social programs and to increase their military actions. Military coups, the consolidation of military dictatorship in Pakistan, Sharon's genocide in the Palestinian territories — events such as these become the norm. On the left, the mass movements take to the street, the entire Palestinian nation resists, Colombian guerrillas strike back and anti-capital demonstrations in Europe grow in size and scope. The electoral Left is marginalized, and the former Centre-Left joins the Right.

One important theoretical point here is that polarization today does not take the form of simple confrontation between left parties and the state. Today the major battles are between the extra-parliamentary left movements and the imperial states and their local clients. Second, the electoral political arena is being bypassed. The Right rules via imperial executive decree and the Left responds in the streets.

The Right takes power via its monopoly of the electoral process and then rules in the interests of big business. The Left mobilizes via its national and international networks, using the Internet, and articulates popular grievances that are ignored by the nominally elected bodies. We are in a period of wars, rising right-wing authoritarian rule, deepening social polarization and increasingly effective extra-parliamentary action. This is a period of permanent wars, coups and empire building without an end in sight. These "forced circumstances" are the driving forces for the resurgence of mass mobilizations throughout Latin America and elsewhere. The political outcome of this polarization is not predetermined: it depends on the political intervention of one or the other antagonists. There are at least four possible scenarios.

Scenario One: The polarization and confrontations are resolved by a return to social democracy. The extra-parliamentary Left grows and threatens the rule of capital but lacks a vocation for power. Out of fear of losing power, wealth and property, the ruling class negotiates with the "lesser evil," a revived Centre-Left, a social pact, sharing the wealth.

Scenario Two: The polarization results in a victory for the Right and Far Right, opening the door to a US world empire based on repressive third world regimes and US-style two-party rule in Europe.

Scenario Three: Left mobilizations and movements, combined with inter-imperial conflicts, trade wars and economic crises, culminate in the Left taking state power and initiating a socialization of the means of production.

Scenario Four: Continued, unresolved polarization without definitive resolution. The US empire is unsustainable because of its economic cost and the weakness of client regimes; socio-political movements oppose dictators and client regimes but are unable to take power; and the

European Union is driven by unresolved class and immigrant-related conflicts.

Faced with these possible scenarios, what is to be done? What can be done to make the third scenario a reality? First and foremost, the extra-parliamentary Left should decisively break its ties to the electoral Left and concentrate on expanding its mass base beyond its original sectoral constituencies, developing a strategy for state power. This requires a total rupture with sectarian left and "spontaneity" ideologues who fragment movements and/or turn them into pressure groups. Second, the extra-parliamentary Left must develop continuity of action, directly intervening in day-to-day neighbourhood, trade union and rural worker struggles. Mass mobilizations at international events must become subordinated to the building of continuous organizations that lead to national class movements. Third, extra-parliamentary movements must confront the fact that the main adversary is American and European imperialism, and not some vague notion of "globalization" or "empire." Ideological clarity is essential in the formulation of an alternative program. The revival of a centre-left electoral force is highly unlikely given the turn to the right.

Even under mass pressure, it is unlikely that the capitalist class will accept a return to a welfare state. Almost surely it will embrace ultra-right solutions. Even if a viable Centre-Left reappears, it will hardly be stable, given the polarized political scene today.

A definitive victory for the Right/Ultra-Right would in most regions take place without a significant mass base. Even military dictatorships resulting from US-orchestrated coups will face the problem of ruling without economic resources (because their reasons for being would be to restore foreign debt payments etc.) and without even the tacit acquiescence of the workforce. The Left must mobilize to prevent the Ultra-Right from coming to power, while not compromising with the Right in any of its forms. Only political independence, the buildup of social power from below, and a vocation for state power will resolve the current polarization in an historically progressive direction.

6. Cod

An Ecological Crisis of Industrial Capitalism

No fish has had such a dramatic history as the North Atlantic cod. The development and history of nations and people on both sides of the North Atlantic, and elsewhere in the world, are bound up with the catching — and eating — of this fish, which even today remains one of the principal sources of food protein in the world. A basic biography of this fish and many accounts and reports of the developments that surrounded its history have already been written (Kurlansky 1997). This chapter will not attempt to synthesize these writings, nor will it seek to extrapolate from their conclusions, and this for two reasons: first, we tend to draw somewhat different conclusions from most of the studies referred to in these publications, and, second, we are particularly interested in what might be termed the "political economy" of the harvesting and consumption of cod.

In the Beginning There Was Cod

> The time may come ... when ... even our stock of cod, if misused, will not prove inexhaustible. Consequently, it would be desirable that everybody ... in the fishing business should know something more about commercial fishes than the best way to catch and market them. (Nancy Frost 1938)

Records show that the English fished on the Grand Banks off "New Founde Lande" as early as 1481, and we know for certain that the Portuguese fished there in 1501. There are also indications that the Vikings visited the waters of Georges Bank and Nantucket Bank in the Gulf of Maine even earlier — perhaps as far back as a thousand years (Kurlansky 1997: 21ff.). But the earliest and historically most significant fishery on the Grand Banks, once the richest fishing ground in all the world, was established by the Basques of Europe. The Basques fished the prolific cod grounds on the Grand Banks for centuries, perhaps as early as 1000 AD, but until the turn of the sixteenth century managed to keep the precise location of the most prolific fishery in the world a secret. Each year, around March or April, a slew of Basque fishing boats would make the perilous journey from Europe to the distant fishing grounds off Newfoundland in search of a prized food fish, which they would first salt and then consume or trade. When Jacques Cartier arrived at the mouth of the St. Lawrence near the Gaspé peninsula in 1534, at what is today New Brunswick and Quebec, he found up to a thousand Basque fishing vessels (Kurlansky 1997: 29). Unlike other explorers of the "New World," wanting to keep a good secret, the Basques had never claimed any of the lands close to their fishing grounds.

The object of these annual visits to the "Grand Banks" was a codfish stock so rich that the waters were literally teeming with them. (In fact, the term "codfish" is loosely used with reference to up to ten families of fish, including more than two hundred species, almost all of which live in the cold waters of the Northern Hemisphere. The gadiform family of "codfish" includes five species: Atlantic cod, haddock, pollock, whiting and hake.) An English Captain Mason, sailing from Bristol, on putting to shore in 1617, observed "cod so thicke ... that we nearlie have been able to row through them" (in Marsh 1992: 5). Alexandre Dumas, in *Le Grande Dictionaire de Cuisine* (1873), with reference to the astounding reproductive capacity of the female cod (many millions of eggs per fish), noted that "if no accident prevented the hatching of the eggs and each egg reached maturity, it would take only three years to fill the sea that you could walk across the Atlantic dryshod on the backs of the cod." With the discovery of this bounty, what had been so long a well-guarded secret was struck with the royal seal and became public knowledge. Owners of fishing fleets from various European ports needed little prodding and took great risks to join the annual race to the Grand Banks — to "Codlandia," or what would become known later as "New Founde Land." Settlements were initially prohibited by British law, but the perils of the annual voyage and the dangers involved in the high-seas fishery,[1] as well as the prerogatives of mercantile trade, led European seafarers and fishers eventually to touch down on *terra firma*. Newfoundland, or the Rock, as it is still called, possessed a coast furrowed with bights and deep coves that offered a base of operations infinitely more stable and comfortable than the bridge of a ship. It also allowed English fishers, with scarce salt reserves, to preserve their catch of Atlantic cod — (*Gadus morhua*, a species of fish called *cabillaud* by European francophones before it is salted, *bacalao* in Spain and *bacalhau* by the Portuguese) — by drying it in the sun on the stony beaches of New Founde Lande. The Basques and other Europeans with access to not only the rich salt deposits of the Mediterranean but also a sun strong enough to dry sea salt, generally preserved their catch in a salty brine ("green cod") before drying it in the sun, thus producing a dried salted form of cod that had a remarkable resistance to spoiling and, when restored through soaking, resulted in a flaky white flesh that is still preferred by many to fresh cod.

For centuries, cod fishing ships from European ports sailed to the rich fishing grounds of the new continent. By 1550 there were at least twenty-five of these grounds, and by the end of the sixteenth century, cod landings on the Grand Banks were already up to a hundred thousand tonnes per year. A century later, landings had doubled, and during the nineteenth century, still with rudimentary technology (dories, line and hooks), the catch ranged from 150,000 to 400,000 tonnes per fishing season.

For years, there were no permanent settlements in New Founde Lande, only annual fishing camps set up to salt and dry cod for shipment back home or to the West Indies, where for years it was exchanged for molasses and rum. In the sixteenth century, however, a number of settlements were established to provide a better base to pursue the cod fishery. Cod not only entered into the slave trade but was the backbone of mercantile trade between Great Britain, North America (Nova Scotia and Newfoundland) and the islands of the West Indies, becoming the staple food for the population of slaves and indentured workers in the Caribbean islands and elsewhere. Cod was the basis of a number of large fortunes and a rich merchant aristocracy formed in New England in the seventeenth century. By the eighteenth century, cod had lifted New England from a distant colony of starving settlers to an international commercial power. The salt cod merchants who constituted the aristocracy in the New England settlements grew rich on the sale of low-quality salted cod to the West Indies (Kurlansky 1997: 78–90).

One legacy of the cod trade is that even today in Jamaica and other Caribbean islands salted (Icelandic) cod still reigns supreme at the level of consumption for all classes of people, being the staple in most islanders' breakfasts and the meal of choice in many restaurants and popular kitchens. In Brazil, another former centre in the trade, *bacalao* is today by far the most expensive menu item in the most expensive restaurants. In Spain, while the prodigious consumption and production of fish and seafood in recent years has to some extent shifted away from cod, for centuries it was the principal catch for Spain's large distant-water fishing fleet and fish merchants.

Cod Then and Now: Where Have All the Fish Gone?

In the fifteenth century, cod fishers from Portugal and the Basque region found the cod so plentiful — individual cod averaging 45–70 kilos — that they could be killed close to shore, with little effort, by a handheld pike. The Portuguese explorer Giovanni Caboto marvelled in 1497 that the waters off the rocky shores of Newfoundland were churning with so many codfish that they made the passage of his ship difficult. In the following centuries, cod fishing was virtually the only reason anyone came to Newfoundland, or settled there.

The most productive cod-fishing area in the vast Northwest Atlantic region was located off southern Labrador and the east of Newfoundland. Thousands of fishers in small craft, using traditional techniques such as traps, gill nets or jigging from a dory, joined fishing boats from Spain, Portugal and France to tap what until recently was the world's most abundant fishery. How abundant? As recently as 1978, the author, accompanying an anthropologist friend on a fishing venture, jigging for cod one early morning, landed a codfish weighing 18 kilos and another weighing even more. However, that was then and this is now. Such cod are history, it being rare today to find one in excess of 4 kilos; they tend to average 2–3 kilos. However, the largest cod fish ever caught, in May 1895, off Massachusetts, measured in excess of 1.8 metres and weighed 96 kilos (Kurlansky 1997: 45).

From the seventeenth century to the 1930s the most common form of cod fishing was to go out to the Banks in a larger ship and then lower small rowing boats or dories, twenty-foot deckless skiffs, with a crew of one or two. Until the 1950s the majority of fishers relied on dories or motorized Cape Islanders, and, for the near and offshore, on bigger yet modestly sized gill netters and longliners. However, this fleet competed with hundreds of large draggers sailing from European ports and crossing the Atlantic each year to take fish from the Grand Banks and as close as twelve nautical miles from the coast. The combined effort in the 1950s yielded annual catches of from 800,000 to 900,000 — even one million — tonnes. Thus, given an average weight of 2.5 kilos, each year 320 to 400 million fish were removed from the ocean.

Could the stocks sustain such a mortality rate? This question was raised by alarmed scientists in the European Community, North America and Japan, resulting in the formation, in 1952 of the International Commission for the Northwest Atlantic Fisheries (ICNAF) on the European side of the Atlantic, and a set of international conservative regulations (Chantraine 1992: 39). However, this effort to conserve the cod stocks in the North

Atlantic had little to no effect on the fierce competition that existed between Canadian trawlers and their European counterparts. In this environment the Canadian government in just five years (1960–65) added to the Canadian fleet 129 trawlers, each with a capacity of 50 tonnes (ADB 1969: 41). In the process, Canada's groundfish trawler catch grew from 136,000 to 325,000 metric tonnes (although European trawlers accounted for 66 percent of the increase in the total catch).

By 1960 the total harvest of cod off the Banks of Newfoundland, Nova Scotia and the Gulf of St. Lawrence totalled more than a million tonnes a year, and it kept on growing throughout the decade to reach 1.9 million tonnes in 1968. However, by then this wild overfishing seemed to have reached its limit, as annual catches in subsequent years began to decline — from 1.5 million tonnes in 1969 to less than 500,000 in the years 1976 to 1978, a level reached in the nineteenth century with a fleet that was a fraction the size and had much more rudimentary technology (Chantraine 1992: 40–41).

The large and growing distant-water fleets from Europe concentrated their efforts on the Grand Banks of Newfoundland, taking up more than 400,000 tonnes of cod annually — more than half of all North Atlantic cod landings. In 1973 the combined effort of the Canadian and European fishing fleets resulted in a collapse of the cod fishery, the first of several that fifteen years later would be used to justify the closing down of the Newfoundland fishery, and with it, the jobs and communities dependent on it.

By the Way of Cod: Collapse of a Fishery and a Rotten Little War

Many efforts have been made to determine the reasons for the collapse of the cod stock.[2] Reasons given by scientists, politicians, industry representatives and fishers themselves have varied from the predations of seals or the changing temperature of the oceans to overexploitation, destructive dragger technology and fishing gear, and a permissive approach to fisheries development to lack of adequate resource management, and government support for the expansionist and profit motivations of private investors within a capitalist system. This last factor has been conceptualized both in terms of "corporate greed" and in more systemic terms, to wit: "Economic growth in modern society is driven by employers' and investors' unrelenting efforts to accumulate more and more wealth in one round of investment and profit-making after another. Those who do not accumulate faster than the pack fall victim to the … competition of other employers and investors. The capitalists' desire to turn money into investment to make more money as quickly as possible becomes not only a goal, but also a goad driving them all. In order that money be turned into more and more and more money, there must constantly be new investment opportunities and production must continually expand. In the fishery, new fish stocks must be found and known ones must be more intensively fished, regardless of the predictable consequences for nature or the people" (Michael Clow, personal communication, 14 June 2002).

Even today, close to thirty years into the crisis, there is no consensus on this issue. There are still those (see Harris 1989) who blame the seal, pointing out that, until the Department of Fisheries and Oceans (DFO) banned the seal hunt in 1983, the cod fishery was on its way to recovery. Each mature seal, situated at the top of the food chain, it is argued, consumes between one and one and a half tonnes of codfish a year. Whether there are between two and two and a half million of them, as at the time the seal hunt was banned, or, as it has been estimated, between four to six million, they certainly have a significant impact on the marine ecosystem — and cod stocks (Chantraine 1992: 96–99).

Another, more critical factor by most accounts was rapacious overfishing, particularly of immature, undersized stock, by fleets of European trawlers. According to George Baker, Liberal Member of Parliament from Newfoundland at the time, this was particularly true in the case of Spanish trawlers, leading to a short and ignoble "Cod War" between Canada and Spain in March 1995. The issue, according to Baker and others in the Canadian delegation of which he was a part, was the harvesting and landing, often in Scotland, of large volumes of immature cod of illegal size even under more lax European rules (Chantraine 1992: 116ff.). Cod of this size could be landed in European ports if, and only if, they were not fished in European waters. In fact, they were caught in waters just outside the Canadian economic zone, on the Nose of the Grand Banks or on the Flemish Cap.

There were various dimensions of this issue. First, the European Community was committed, both in principle and in practice, to the conservation of depleted stocks and the regulation of the fishing effort, but at the same time it was engaged in a program of fleet modernization and expansion. Second, because they were less developed economically than England, Germany, Benelux and France, and because fishing represented a greater percentage of the GNP in their countries, Spain and Portugal had a relatively greater say in the European and international agencies that regulate fishing, and they were also given relatively generous catch quotas. In any case, it was difficult to properly inspect catches and enforce regulations, such as the use of minimum mesh size in nets, and a number of Spanish vessels boarded by Canadian inspectors in Canadian territorial waters and the Northwest Atlantic Fisheries Organization (NAFO) zones bordering these waters were found to be in breach of these regulations. In addition, evidence came to light about the processing of undersized fish, harvested by Spanish trawlers, in plants in Scotland. In the "war" that ensued, with Spain defending its historical fishing rights on the Grand Banks of Newfoundland, the blame for the dire straits in which the Atlantic fishery found itself shifted from *las focas* (the seals) to systematic overfishing by European, and especially Spanish, fleets of freezer trawlers.

But how do the voracious eating habits of the seal, the landing of baby cod, "corporate greed," or capitalism, and the gross overexploitation of depleted resources factor into the ecological collapse of the northern cod and the "great destruction" of fishing as a way of life? The historic evidence is, generally speaking, as follows: First, the boom in cod stocks appears to have begun to wane in the mid-1950s when the Newfoundland Banks or "deep sea" schooner and inshore small boat fishery, established back in the nineteenth century, was displaced by a new monster breed of factory-fishing vessels. Modelled on distant-water whaling ships, these new factory trawlers came from countries, thousands of miles away, in search of herring, haddock, capelin, redfish and, of course, the valuable Northwest Atlantic cod. Up until the late 1970s these distant-water factory trawlers, 450 feet long and with a 4,000-tonne capacity, set and hauled their colossal nets from the stern, quickly processing and deep-freezing nearly all the fish they caught, working around the clock in all but the worst weather conditions.

The "Great Destruction" and the Predations of Corporate Capital

With the increased effort by distant-water fleets, catches and landings of northern cod increased from an annual average of 25,000 tonnes in the early 1950s to a peak of 800,000 in 1968 (DFO 1994: 19). This represented about 48 percent of all fish harvested and landed in the North Atlantic fisheries, with Canadian fishers accounting for 28 percent (ICNAF 1996). With the declining cod population subjected to unprecedented pressure, by 1975 the overall catch declined from this peak to 300,000 tonnes. Concerned that stocks were being reduced to below their reproduction level, the Canadian government in 1976 passed legislation to extend its jurisdiction, banishing foreign fleets to the "high seas," but at the same time allowing the newly capitalized offshore fleet of Canadian trawlers to step up its fishing efforts. This was particularly the case for the investors and merchants who owned the corporate giant National Sea Products. In 1977, in the context of an extended offshore economic zone (two hundred miles, but short of the rich edges of the continental shelf where foreign fleets continued to fish), the corporate executives of National Sea decided they wanted access to Newfoundland's northern cod stocks. Instead of investing in Newfoundland's inshore fishery (the traditional users of this resource), National Sea set out with substantial federal subsidies to build a new "distant water" dragger fleet; other draggers were added by the Lake and Monroe corporate interests in Newfoundland. At this point, Ottawa spared no effort to ensure the success of this "modern," capitalist corporate fishery, using every conceivable device in its considerable arsenal to support the trawlers. All this effort, however, was to no avail. In 1982, the government issued a report (DFO 1982) that pointed towards "a promise of abundance" for the Newfoundland economy in the context of its extended jurisdiction and the entry into the field of new corporate players who knew how to play the game for cod fish and profits. But just two years later, Canada's entire east coast offshore dragger sector went bankrupt. Although Ottawa has continued to bail out the corporations at great cost to the public purse — a cost, which, unlike the income transfers to the traditional inshore sector, has always been downplayed by the government — the corporate sector of the east coast fishery remains in crisis. The unfortunate side effect of this failure of corporate capital is that the relatively efficient, non-destructive and more sustainable inshore fishery was dragged down with the unsustainable and destructive offshore corporate fleet and then blamed for local resource mismanagement. In 1991, at the precipice, and blind to the impending crisis, Ottawa deliberately chose to have 60,000 tonnes of northern cod caught by only 500 "draggermen," rather than spread it among the more than 10,000 inshore fishers, who, in addition to sheer numbers, had an historical and moral right to this fish. Not that its dragger-oriented approach could make much difference at this point: within a year the government was forced to close down the entire cod fishery and with it the livelihoods of the fishers, fishworkers and their families, and the viability of their communities.

A Cod Living: The Social Relations of Fish Production

Like the North Atlantic cod fishery, marine fisheries worldwide are characterized by a fundamental dualism in the form of small-scale inshore fisheries coexisting with large-scale industrial fisheries based on corporate capital. Development efforts and government initiatives over the years have focused almost exclusively on support of the large industrial and corporate fisheries, presumably in the belief that small-scale inshore fisheries were only a temporary feature of a transition from a traditional to a modern industrial form of development. However, the traditional, small-scale inshore fishery — usually referred to as an "artisanal" fishery — forms the backbone of most local economies in coastal zones across the world. In 1980, it was estimated, they employed up to 90 percent of all fishers, and today, two decades later, there are still about ten million small-scale fishers landing close to 20 million tonnes of fish annually, about one-half of the world catch used for human consumption (Panayotou 1982: xx, 1). In many areas the fisheries constitute virtually the only source of employment and income for the vast majority of the local population and the only industry for thousands of small communities strung along the coast.

As for the cod fishery in Atlantic Canada, it is estimated that at the time of the first signs of its possible collapse, in the mid-1970s, 15 percent of all labour in Newfoundland was connected to the cod fishery and one out of every four of the population was directly or indirectly dependent on the harvesting or processing of cod for their livelihoods. Along the entire coastline of Atlantic Canada the cod fishery in the mid-1970s employed up to 47,000 actual fishers and about 20,000 workers in fish-processing plants (Chantraine 1992: 58). About 75 percent of all coastal communities participated in the fishery, and about 20 percent, comprising a total of 250,000 people, had no industry or source of income other than that generated by the fisheries — mostly cod. Later studies by the Royal Commission on Employment and Unemployment show that many outport communities in Newfoundland, and to a lesser degree in Nova Scotia, continued this dependence on cod fishing well into the 1980s and 1990s.

The sad saga of Newfoundland, played out with numerous permutations in other parts of the world, is that the collapse of the cod stocks not only undermined the economy but destroyed an entire population's identity and historic way of life. Imposed cessation of their primary economic activity has been a very bitter pill for Newfoundlanders to swallow. Nor has the sugar-coating of half a billion dollars in palliative economic aid made things easier: getting "the package" (between two and four hundred dollars a week) to sit back and wait for the return of the cod is cold comfort to thousands of islanders and scores of communities that had been dependent on the harvesting, processing, sale and consumption of cod. For one thing, pride cannot be bought, and islanders are a proud people with a rich heritage and culture. And one of the best ways to kill a person, or a people, it has been said, is to pay them to do nothing.

As for the Newfoundlanders' culture, the people who attached themselves to the "Rock," in their living off cod, acquired the resilience and solidity of the place. Over three or four centuries (St. John's is North America's oldest city), Newfoundlanders acquired not only strength, endurance, independence and courage, but also the altruism, sense of community, equanimity and humour needed to survive in such harsh conditions. These qualities were woven into a pattern of national identity, an insular mystique, that has survived the conditions of its attachment to Canada since 1949 but will surely crumble in the absence of the activity that has sustained it over the years. Cod fishing is an intimate part of the psyche and culture, as well as economy, of Newfoundlanders.

The human tragedy resulting from the industrialization and capitalist development of the fishery since the 1960s and 1970s, as well as the earlier infamous government programs to resettle the population away from isolated coastal communities and into urban centres where social services can be more easily provided — or eventual migration "down the road" to Alberta or Toronto — has culminated in the withering away and progressive extinction of not only cod stocks but the inshore fishers themselves, the historic guardians and managers of the fishing resource. Since the 1980s, particularly in the wake of the moratorium on cod fishing — originally for eighteen months but still in place at the time this was written — this process has greatly accelerated. The vigorous small communities that make up the Rock's social fabric and economy, already badly wounded, are everywhere under threat of extinction. A once proud people has been forced to its knees by politicians and capitalists. As argued in 1993 by Conrad Black, the denationalized and now knighted scion of Canada's corporate and media elite, "the country [Canada] can no longer afford to support the public assistance [transfer payments] to people … in their marginal and dying communities: they should be encouraged [or forced] to migrate to where they are needed — where the jobs are [Ontario and Alberta]" (Black 1995: 158–70).

Good Cod!: The Harvesting and Processing of a Depleted Resource

In the harvesting sector, there were essentially three fisheries in the North Atlantic, each with its distinct technology and gear, and each with a specific mix of production relations. In this mix (offshore, nearshore, inshore) the offshore "draggermen," made up of corporate capitalist enterprises, harvested cod for processing in plants owned by a small number of big merchants who distributed the catch through outlets they also controlled. Although many fishers worked in small groups for themselves, and some worked for wages on trawlers, most did so as part of a crew, receiving in return for their efforts a share of the catch, the captain usually receiving an additional boat's share, as owner of the vessel. These fishers, most of them operating in the inshore or near-shore fishery, were the backbone of the industry. Thousands of small-boat operators with simple or artisanal technology harvested cod, with traps set close to shore or by hook and line jigging from small dories, bringing in the catch each afternoon for sale on the dock to middlemen or company agents, who were also dependent on the inshore for their supply of sea products for processing or sale in diverse markets.

Offshore, however, fishing was dominated by large trawlers and draggers that move at great speed and drag behind them enormous net-systems that sweep up everything in their path, regardless of fish quotas, and in total disregard to the environment. Inshore artisanal fishing, in contrast, was based either on traps or handlining, jigging with handheld lines and hooks that more often than not did not even require baiting.

Most of the actual harvesters — the fishers — were (and are) men, while most workers in the processing plants scattered along the rocky shoreline of bights and coves are women, often the wives and daughters of the fishermen (Macdonald and Connelly 1983). The fishing industry, so constituted, is in effect the only industry for hundreds of small communities strung out along the shorelines of Newfoundland and Nova Scotia. In Newfoundland, part of the Canadian federation since 1949, the cod fishery once provided a direct source of work for up to 47,000 fishers and another 20,000 or so additional individuals in the processing sector. It is estimated that up to 40 percent of all Newfoundlanders and their families and communities at one point, and perhaps right up to the 1980s and the 1992 moratorium, were either directly or indirectly dependent on the cod fishery before it finally collapsed.

The Government Goes Fishing: Where Have the Fish Gone?

It has been said that in government archives there are probably more reports, summaries, policy statements, working documents, statistics, analyses, task force reports, commissions (royal and otherwise), directories, papers and studies on the fisheries than the cod caught in any one year. The sad thing is that, since 1920, all the reports and the noble intentions which gave rise to them have come to just about the same thing: nothing. Indeed, the 1928 *Report of the Royal Commission on the Quebec and Maritime*

Fisheries sought a permanent solution to the "fisheries problem," or to "suggest, at least, methods of permanent relief rather than ... temporary palliatives." At the time, however, it was noted that, in spite of exhaustive studies conducted in the past and to that point, "the difficulties ... are so many, so varied and so intricate that their complete and final removal will require [from the DFO] patient and perhaps prolonged endeavour" (Canada 1928: 85).

Indeed, the 1976 document, *Canadian Policy for the Commercial Fishery,* confirmed this view (Fisheries and Marine Service 1976), as did *Navigating Troubled Waters,* the report issued six years later by the task force chaired by Michael Kirby (1983), one of Atlantic Canada's few (and perhaps only) contributors to David Rockefeller's Trilateral Commission. The Royal Commission on Employment and Unemployment in Newfoundland, chaired by the sociologist Doug House, came to a similar conclusion, namely that the cod fishery constituted a problem without an easy or apparent solution. The 1982 Kirby task force was at least honest in its assessment, if not diagnosis or policy prescription: "Despite the fact that the problem was identified at least 54 years ago[3] ... it is distressing that the conclusions of this Task Force are substantially similar to those of the Royal Commission and show that very little has been done to attack this basic problem." And yet these commissioners dared to reiterate, without any apparent fear of ridicule from the fishers who had been weathering the crisis for some twenty years, a view stated in the government's *Canadian Policy for the Commercial Fishery* (1976), and they did so in the following terms:

> The Canadian fishing industry has good potential for expansion. It is situated close to fishing territories capable of becoming the most productive in the world, and to very attractive food-consumption markets. The extension of the national territorial jurisdiction for the fisheries to at least two hundred miles from the coast can only improve the prospects for a well-established industry that processes its fish on shore.

The issue, both for the authors of *Canadian Policy* and the Kirby report (1983), six years later, was "the materialization of [the excellent] prospects" for the fishery. In this regard, the *Canadian Policy* document wrote of the need for "a new direction in management policy and development of the fishery" while the report of the Kirby commission sought to articulate a new policy for the Atlantic fishery, in terms of a troubling paradox: "On one doorstep we have one of the world's great natural fisheries resource bases.... On another ... is the United States, a major and accessible market for fish." As for the widely perceived crisis, lived for close to twenty years by the fishers and their communities, the issue was viewed as not one of a "new policy" but rather better management — one of "navigation in troubled waters." In this connection, the solution proposed by the Kirby commission was no different from that of the *Canadian Policy for the Commercial Fishery*, namely, (1) no longer ...to push the biological yield to the maximum but to encourage better use of society's resources (sustainable development); and (2) to allow fundamental decisions on management of the resource and *an expansion of the industry* to be taken jointly by the industry and the government.

Of course, by "industry" the task force had in mind large, vertically integrated companies such as Fisheries Products International (FPI) in Newfoundland and National Sea Products in Nova Scotia. In fact, Kirby would soon be appointed to the board of National Sea. The priorities of industry clearly came to dominate fishery policy in official terms in the 1980s. There is no question about this. For one thing, the comprehensive regulatory frameworks of earlier years were replaced by the commodification of licences and the privatization of fish quotas (the total allowable catch, or TAC], beginning, of course, with the large players in the industry. In short order the corporate, or dragger, sector of the industry was expanded, picking up the slack in the reduced TAC in both the inshore fishery and the foreign fleets. And in equally short order the fish stocks disappeared, the major corporate players in the industry went belly up and the DFO managed the Atlantic cod fishery out of existence.

A key part of the study of the state of the resource had to do with calculating the spawning biomass of the cod stock. Since cod take seven years to mature sufficiently so as to be able to spawn, the size and health of this biomass is critical. It is calculated that 1.5 million tonnes are required for a healthy stock. However, government scientists found that the spawning biomass in 1988 had been reduced to 40 percent of this level, with serious signs of impending decline — in one scenario, down to only 275,000 tonnes, a level at which, according to the Interim Harris Report (1989), there would be no more fish in the near future. In consequence, that report recommended an immediate cut in the TAC to 125,000 tonnes and then 100,000. But notwithstanding this rather pessimistic conclusion drawn by the Harris commission, and the even more pessimistic cries of inshore fishers, as well as evidence that the actual spawning biomass of the cod stock could be as low as 280,000 tonnes, perilously close to the precipice, the Dunne task force, set up by the government to act on this conclusion, recommended a constant catch of 200,000 tonnes (to secure "industry stability"). This was in 1989. By 1992, however, just ten years after the Kirby commission's report on the positive prospects for the sustainable development of the fishery — and in the broader context of the Rio de Janeiro Earth Summit — the Canadian government imposed a total moratorium on cod fishing, not only by the destructive draggers but by the more ecologically minded, and efficient hook-and-line fishers. [4] The crisis was upon the fishers and their families and communities. In a belated response to this crisis, the Canadian government in July 1999 closed Newfoundland's waters, the Grand Banks and most of the Gulf of St. Lawrence to the harvesting of groundfish of which the most sought after was the erstwhile abundant cod.

Trawling for Profits: The End of a Long Road

The collapse of the cod stocks and the fishery to some extent appears as part of a global trend, reflecting forces that are operating in other fisheries all over the world. The trend is clear enough. As noted by Peter Weber (1993), in a World Watch report, *Abandoned Seas: Reversing the Decline of the Oceans*, "over fishing has precipitated declines in individual stocks throughout the world.... The catch of [the] four [most] commonly-eaten, average-value fish (Atlantic cod, Cape hake, haddock and silver hake) fell from five million tonnes in 1970 to 2.6 million in 1989." The overall harvest in ocean products over this period, and since, has actually increased in both market value and volume. But, Weber notes, this is because "fishers have managed to keep the marine fish stocks climbing ... by abandoning fished-out stocks and pursuing new species ... typically lower-value fish that were previously undesirable and unwanted" (Weber 1993: 32–33).

Notwithstanding the persistent growth of the industry, based on the worldwide harvesting, processing and provisioning of fish and seafood, fishing as an industry, occupation and way of life is everywhere in serious trouble if not crisis. According to the Food and Agriculture Organization (FAO 2000: 1), the growth is largely accounted for by increased production of fish for human consumption. By weight, China's production of fish accounts for 32 percent of the world total. Other major fish production countries include Japan, India, the USA, the Russian Federation and Indonesia, as well as the EU. Despite the crisis in key sectors, total fisheries production (and trade) across all species and sectors has steadily increased over recent years, on an absolute but not per capita basis, both in the "capture" and aquaculture fisheries. In 1998 this growth trend was halted and temporarily reversed, basically as a result of a "climate anomaly" (El Niño) primarily affecting production in the Southeast Pacific (down from 17 million tonnes in 1996 to 8 million in 1998). According to the FAO, the number of fishers and fish farmers worldwide increased from an estimated 12.5 million in 1970 to around 27 million in 1990 and 36 million in 1998, at which point overall numbers seemed to stabilize and have perhaps declined (FAO 2000: 3–4).

Records kept by the FAO (2000) indicate that, of the world's fifteen main fishing regions, four are depleted and nine are in trouble. This global fisheries crisis, according to the FAO and other international agencies, can be traced back to overharvesting and poor resource management decisions, designed to satisfy short-term economic and/or political objectives rather than to protect the marine environment and conserve fish populations (Greenpeace 2002). In this regard, even countries such as Canada, where relatively advanced fisheries management systems have been in place for many years have, according to a Greenpeace report (2002, "almost without exception, failed to control the conditions and stem the abuses that lead to over fishing and destructive environmental impacts." Indeed, this report adds, "in many countries, governments have played an important part in fuelling the expansion of excessive fishing capacity and overexploitation by providing lucrative subsidies, taxpayer funded handouts." On a global scale, the report notes, these "destructive subsidies" run up to $50 billion a year. As a result of this and other such examples of fisheries politics geared to the profit imperative or commercial interests, "nature's limits have been breached by too many fishing vessels catching too many fish, very often in wasteful and destructive ways" (Greenpeace 2002; FAO 2000).

As for Canada's Atlantic Provinces, the fisheries crisis can be traced back to at least 1973. By then, overfishing had already plunged the region into a serious crisis, which they weathered only with massive aid from the federal government, extended as a short-term measure to support the fishery industries until the stocks recovered. Taking into account the devaluation of the Canadian dollar, the aid package for the eighteen-month moratorium on cod fishing cost the public purse a half-billion dollars spread over three years. To secure this recovery, a number of conservation and other measures were taken by the government, most particularly the extension of the economic zone over which it had exclusive jurisdiction to two hundred nautical miles from the coast. With this jurisdictional extension the Canadian government implied that foreign overfishing was the crux of the problem. In any case, it was followed by a program designed to capitalize the industry, extending additional credit and licences to Canadian fishers, particularly in the corporate sector, to expand their fishing effort in this extended economic zone. To make fishing trips more profitable, more and larger trawlers were brought into play, armed with larger draggers, and upgraded, higher tech fishing gear, especially affecting fish location and catching power.

This increased fishing effort and these technological innovations had a predictable and adverse effect on fish stocks and the ecosystem of the seabed, the spawning ground for the cod, which by all accounts were ravaged and nearly destroyed by the trawling process. Dragging immense "rollers" along the seabed tears up all before it, including spawning stock and its habitat (see Marsh 1992: 32ff). In this context, Canada's recapitalized and government-supported dragger fleet displaced the foreign fleet within Canada's newly extended economic zone, while the foreign fishing fleet redoubled its efforts on the Flemish Cap, the Nose and the Tail of the Grand Banks, and the continental slope, where the cod migrated in winter, escaping Canada's exclusive jurisdiction but not the rapacious (and improved) catching power of the international fleets on the high seas. Some of the ships in these fleets — the giant floating fish factories of the ex-Soviet Union, Germany, France and Spain — were enormous and able to raise fish by the tens of tonnes at a time with colossal winches, chains and cables. The cod had no chance to recover. The overall effect was continued pressure on fish stocks and devastation of the seabed, ripped up by gear trawled at great speed across the ocean floor. Statistics on stocks and landings in subsequent years tell the story.

Marked by the implementation of new laws and strict catch quotas per species and fishing zone, the 1970s added a new doleful refrain to the traditional litany of fishers. "If there are fish, there's no market, and if there's a market there are no fish" was now followed with "and when there are fish and markets, our hands are tied by regulations." These regulations, of course, were required to avoid a catastrophe.

The Canadian government regarded the extension of its exclusive jurisdiction in 1977 as an opportunity, if not a panacea. At the time, cod stocks were particularly low and the objective of the government in declaring a two-hundred-mile limit was, ostensibly, to implement a new regime of regulation and conservative management of the stock. Indeed, it appears that the stock of cod did indeed revive somewhat during the early 1980s, and in 1982 the DFO published a paper entitled "Northern Cod: A Fisheries Success Story." Whether DFO officials or the government actually believed this to be the case or whether it put on blinders, falling prey to political pressures from "the industry," is unclear. What is clear, however, is that the two-hundred-mile limit was not as much a conservation measure as a protectionist measure for Canada's fisheries, a means of rescuing the near-bankrupt offshore fleet of several seafood companies. In this context, the government's take on the northern cod ("a fisheries success story") was used to launch a major program of capitalization and licence expansion to the offshore fleet, and to some extent, the near shore, bringing about within the space of a few years another major crisis — and a total moratorium on the cod fishery.

What Went Wrong

In the space of these years, the government maintained its regulatory regime but gave relatively free reign to three large corporations formed to harvest, process and sell fish. Under the government's plan to bail out and rescue the corporate offshore fishery, Newfoundland's seafood companies were merged into the conglomerate Fisheries Products International. In addition, public funds were used to resuscitate Nova Scotia's National Sea Products. By the late 1980s, ten years after the two-hundred-mile limit had been declared and Canada's ports closed to foreign vessels (the Portuguese were expelled from the Grand Banks in 1986), both FPI and National Sea prospered, while the inshore found their catches dropping off year by year. These fishers complained vociferously to the DFO, but to no avail. The government's priority was to make its investment in the offshore another success story.

Meanwhile, government researchers looking for the cause of declining inshore stocks, turned away from overfishing to the rapacious eating habits of the seal and changes in ocean temperatures. For some years the annual harvest of seal pups, under pressure from environmentalists all over the world, was boosted by the argument that a major cull of the predatory seal population was required to counteract its voracious appetite for immature fish (Rogers 1995: 150). Today the annual seal hunt remains a critically important source of income for hundreds of former cod fishermen.

Notwithstanding this concern about the predatory seal and its voracious eating habits, there is little or no question that the chief culprit of the disappearance of the cod is destructive technology and overfishing in the corporate offshore sector and gross mismanagement of the resource by the government itself. However, beyond these and other immediate causes of the collapse of the cod fishery, the ultimate culprit is the entire system, geared as it is to corporate greed in the rapacious search for profit. The evidence on this point is clear: wherever the common resource is managed by communities of direct producers in their own collective and long-term interest, the technology and social relations of fish production tend towards a sustainable development of the resource and livelihoods. But whenever corporate interests and capitalism prevail, the end result is an economy in crisis and a people in dire straits. All over the world the story is the same. Certainly, fishers themselves in the community-based inshore fishery have no doubts on this score. Everyone in the industry or communities, old and young, interviewed on this issue, with the exception of DFO officials (we did not survey the opinions in the corporate sector), concurs with this view. Scientists, like environmentalists and fishers themselves, have, in fact, over the years issued numerous warnings to the effect that failure to take appropriate steps to reduce the current level of fishing mortality, and to abandon the deadly technologies and the predations of corporate capital in the industry, would lead to a significant continuing decline in the spawning population of northern cod (see, for example, Harris 1989). From this perspective the decline and collapse of the fishery was both inevitable and predictable — and, in fact, was predicted years before the belated laments and inadequate reactions of the government.

How did the government respond? Beyond commissioning round upon round of studies and reports, the government responded in three forms: (1) by extending its jurisdiction over a two-hundred-mile offshore fishing zone and increasing its surveillance of foreign fishing; (2) by imposing a new regulatory regime in the fisheries based on allowable catch quotas; and (3) by supporting corporate capitalist enterprise in the industry with additional licences and catch quotas for a fleet of recapitalized draggers. It took another ten years, by which time the stocks off Newfoundland's east coast had totally collapsed, for the government to take action and declare a complete moratorium on cod fishing. As a result of this action, more than forty thousand fishers lost their jobs or source of livelihood, and hundreds of communities that could not adapt to the new crab and shrimp fisheries became virtual wards of the state, totally dependent on welfare transfers. Newfoundland and Nova Scotia are by no means alone in this development. For example, in Spain, which still has Europe's largest fishing fleet and, because of its unusually high per capita consumption, its largest market, few cod are landed anymore, even by the Basques who began it all. The grand *bacalao* companies that owned their own trawler fleets landed salt cod from the Banks and sold it all over the world have all closed down, with a consequent loss of jobs in both the harvesting and processing sectors.

By 2002, a decade into the moratorium, there was absolutely no sign of recovery in what was once the world's most abundant fish stock. In this connection, the Trawler and Fishermen Association (TFA), composed in part of ex–cod fishers, and which in 1989 took the Canadian government to court over its gross mismanagement of the fish stocks, as recently as May 24, 2002, despaired of these stocks ever rebounding. Unable to account for the failure of stocks to recover after ten years of no fishing, the Association recommends a continued adjustment to the new commercial shrimp and crab fisheries that have opened up over the course of the decade, in effect giving up on cod. For the Newfoundland fishers represented by this Association, the dreaded day when the last good catch of codfish is pulled from the ocean has come and gone.

The Demise of Cod

But, of course, the dreaded day of the last cod has not come everywhere or for everyone. It is still possible to find the odd fish here and there. But the economy based on king cod, and, in Newfoundland, the way of life and culture built upon it, has disappeared. Most fishers in the province, those who in drastically reduced numbers have clung to fishing as an economic activity and way of life, have turned to other species of groundfish, shellfish or lobster — particularly crab and shrimp — as well as the seal hunt. In 2002, at the time of this writing, the number of individuals directly dependent on the cod fishery had shrunk to less than one quarter of the number of fishers in the heyday of cod. The fishery that once sustained more than a thousand communities in the Atlantic Provinces is but a shadow of its former self. With a massive exodus of their most productive members, the small communities built around cod have been converted into quaint stops on the tourist trail, captured on postcards or photo prints. The vast majority of families of fishers and fishplant workers in these communities have been forced to adjust, in small numbers, to the limited opportunities in the new fisheries or, in large numbers, to migrate to the urban centres in the region or further "down the road" to Central Canada or further west. Another way of life has been consigned to the dustbin of history, the victim of a rapacious system that rewards *greed* and apportions the benefits of resource utilization more to vertically structured *corporations* than to community-based enterprises. Indeed, the tragic fate of the cod is principally due to the marriage of these two factors–that is, to corporate greed.

What to Do?

> Fisheries management should belong to those people whose lives are dependent upon it and not just to the masters of industry. The only hope ... is to protect the resource from the rapacious corporate interests of those who think only of profit and forget that the inshore fishery is the heart and soul of Newfoundland. (Marsh 1992: 169)

The market for cod over the centuries has been fuelled by the need for a readily available form of dietary protein at low cost.[5] In the case of the slaves and their descendents in the "West Indies," cod served a vital role as a means of subsistence. Over the centuries, cod became a protein and food source of choice for all classes of people in countries all over the world, particularly for the population on both sides of the Atlantic Ocean — in Newfoundland and the Maritime Provinces of Canada, and in the Basque region and Catalonia. In Brazil, cod has been replaced by other sources of fish and animal protein, but it remains the food of choice for the best, and the more popular, restaurants that serve the population. In the broader context of world fisheries production, the history and consumption of cod intersects with the history of diverse fish species and an industry that is in most places, if not everywhere, in crisis. In this context, the story of cod has been (and is being) played out on a series of larger and smaller scales. Very few sectors of the industry are immune to crisis, chasing fewer and fewer fish with greater effort but smaller results. The statistics on the worldwide fishing "industry" tell this story clearly, and the testimonials of people who live this sad story are many.

Drawing upon a seemingly inexhaustible ocean to provide protein for the world, the capitalist industrialization of the global fishery in the years that followed the Second World War led to a doubling of the catch of fresh fish to 20 million tonnes, to an increase by a factor of ten of the catch of frozen fish (13 million tonnes), and to rapid expansion of the production of fish meal and oil (20 million tonnes). Cod played an important part in this development, and a good deal of the exploitation by an international distant-water fleet took place in the Northwest Atlantic until the ecological collapse of the early 1970s. What to do, and eat? And how to make a living in coastal zone communities north and south of a growing divide, in a globally unsustainable capitalist economy in which people are separated from the global commons and any possible means of direct production (and employment), which are privatized in the interest of a few and at a cost to many?

Is there a *solution* to these and other problems *within* the capitalist system in place? Can the vital nexus between communities and their common resource base, broken under conditions of private property in the means of production, be restored? There are various models for such a restoration of popular forms of sustainable development and livelihoods, but they are all predicated on opposition to, resistance against and successful delinking from the seemingly intractable processes of modernization and capitalist development that dominate the world economy.

In his analysis of the regulatory regime established for the east coast fishery, Ralph Mathews (1993), among others, criticizes the DFO for its unquestioned assumption that available resources needed to be commercialized and could not be properly managed except on the basis of private property — that the solution was the privatization of the commons and more government regulation. This solution, and the mindset in which it is invariably proposed, flies in the face of a mounting body of evidence concerning both the fisheries in Canada and the development of coastal zone communities across the world: that small communities of direct producers and their families are much better managers of common resources than industry or government. The tragedy of the commons, both in Atlantic Canada and elsewhere, is precisely that this well-established capacity of small communities of direct producers and workers to manage their common resources, and secure the sustainable development of the environment and their livelihoods, is undermined by regimes of capital accumulation, and modes of regulation put into place by governments. In this context, the only viable solution to the crisis confronted by fishers and their communities, and workers and their families, in coastal zone communities across the world is to socialize their means of production — for producers and communities to regain control over the commons, and for workers to regain control over their workplaces. And the only apparent path towards this solution is collective action by producers and workers, their families and communities, against the predations of capital and the incursions of government and state agencies into the resource base of their local communities. This will require a long struggle, but there is no other way out of a deepening economic and ecological crisis.

Fish remains a critical source of food protein in a hungry world with a growing population. Markets for fish and seafood, whether fresh, salted or cured, frozen or otherwise processed, continue to expand, even under conditions of impending ecological disaster. One reason for this is the ready availability of food protein provided by fish and seafood. Cod, for example is more than 18 percent protein. Another is the steady expansion of commercial fishing as an industry, if not an occupation and way of life. But it would appear that the day of cod has come and gone, at least in Newfoundland. Even with the closure of the Grand Banks, worldwide more than six million tonnes of gadiform fish (cod, haddock, pollock, hake) are caught every year, and more than one half are *Gadus morhua*, Atlantic cod. By the mid-sixteenth century, 60 percent of all fish in Europe were cod, caught mostly in the North Atlantic by fishers from Spain, Portugal and France (Kurlansky 1997: 51). Today, however, although still prized, Atlantic cod survives primarily as an expensive delicacy, and in most places it has been replaced by its less desirable cousins — haddock, pollock and hake. In Nova Scotia and Great Britain, as well as New England, haddock is actually preferred over cod — in the form of fish and chips. But tradition and habits die hard. There is no substitute for cod in the Caribbean or Brazil, or, for that matter, in Spain, the country traditionally with the highest per capita cod consumption. But cod is no longer king, not even in Spain. Despite the hope among fishermen that cod may some day return in greater numbers, its heyday and reign is over. The history of cod, a fish that helped to shape the world, appears to have run its course.

Part II

POLITICAL DYNAMICS OF ANTI-GLOBALIZATION

7. Latin American Peasants against the State

One of the ironies informing the study of peasants since the 1970s is that, while a plethora of analyses of both the peasantry and the state exist, there is still no adequate theory of the relationships between them over time. Numerous monographs chronicle the history of the state in terms of its formation, support and reproduction as a macro-level political institution, and the history of the peasantry as a socio-economic category with (or without) its history in specific micro-level contexts, but — except when peasants and the state are engaged in violent conflict with one another or against a third party — neither feature in each other's history except peripherally, as a fleeting appearance in someone else's grand narrative. This is why the first part of this chapter will briefly examine the debate on the state, evaluating the adequacy of diverse views and arguments in explaining peasant/state relations in Latin America.

In the second part of the chapter, we will we discuss the practice of the state, specifically the dialectic between the state and the peasantry in Latin American history as seen "from above," a relationship that has been complex and changing. It is a truism, albeit an important one, that the role of the state with regard to the peasantry is deeply influenced by the type of production unit that is dominant and its relation to the market. The role of the state vis-à-vis the *latifundio,* with its smallholders, tenant farmers, sharecroppers and migratory forms of landless or near-landless workers, is significantly different from that involving the plantation system, with its seasonal but "stationary" wage-labour force. In the second half of the twentieth century the rise of a quasi-industrial bourgeoisie, sharing power uneasily with labour and sectors of the agricultural elite, redirected the role of the state towards the promotion of import-substitution industrialization financed by the export earnings of the agro-export sector. The role of the peasantry within this scheme — the "subordination of agriculture to industrialization" — was designed to supply cheap labour to the cities and low cost food for the urban labour force. The state was compelled to introduce a series of social and political reforms that would not only accommodate the interests of the agrarian and industrial bourgeoisie, and incorporate the urban middle and working classes into the economic and political system, but also stave off pressures for more radical change.

With the advent of neoliberalism in the 1980s the relationship between the state and the peasantry took another turn. Under the neoliberal doctrine of free markets, structural adjustment and globalization, the reversal of previously instituted reforms is accompanied by a massive displacement of small and medium-sized rural producers and rural workers at a time of declining urban-industrial employment, engendering a new set of conflicts and confrontations between the peasantry and the state.

The third part of the chapter will explore the "from below" responses of the peasantry to the "from above" imperatives of the state. Considered are three specific agencies involving peasants: repression, displacement and revolution. The generally repressive role of the state vis-à-vis the peasantry is contextualized, so as to identify its particular and changing forms. In this connection the displacement of the peasantry from the land, and from the agricultural sector entirely, and its increasing movement across national boundaries, is not simply a matter of "individual choice," but rather of a systemic imperative driven by state policy defined by the dominant classes. The long-term and large-scale direct and indirect involvement of the state in the exploitation, repression and displacement of the peasantry has engendered rebellions, reforms and revolutions in which peasants have been the major protagonists. In colonial Peru, Haiti and Mexico, the enslaved, indentured and enserfed rural labour force challenged colonial state power throughout the eighteenth and early nineteenth centuries. In the late colonial or post-colonial liberal reform period in Central America (El Salvador, Honduras, Nicaragua, Guatemala), the state-instituted legislative, policy and repressive measures to control rebellious peasants, indigenous peoples and landless rural workers protesting state actions, and bring them into line with the interests of the landed oligarchy (Wheelock Román 1975; Gould 1983; Amador 1990: Mahoney 2001). And in the twentieth century, social revolutions in Mexico (1910), Bolivia (1952), Cuba (1959) and Nicaragua (1979) had peasants playing a major role in overthrowing the state. In other contexts, peasants and landless workers were major actors in stimulating the development of a comprehensive, albeit limited, agrarian reform program. This was the case, for example, in Chile (1965–73), Peru (1958–74), El Salvador (1980–85), Ecuador (during the late 1960s into the 1970s) and Brazil (1962–64).

The fourth part of the chapter examines the power and limitations of peasant movements in their struggles with the state. The key issues raised concern how the state has affected the peasantry, and the degree to which the state has been a friend or enemy at different times and in different countries over the past half century. From the mid-1980s onwards, peasant and rural landless workers movements, as well as rural guerrilla movements, have moved onto the centre stage of a protracted struggle throughout Latin America against neoliberalism and its imperial backers. In this struggle, the reforms and revolutionary changes wrought by the peasantry have been vulnerable to reversals, and peasants have suffered harsh repression, being forced to migrate in large numbers from their communities as the result of changes in the configuration of state power. The unfolding of this process is particularly clear with regard to developments in Brazil: as a consequence of neoliberal structural adjustments to the economy, it was estimated by the Instituto Nacional de Colonização e Reforma Agrária (INCRA) in 1999 that in five years more than a million landless or near-landless peasants or workers would join the five million or so that had migrated to the cities from 1986 to 1996, a year into Fernando Henrique Cardoso's presidency (FAO 1998: 23).

The State in Theory

In Latin America, as elsewhere, the state has been and is essential to the operation of markets and the defence or transformation of the dominant social relations of production. In each specific form of agricultural production the state has been instrumental in the foundation, extension, reproduction and transformation of the system involved, benefiting some classes — most often the large landowners — and disadvantaging others (mainly workers and peasants). The essential theoretical point here is that the market is inexorably linked to an "activist state," whether the principal agricultural unit be the large landed estate (the *hacienda* or *latifundio*), the plantation, the family farm, the peasant economy or a combination of these production systems. Before examining the latter, however, it is necessary to consider the state in theory, and why there is still no adequate framework for understanding peasant/state relations.

Much recent theory about the peasantry has tended to oscillate between two competing and politically very different perceptions. One view regards the peasantry as an entirely passive entity: it is either the disempowered object of various kinds of state agency (legislation, taxation, agricultural production regimes, systems of regulation, macroeconomic planning) emanating from above and elsewhere, or the equally disempowered recipient of state patronage and inputs. The rival view sees the peasantry as an active and empowered entity, whose grassroots agency contests both the effects of state action (through revolutionary mobilization and rebellion, everyday forms of resistance) and what is received or on offer from the state (economic resources, infrastructural developments etc). This distinction is perhaps accurately reflected in the current epistemological gulf between varieties of Marxism and postmodernism. For Marxists the peasantry is mainly an economic category that corresponds to a transitional or archaic organizational form, destined to vanish into the dustbin of history, whose presence on the world stage is affected now in other disguises (as a rural proletariat, as an urban lumpenproletariat trapped in the proliferating informal sector or as "wage labour equivalents" everywhere).

In much postmodern theory about the so-called "third world," by contrast, the peasant is conceived mainly as a cultural category, whose identity as the disguised "other" of Eurocentric metanarratives has been rescued by, among others, exponents of post-colonial, post-development frameworks and the subaltern studies project, and given new life as the emblem of an irreducible "alterity" that is erased by misguided or inappropriate economic development. Not the least problematic aspects of this approach are the following. First, postmodern analysis of acts of resistance privilege the element of identity-based particularities, which — when ethnicity replaces class — brings them into the orbit of conservatism and even the political right. Second, the acts deemed by postmodernism to be empowering are invariably localized and/or small-scale, an approach that avoids posing questions about the role/function/reproduction of the state apparatus. And third, by refusing to address both the issue of class, and therefore the instrumentality of the state through which a class exercises power, postmodernism leaves the state intact, for either a landlord class or a bourgeoisie to use against peasants.

For its part, theory about the state has generally avoided issues to do with the peasantry. In the case of non-Marxist theory, where peasant/state relations are considered, they have invariably been viewed through the prism of establishing or re-establishing nothing more than bourgeois democracy. Thus the focus of an early and important analysis (Moore 1966) was on the way in which the process of agrarian transition led either (in the case of Asia) to communism or fascism, or (in the case of France, England and North America) to capitalist democracy. More recent analyses that plough the same political furrow have as their objective not the establishment but rather the *re*-establishment of bourgeois democracy and its capitalist state. Here the focus is on resistance by new social movements, leading to the "redemocratization" of the existing state apparatus (Fox 1990; Hartlyn 1998; Lievesley 1999; Grindle 2000; Haagh 2002), in the process forming a "civil society" that enables "good governance" or "hegemonic" rule to occur (Scott 1976, 1985; Nugent 1998; Joseph and Nugent 1994). Linked to this are two other approaches with similar objectives. The first is the Gramscian notion of "hegemony," whereby control of the state is achieved by constitutional (i.e., parliamentary) means, a method that was tried and found wanting in Chile during the early 1970s. The second is the currently fashionable concept of the "weak" or "failed" state (particularly in Africa), where the object is similarly to constitute or reconstitute the formal apparatus of the bourgeois state (Sandbrook, 2000; Rivera, 2001). Insofar as peasants and agricultural labourers are included within the ranks of these new social movements, and participate in the resistance mounted by such mobilization against the weak or failed state, the inference is that the rural poor necessarily benefit from such agency.

The absence of peasant/state relations from much of Marxist theory about the state has been due in part to the fact that the focus of the latter over the past three decades has been on the formation/reproduction/role of the state either in advanced capitalist societies or in areas of the so-called "third world" where capitalism is well established (Holloway and Picciotto 1978; Jessop 1990; Clarke 1991; Barrow 1993). In neither of these kinds of context has a consideration of peasant/state relations been paramount, not least because epistemologically the presence of capitalism has tended to exclude the existence of peasants, and vice versa. For those Marxists with an interest in underdevelopment, therefore, the theoretical decoupling of third world capitalism from the peasantry meant that the political object of agrarian struggles was to unite peasants in what was deemed to be a pre-capitalist countryside with elements of the "progressive" national bourgeoisie in the towns against a "feudal" (or "semi-feudal") landlord class and its colonial state. The aim, in short, was for the peasantry to help the urban bourgeoisie to achieve power, so that capitalism could then be established or "deepened" in rural areas. Just as the focus of non-Marxist theory about the role of the state is on the weak or failed state — the object being to attain or re-attain bourgeois democracy and capitalism — so for Marxist theory the focus has been on the strong (or in the case of Latin America, the "bureaucratic authoritarian") state, seen as an impediment to the realization of bourgeois democracy, and thus to a socialist transition. The 1970s saw a gradual change of emphasis, the idea of a "strong" and class-specific state giving way to the concept of an "autonomous" state; the rule by class of class associated with the strong state was accordingly replaced with the notion of a "plural" state, through which no particular class was powerful enough to be able to rule. During the 1980s and 1990s this trend saw its apogee in postmodern theory, which denied both the efficacy of class and, consequently, state instrumentality.

Ironically, therefore, the development in Marxist theory of notions such as an "autonomous"/"plural" state resulted in a *de facto* merger with non-Marxist theory: both now subscribed to a non-instrumental view of the state, against which were arraigned not specific classes but rather multi-class new social movements, henceforth pursuing not revolutionary aims (the overthrow of the existing social order) but engaged rather in everyday struggle in and against the state. It is time, therefore, to remind ourselves of two things: not just that the role of the capitalist state is essentially a coercive one (the enforcement of *class* rule), but also that in Latin America, historically and currently, the target of this particular kind of non-hegemonic instrumentality has been and remains peasants and workers. The threefold object of the presentation which follows is accordingly to reinstate the agency of the state, to link this to the enforcement of class rule over peasants and workers, and to connect the latter with challenges by peasants and workers to class rule and state power. From the state in theory, therefore, we turn to the state in practice.

Agricultural Systems and the State

The origins in Latin America of the earliest form of large-scale agricultural production, on the landed estate, were based on three combined processes enacted by the colonial state: (1) the forcible seizure of the land; (2) the coerced conscription of labour belonging to indigenous populations, small producers or imported slaves; and (3) the development of a marketing and transportation infrastructure to facilitate exports (Bauer 1975; A. Pearse 1975). A patrimonial state, a mercantilist economy and a *latifundio/hacienda* land tenure system served to fuel the European, and later US, accumulation process, which in turn generated nineteenth-century forms of industrial capitalist development and its adjunct, the old imperialism of exchange of raw materials and cheap labour for manufactured goods.

Rural Labour Regimes and the State

The key to the whole system was the availability and exploitation of labour power, achieved via state coercion of workers, primarily of native peoples and African slaves (Chevalier 1963; Bowser 1974; Florescano 1975; Rout

1976; Góngora 1975; Duncan, Rutledge and Harding 1977). Exploitation in this context was generally based on the expropriation of surplus in the form of rent rather than profit, and was more "extensive" than "intensive" — that is, an extended workday predominated over technological change. Given the abundance of land vis-à-vis people, and the labour conditions of superexploitation, the only means by which the *latifundio* (and with it the whole export-mercantilist system) could operate and expand was through a system of overwhelming force and total state control.

The internal structure of the *latifundio* was based on a closed social system in which all of rural labour-force interactions took place within the *latifundio* and with the "patron" — the boss (landowner, overseer or manager) — thus isolating the dominant class from the multiplicity of commercial, financial and manufacturing activities which might foster discontent, flight or rebellion. To retain rural labour involuntarily within this allegedly paternalistic and closed social system, violent coercion was routinized, indiscipline was arbitrarily punished and protest was savagely repressed with exemplary violence. The impressionistic view, held by some scholars, of "reciprocal relations" and mutual obligations based on an apparently harmonious "moral economy," derived from the tightness of this control and its "normalization" inside a closed social system where obedience was enforced under the threat (rather than actualization) of violence. The appearance of everyday normality was maintained by the ever-present threat, and only occasional reality, of a machete beheading (Taussig 1986; Mallon 1983; Mendes 1992).

Two theoretical points need to be understood here. First, the existence of coerced labour was not, as is sometimes supposed, part of the organic evolution typical of feudal or semi-feudal systems. Rather, local and world market opportunities, and diverse and growing economic activities, encouraged large landowners to resort to coercion and total control as a means of maximizing exports and trade, securing thereby a supply of labour under conditions of an unfavourable land/people ratio. The object was to pre-empt or prevent competition for workers, which, if permitted, would raise the cost of labour. This is not to say a market in labour power was non-existent, but that where it did exist it was controlled by landowners, who frequently exchanged among themselves the labour power of their own workers (tenants, poor peasants and their kinfolk), an arrangement that operated independently of worker consent. Second, and for this very reason, the system of "feudal," "paternal" or "reciprocal" relations on large estates was little more than a facade for forced labour, a form of control made necessary by the desire of most labourers to secure their independence and own plot of land, as evidenced by the history of escaped slaves in Brazil, Guyana and elsewhere in the Caribbean, and the search for refuge by Indians in the Andes and Central America.

The plantation system, in fact, was a rationalization and transformation of the *latifundio*-based agricultural system (Barraclough 1973). In no case were these two systems ever in contradiction, either in violent civil wars or in bitter and prolonged political conflicts. The plantation system functioned adequately with different kinds of workers: slave, indentured and wage-labour (Best and Levitt 1975). In all these labour regimes, the state's virtual monopoly over the means of violence in securing the prevailing social relations of property in land and other means of production severely limited either the formation or reproduction of an independent peasant economy. The peasantry, in effect, served as a huge reserve army of labour, subsisting on tiny plots of land adjoining larger productive units, thereby enabling what neoliberal ideologues call "flexible production." Employed only during planting and harvesting, they subsisted on their own plots in the "dead season," saving their landlords the cost of their social reproduction (Veltmeyer 1983; Meillassoux 1981). Nevertheless, the small holdings served as a meeting ground for organization and occasional large-scale land seizures and protests; the social advantages to the landowners of this arrangement had a political price.

Theoretically, the transition away from coerced labour led not to a wage labour system, or to a peasant economy, but rather to a system of wage labourers who were also peasants. When they rebelled against their landlords, therefore, it was as workers, but their demands on such occasions were those of peasants — for land. The role of the state in such circumstances was to facilitate land use for specialized production of exported commodities and, given the precariousness of the commodities produced (their harvest time was short), to apply the maximum force needed to ensure that labour produced "just in time." Given the fact that the plantations were largely foreign-owned, particularly by investors from the imperial country (the United States, Britain), the state operated as a "*comprador*" institution: its economic activities were geared toward facilitating the movement of capital and commodities, and policing the workforce composed of peasants.

Policing involved repression, which in an important sense has been a constant in the history of state/peasant/landlord relations, notwithstanding occasional shifts in state power to pro-peasant regimes. However, the level, intensity, content and purpose of state policing have all metamorphosed with changes in the dominant form of agricultural production. Policing under the *latifundio* system was essentially local, supplemented by state power in cases of "emergency" involving widespread rural rebellion. The purpose was to maintain the "closed social system" of the *latifundio* in which tenants and labourers only interacted with the patron, minimizing external (and "politically contaminating") linkages. The only exception here would have been the military conscription of peasants, who, because of their contacts with the urban centres, frequently became the bearers of dissident views. In effect, policing under the *latifundio* system was directed towards immobilizing the peasantry, confining them to a closed social system.

In the plantation system, however, the role of the state was twofold: (1) to provide a certain flexibility of movement while at the same time trying to limit contact between rural and urban labour; and (2) to ensure a docile and stable peasantry by providing it with subsistence farming during the "dead season." While local policing continued, therefore, the great concentration of landless labourers, their greater accessibility to "outside" ideas and organization, and their capacity for concerted large-scale action all led to a greater degree of "national-state military intervention." Local military officials, judges and prosecutors, all of whom were politically and socially intertwined with plantation owners, were in the course of employer-worker disputes frequently called upon to set in motion and legitimize the use of state violence and subsequent punishment (detention without trial, imprisonment). The crucial strategic weakness of the plantation owners was the vulnerability of their crops during harvest season: a strike of only a few days' duration could lead to the reduction or destruction of a harvest. This fact was well understood by the rural organizers of the plantation work force. Given this strategic asset favouring the workers, plantation owners turned to the state for help and solicited its repressive intervention — "exemplary" and preventative violence — so as to pre-empt or prevent any action at harvest time.

Plantation markets were largely international, American or European, and as tropical production sites multiplied and competition intensified, working conditions deteriorated and new lands were expropriated from untitled local producers. In this political situation, market dynamics led to intensified conflict between peasants/plantation workers and the owners of expanding plantations. Once again, the state played a crucial role. First, evicting *de facto* peasant squatters, using the judicial device of "untitled land"; and second, pushing displaced peasants onto reserves set aside for indigenous peoples, thus opening up additional land for agriculture in the future. The state also promulgated labour legislation outlawing the right to strike during the harvest season and subsequently institutionalized (i.e., "normalized") collective bargaining between plantation owners and domesticated leaders of the plantation work force.

Agriculture and the 1930s Capitalist Crisis

The plantation model of agrarian development was so successful that it spread from one section of the Latin American imperial domain to another; because it was an advanced system of agricultural production, however, it was ironically prone to economic crisis. That which occurred during the 1930s had an enormous impact on agro-export production systems, leading to a virtual disintegration of export markets and the emergence of popular rebellions in the context of widespread hunger. In a manner reminiscent of what happens today (not just in the third world but also in metropolitan capitalism), the 1930s capitalist crisis was — as Marxists argued then and have argued since — the effect of over-accumulation, overproduction and the consequent devalourization of existing means of production, a combination that in turn precipitated a financial crisis in the banking sector. With the collapse of export markets, and commodity prices hitting rock bottom, the crisis of the 1930s dealt a powerful blow to plantation agriculture. Some foreign owners sold their large rural properties to the local elite, while others retained their holdings but subcontracted them to local farmers; still others abandoned their lands in part to peasant squatters. All plantation owners faced varying degrees and forms of rural insurgency and peasant uprisings, and many of them diversified their portfolios, diverting investment into urban real estate, finance and, in a few cases, newly protected "import-substitution" industries. Although the state played a crucial role in the suppression of rural uprisings, it also — and equally importantly — facilitated the transition to new forms of agricultural production and urban sites. Not surprisingly, therefore, the 1930s crisis and the consequent economic decline of the liberal agro-export sector had a major impact on peasants and rural workers in Latin America.

The 1930s crisis of the liberal agro-export system led to the emergence of a new "import-substitution" model, which harnessed agro-exports to local industrial production without changing the domination of the agricultural elite over the peasantry and the rural labour force. In effect, the ascendancy of the urban bourgeoisie and petty bourgeoisie involved a trade-off in which the agrarian oligarchy accepted its political subordination in exchange for continued control in the rural sector. Agrarian reform — supposedly a "democratic demand" of the "progressive bourgeoisie" — had no part in the social pact between the urban bourgeoisie and the agrarian oligarchy. In any case, politically, the period from 1930 to 1964 in the case of Chile, and within more or less the same time frame in other countries, saw the gradual decline of the agrarian oligarchy as industrialization advanced and capitalism more fully penetrated the countryside, converting important elements of the landed oligarchy into an agricultural bourgeoisie committed to a more complete capitalist transformation of agriculture (Orlove and Custred 1980).

In this kind of situation, the role of the state was twofold: first, the state was committed to industrialization based on a process of import substitution, transferring resources and investment capital from mining and agriculture into urban-centred industry; and second, it ensured the availability of cheap foodstuffs and other wage goods.

The import-substitution model without agrarian reform led to the first wave of rural to urban migration, beginning in the late 1930s and 1940s and accelerating from the 1950s onwards. In this new situation the federal state channelled resources into industry, allocating foreign exchange earned by the primary sector to the importation of capital and intermediary goods for the burgeoning consumer goods industries. At the regional or local level, the big landlords retained control over state power and so managed to pass the "costs" of their political subordination onto the peasantry. In the same context, while Marxist or Communist parties endorsed the notion of a worker-peasant alliance, in fact they were generally seeking alliances with the so-called "national bourgeoisie" in pursuit of a *productionist* strategy, or were engaged in strictly *workerist* struggles and organization. The emergence of peasant-based movements in this context owed little to the urban-based left or populist parties — at least to their mainstream leaders and organizations (some local organizations and individuals excepted).

The State, Capitalist Modernization and Agrarian Reform

In a very real sense the economic crisis of the 1930s, as it affected the agrarian sector in Latin America, was not itself "resolved" until the 1960s, when a program of land reform was initiated by the state. This was done as a defensive response to the lessons of the 1959 Cuban revolution and was thus designed to prevent the emergence of more radical demands for change among the peasantry. In this political climate the state in almost every country initiated a broad program of agrarian reform, an additional political objective being to incorporate the peasantry within a dual agenda, i.e., not just to divert existing and future dissent into constitutional channels, where it might be more easily co-opted by the state, but also to bring smallholders into the orbit of a specifically capitalist development project, thereby offering them a rival to the socialist alternative. Generally speaking, under the rubric of agrarian reform legislation designed to modernize agriculture, the ownership of productive tracts of land has been further concentrated, redistribution occurring only within the peasant sector itself, leading to a process of internal differentiation. The latter has involved the emergence of a small stratum of rich peasants, some of whom are converted into rural capitalists, a somewhat larger middle stratum of self-sufficient peasant farmers with productive capacity for the domestic market, and a rural proletariat composed in most instances of a mass of semi-proletarianized — that is, landless or near landless — migrant workers. In most contexts, however, these attempts at accommodation and co-optation, including unionization from above and the setting up of parallel or government-controlled peasant organizations, either failed or were only partially successful: usually they tended to unleash class conflicts that continued into a more radical phase of land reform (Kay 1977). For this and other reasons, Latin American governments at first instituted a land reform program, but then devoted their energies to preventing its radicalization, using a combination of strategies ranging from corporativism (unionization from above), attempts at controlling peasant organizations, by co-opting their leadership, to outright repression (Thorpe et. al. 1995).

In each phase of capitalist modernization — that is, in the transition from *haciendas* to plantations, and from export-oriented to import-substituting industrialization — the state has played a crucial role in promoting, financing and protecting the dominant "modernizing" classes from the threat of peasant and rural worker movements, forcing the rural proletariat and peasantry to bear the costs of "transition." These dynamics reappeared in the 1980s in the context of a transition towards a neoliberal world order facilitated by the so-called "globalization process." Among the categories disadvantaged by the application of neoliberal measures in Latin America, the peasantry and rural workers have been the most adversely affected (Veltmeyer and Petras 2000).

From Neoliberalism to Neomercantilism

With the advent of neoliberal reforms in the 1980s and 1990s, governments in the region acquired a new set of weapons in their confrontations with peasant-based and/or peasant-led organizations and movements, and in short order, according to some observers, the era of radical, and even liberal, land reform was over (Lehmann 1978; Kay 1999). This is at least how it has appeared to those in control of the state apparatus and to economists who serve the state as policy advisors. In short, the issue in agriculture was no longer one of redistributive land reform, let alone new non-individualistic or non-private property relations, but rather modernization and capitalist development (i.e., productive transformation), a process to take place without a change in property relations or nonmarket redistribution of agrarian resources and assets. To this end, governments in the region enlisted the support of non-governmental organizations (NGOs) to encourage peasant organizations and communities to make greater use of the "market mechanism" (land titling, land banks etc.) and, in their politics, to eschew direct action and utilize instead "the electoral mechanism" — in other words, to adopt peaceful and legalistic forms of struggle in pursuit of their interests (Amalric 1998; Chambers and Conway 1998; Ghimire 2001).

The reality of today's world economy has little to do with "free markets" and even less with a "globalization" in any of its permutations (Petras and Veltmeyer 2001a). The world is now divided into three competing and cooperating imperialisms, headed by the US and including the European Union (EU) and Japan. The nature of these imperialisms is essentially neomercantilist, although their interests are cloaked in rhetoric of a "marriage [between] the free market and liberal democracy" (Domínguez and Lowenthal 1996). Neomercantilism puts the imperial state at the centre of economic activity — much to the disadvantage of rural producers in Latin America, particularly smallholders and rural workers. The essence of neomercantilism is its two-pronged strategy: at home, state protection of domestic capitalists who are not competitive, and, abroad, the forced opening of markets in the third world under conditions that are prejudicial to other imperial competitors. Among the most protected and state-subsidized sectors is agriculture. Imperial policymakers spend tens of billions of dollars, Euros and yen directly and indirectly subsidizing producers and exporters, while establishing a variety of protective measures, from explicit quotas on agro-imports to so-called "health concerns," to curtail or exclude imports from competitors and third world countries.

Latin American peasants and rural labourers have been undermined by this neomercantilist system in a number of ways. First of all, the subsidies allow agro-exporters, via subsidized electricity, water and extension programs etc., to sell cheaper than peasant and farm producers in the third world, thus driving millions of peasants into bankruptcy. Cheap food imports supposedly produced by more "efficient" (i.e., subsidized) US farmers drove more than two million Mexican and Brazilian peasants off their farms in the 1990s (Petras and Veltmeyer 2001b). While the United States and the EU heavily subsidize their food and grain exporters, the IMF and World Bank demand budget cuts and free trade from Latin American countries, leading to precipitous declines in budget funding for agriculture and the flooding of domestic markets with cheap, subsidized imports.

State-imposed overt and covert quotas on farm imports into the EU and the US undermine potential agro-exporters in Latin America, who, in turn, cut back on the work conditions, payment and employment of rural workers, increasing the number of rural destitute. The non-reciprocal nature of the trading rules "agreed to" by Latin America regimes reveals the "colonized" nature of these states. These colonized states play a crucial role in opening the gate for foreign imports, and cutting credit and investment funding in agriculture (except for a few specialized sectors that complement EU and US needs). In addition to draining resources from the countryside to meet foreign debt obligations to EU and US bankers, the colonized states in Latin America are also assigned several other crucial roles: to police displaced peasants and destitute rural workers, denationalize landownership, and privatize enterprises in key economic sectors.

Having examined the way in which the state in Latin America has ordered and re-ordered agriculture "from above" — first in the interests of a landed rural oligarchy, then on behalf of an agrarian bourgeoisie and more recently to favour foreign and domestic agribusiness enterprises — it is necessary to consider the "from below" response of peasants and rural workers to all these developments, and their resort, at different conjunctures, to rebellion, revolt and revolution.

Rebellion, Revolt and Revolution

From the very beginning of colonialism and throughout its history — the Spanish and Portuguese conquests and subsequent military incursions by British, French and US forces — the peasantry has been the mainspring of popular rebellion, revolt and revolution in Latin America. While the forms of popular rebellions varied and took on the appearance of archaic or millenarian movements by primitive rebels, the reality was much more complex, both in substance and motivation (Hobsbawm 1959).

The Modernity of Peasant Agency

The early rebellions, symbolized by the uprisings led by Tupac Amaru, were attempts to oust the Spanish colonial rulers and restore elements of pre-Columbian society. The key issue was not the non-viability of the latter, but rather the thrust of the popular rural uprising aimed against imperial power. One cannot simply impose on this rebellion an archaic restorationist symbolism, since peasants rebelling to free themselves from labour-service obligations (*mita* or *repartimiento*) and other extra-economic coercive mechanisms of the *encomienda* system, or from the burdens of tenurial labour-rent (*inquilinaje*, *ponguaje*, *huasipunguero*), created the possibility of constructing a peasant-based subsistence agricultural system (Pearse 1975). But, as Bauer (1975) points out with regard to Chile, the constraints and oppressive conditions of the precapitalist (and premodern) agrarian structure informing the *latifundio/minifundio* complex, and the prevalence of tenurial relations binding the smallholding peasantry with only usufruct rights to a landlord class (the *hacendados*), for the most part prevented the evolution of an independent and modernizing peasantry.

The clearest example of the inherently modernist tendencies of an enslaved rural labour force is found in the Haitian Revolution at the end of the eighteenth century. The anti-slavery revolution was also anti-colonial and, at least among the masses, strongly influenced by egalitarian sentiments favouring land redistribution. The subsequent wars of independence in Latin America operated on two levels: struggles by merchants and landlords to secure state power (i.e., political independence), to liberalize the economy, expand trade and appropriate native lands, and, on a different plane, struggles by slaves, peons and smallholders to secure access to land and free themselves from coercive and exploitative social relations of production binding them to landlords (i.e., socio-economic emancipation).

The post-Independence era during the nineteenth and early twentieth centuries was a period of repression coupled with modern rebellion. By that we mean the following dialectical process. On the one hand, the dominant rural oligarchies engaged in "primitive accumulation" involving the seizure of native communal land and the abolition of legislative protection against the exploitation of rural labour, particularly that of indigenous peoples. On the other hand, the popular rebellions were "modern" not in an ideological or programmatic sense but with reference to their collective attacks on the oligarchy's monopoly of landownership, state power, trade and credit. The reclaiming of territory and defence of pre-existing native property rights (usually community-based or cooperative in origin and function) prefigured and were, in effect, dress rehearsals for the modernist claims that have been made by indigenous peasants in Bolivia, Ecuador, Mexico and elsewhere in Latin America for self-determination, autonomy and social justice. Local or decentralized forms of rebellion were a characteristic of all "early modern" urban and rural revolts in the nineteenth century. The key point is that peasant/peon revolts were, in substance, blows against a liberal export model of agricultural development linked to world markets, as opposed to production and trade of foodstuffs for local markets.

The savage repression that accompanied the seizure of land and control of post-slavery labour was met by mass resistance in Mexico and elsewhere. The successful repression by the state of these mass collective mobilizations had as its aftermath the fragmentation and dispersal of the dispossessed peasantry and the formation of bands who were later dubbed "primitive rebels," a label which, as Wolf (1969) points out, obscures much more than it reveals about the sequencing of collective action. While there is no question that the armies of the oligarchic government were formed by peasant and peon conscripts, and that there were varying lapses of time between revolts and rebellions, nevertheless there were oral traditions that transmitted tales and legends of earlier periods of emancipatory struggle, between generations and throughout the region.

The modernist nature of rural revolts was confirmed by the Mexican peasant revolution of 1910 (Knight 1986; Hart 1987; Katz 1988). By the end of the eighteenth century, Mexico had gone furthest in terms of integration into world markets, penetration by foreign capital and formation and dissemination of liberal ideology — *los cientificos* — cultivated by the Profiriato. The brutal forms of torture and labour control, graphically portrayed in the novels of B. Traven and the popular prints of Posada, were not part of an archaic (or "feudal") dynastic order exercising a benign form of authority over the Mexican countryside and its denizens, but the means of maximizing profits for modern capitalists in Europe, North America and Mexico City. At least with regard to its popular sectors, then, the Mexican revolution was not merely a land reform movement but had an anti-imperial character. It was, in fact, the first major revolution against burgeoning US imperialism. Ironically, the trajectory of the Mexican revolution highlights both the tremendous revolutionary potentialities and the strategic weakness of the peasantry, particularly with regard to state power.

Even though the peasantry has formed the backbone of virtually all revolutionary armies, its basic economic interests have found expression in only a few regional armies, for example, the Zapatistas. While the peasant armies were successful in overthrowing established power, they continually resorted to "pressuring" the urban-based political regime to implement political pacts. The state thus became a point of "mediation" between conflicting bourgeois and peasant demands, not a strategic resource to be reconfigured and transformed in the service of a new peasant-based economy. At the peak of each peasant revolutionary mobilization, the bourgeois state responded with concessions and promises, even radical legislation. But after the bourgeoisie and military regrouped, and peasant mobilization weakened, the state either reversed the reforms or failed to implement them.

Mass collective action that mobilizes against the state, displaces incumbent office holders and secures concessions via pressure, without changing the class configuration of the state, has been a characteristic feature of peasant movements throughout the twentieth century. Nevertheless, the nature, leadership and the demands of rural-based movements have changed over time.

Peasant Revolt, the State and Revolution

In the 1930s, significant peasant-based mass movements emerged in Mexico, El Salvador, Nicaragua, Colombia, Brazil and Peru (Stavenhagen 1970; Landsberger 1969, 1974). Rural workers, particularly sugar workers in modern plantations in Cuba, the Dominican Republic and Puerto Rico, as well as Guyana and elsewhere in the Caribbean, engaged in class warfare. In each instance, extremely violent and repressive measures were taken by the state, and these rural rebellions were suppressed or destroyed. In the exceptional case of Mexico under Lazaro Cardenas, agrarian reform was extended to include hundreds of thousands of poor rural families. In El Salvador the peasant uprising was crushed and some 30,000 were killed, and a similar "development" occurred in Ecuador, and with the same devastating effects on an incipient class struggle (Dunkerley 1992). In Nicaragua, the Dominican Republic and Cuba, the US occupation army and its newly anointed tyrant-presidents — Anastasia Somoza, Rafael Trujillo and Fulgencio Batista — slaughtered thousands, decimating the burgeoning peasant and rural workers movements. In Brazil the Getulio Vargas regime defeated Luis Prestes' rural-based guerrilla army while pursuing a strategy of national industrialization. In Chile the Popular Front of radicals, socialists and communists aroused and then abandoned the peasant struggle, together with demands for agrarian reform, in an implicit gentlemen's pact with the traditional landed oligarchy (Kay 1981; Loveman 1976).

In the best of cases, peasant-based revolutions have been able to secure extensive institutional reforms in the agrarian sector, namely, land redistribution. In Mexico, agrarian reform was a sporadic and prolonged process that began in the early 1900s and reached its high point in the 1930s (Silva Herzog 1959; Tannenbaum 1968). In Bolivia the 1952 revolution of miners and peasants led to a sweeping agrarian reform that resulted in the expropriation of most large estates (Lora 1970; Dunkerley 1984). In Cuba at the end of the 1950s the victory of the 26th of July movement led by Fidel Castro ended with the confiscation of most of the US- and Cuban-owned plantations, and the land was either collectivized or distributed to smallholders (McEwan 1981). In Peru during the 1960s, Chile over the 1966–73 period and Nicaragua from 1979 to 1986, substantive land distribution took place, largely as a result of mass peasant mobilizations and direct action (Cotler 1978; Kay 1981, 1982; Midlarsky and Roberts 1995; Vilas 1995).

However, with the exception of the 1959 Cuban Revolution, these advances by peasants and landless workers suffered severe setbacks over the medium and long term. The key problem was always the relationship of the peasant movements to the state. In practically all the revolutions the agrarian reforms listed above were reversed. In Mexico, Bolivia and Peru, a prolonged process of state disinvestment in the reform sector culminated in legislation that provided incentives to agro-export monopolies, alienating community lands (the *ejido* in Mexico) and stimulating cheap, subsidized imported foodstuffs. The politics of alliances, in which the peasantry was generally subordinated to the urban petit bourgeoisie and bourgeoisie, would often secure an initial round of redistributive reforms and state assistance. Subsequently, peasant movements tended to fragment and divide along an official and oppositional line, by which the former became a means to transmit state policy; the state either played upon or actively created these divisions. The inability of a peasant movement to transcend its sectoral and/or "economistic" consciousness confined it to militant "pressure group politics" in which other urban classes took hold of the reins of power, using the peasant movement as a battering ram to clear the way for a kind of capitalist "modernization." Only in the case of Cuba was the peasantry able to consolidate its position and prosper, largely due to the socialist nature of the urban leadership and its efforts to invest in and develop the countryside as the "motor of development."

The second factor leading to the decline of the agrarian reform movements is intimately related to the first: the lack of state investment in the infrastructure, credit, marketing and extension of services essential for the development of cooperatives or individual land-reform beneficiaries. The "maximum act" of the state was the awarding of land titles in ostentatious ceremonies. The promise of future investments never materialized or, as in the case of Mexico and Chile, was selectively distributed as part of an electoral patronage system. In the case of Nicaragua during the 1980s, the US-Contra war destroyed many of the state-sponsored agrarian reform support services, while forcing the Sandinista regime to reallocate budgetary funds from agricultural development to military defence (Walker 1997). Lacking credit, the beneficiaries were hard pressed to finance capital investments; lacking roads and transport, they could not market at a profit. The high costs of private credit and transport ruined many rural households that had benefited from earlier land redistribution, and the lack of state investment in irrigation facilities, plus the state sanctioned usurpation of water rights by better-off members of the new agrarian classes, undermined growth. With the advent of neoliberalism, the elimination of price supports and subsidies, together with the importation of cheap foodstuffs, delivered the *coup de grâce* to the descendants of the initial land reform beneficiaries (Vilas 1995).

Counter-revolution and the State

Over time, the state turned increasingly to stimulating the reconsolidation of landownership and the promotion of agro-export sectors. For example, in northern Mexico, the Santa Cruz region of Bolivia, Peru, Nicaragua and especially Chile, land reforms were reversed, and old owners recovered their land while new ones purchased their holdings, all with the support of counter-revolutionary or counter-reform regimes (Teichman 1995). This process of land reconcentration and reform reversal was itself facilitated by the co-optation of peasant leaders and the incorporation of bureaucratized peasant organizations as a subordinate component into the party-state. This, for example, was the case in Mexico with the PRI (Partido Revolucionario Institucional, or Institutional Revolutionary Party), and in Bolivia with the MNR (Movimiento Nacionalista Revolucionaria, or Revolutionary Nationalist Movement).

The key theoretical point here is that, with the exception of Cuba, revolutionary peasant movements have been unable to seize state power and recreate the society and economy in their own image — at least in a manner that consolidates and expands both their social forces and political interests. Armed peasant revolts with revolutionary programs have seen their leaders accept the blandishments of the urban elite, concern themselves with modernizing reforms ("land titles" etc.) or succumb to the temptations of capital and patronage (Brass 2000). In the case of Nicaragua during the 1980s, Chile in 1973, and the Dominican Republic in 1965, armed US intervention — via Marines or mercenaries — was an important factor in the destruction of pro–land reform regimes and the institution of corporate agribusiness (Kay 1977, 1981; Vilas 1995; Walker 1997).

The crux of the problem can be summed up thusly: *The principal vehicle for any agrarian reform programs in Latin America has been peasant influence on the state; the principal weakness, by contrast, has been the failure of the peasants to consolidate state power so as to sustain reform and make it irreversible.* In both its positive and negative outcomes, therefore, the fate of Latin American peasant movements is inextricably and unavoidably bound up with the state. The point is that a revolutionary vision that takes account of the links between agriculture and the commercial, financial and monetary system is essential. The only successful case of revolution in consolidating the position of land-reform beneficiaries has been Cuba, which managed to transform the urban economy within the context of a far-reaching and radical agrarian reform program. The question is whether the new and dynamic agrarian movements that now dominate the political landscape in the Latin American countryside have learned the lessons of the past.

Contemporary Rural Mobilization and the State

By the end of the twentieth century, a new configuration of dynamic rural movements took centre stage in Latin America (Petras 1997; Petras and Veltmeyer 2001c). Such movements are found throughout Latin America, including in Ecuador, Bolivia, Paraguay, Brazil, Colombia, Mexico, Guatemala, the Dominican Republic, Haiti and, to a lesser degree, Peru, Chile and northern Argentina. Significantly, it is these peasant movements — frequently with a significant indigenous component — that have led the opposition to neoliberalism.

As in the past, the growth and radicalization of the major peasant and indigenous movements is intimately related to state policies. In Mexico, for example, the inauguration of the North American Free Trade Agreement (NAFTA) sparked the uprising by the Zapatista Army of National Liberation (EZLN) in 1994 (Harvey 1994, 1995). Similarly, the major Indian-peasant uprisings and takeovers of Quito, the capital of Ecuador in January 2000 and a year later were in large part responses to the neoliberal policies implemented by the national government (Ceriza 2000; Lluco Tixe 2000; Lucas 2000; Macas 2000a, 2000b; Hernandez 2001). In Brazil the Landless Workers Movement (Movimiento dos Trabalhadores Rurais Sem Terra, or MST) has combined land occupations and mass demonstrations in order to put pressure on the government to legalize and finance the redistribution of land (Petras and Veltmeyer

2001b; Robles 2001). Movements employing similar tactics, such as Federación Nacional Campesina, have formed in Paraguay, where direct-action land redistribution tactics are combined with confrontations with the state to legalize and finance agricultural credits and inputs (*Informativo Campesino*, no. 91, April 1996; Fogel 1986). In Bolivia, Colombia and Peru, peasant movements have been in the forefront of the struggle to develop or maintain alternative crops (for example, coca) as a source of livelihood in the face of neoliberal free market policies that have inundated local markets with cheap imports. The military and their paramilitary auxiliaries, with the active support and approval of Washington's client regimes, have spearheaded the US-directed offensive against coca farmers. The irony is that client regimes and their generals have been the major drug traffickers in the region, and leading US and EU banks have been the major launderers of drug money.

However, most important is the fact that the contemporary peasant movements mentioned above differ substantially from those of the past. First, they are all independent of electoral parties and urban politicians. Second, their leaders are not part of and subordinated to a bureaucratic apparatus but are products of grassroots debates and accountable to popular assemblies. Third, they link sectoral struggles with national political issues. For example, the MST in Brazil calls for agrarian reform, nationalization of the banking system and an end to free market policies. The same is true for CONAIE (National Confederation of Indigenous Peoples of Ecuador) and other movements. Fourth, most of the movements have developed regional linkages (via CLOC, or Coordinadora Latinoamericana de Organizaciones del Campo) and international ties (Via Campesina) and frequently participate in anti-globalization forums and demonstrations (Edelman 1998; Desmarais 2002). Fifth, the new peasant movements have been assiduous in their search for urban allies and building electoral strength in national parliaments. Finally, these movements have learned much from each other, particularly in terms of tactics — for example, the widely practised action of setting up and maintaining roadblocks (*cortas de ruta*) — that are now used even by recently formed movements of unemployed urban workers in Argentina.

Because the neoliberal economies depend on mining, forestry, agro-export enclaves, assembly plants and external markets and finance, they have weakened the economic positions of not only the peasantry but also urban workers: food imports lead to "depeasantization," which ensures that peasant dispossession unloads more surplus labour onto an already flooded urban labour market. In response, peasants have resorted to massive and direct forms of action, involving, among other things, the cutting of major highways, blocking the circulation of essential commodities, reducing foreign currency earnings available for debt payments and putting pressure on overseas lenders. Roadblocks by peasants and rural workers are the functional equivalent of strikes by workers in strategic industries: they paralyze inward and outward flows of commodities destined for production and trade.

The deepening of the economic crisis, particularly severe in rural Latin America, has had two major consequences, both particularly evident in Colombia. First, there is the radicalization and expansion of the struggle in rural areas, particularly the growth of guerrilla armies, now totalling more than 20,000, of mostly peasant fighters. Second, the number of agrarian producers involved in the struggle has increased. At the end of July 2001 in Colombia, farmers, peasants and rural workers joined together in a national strike, blocking major highways in protest over debts, cheap imports and lack of credit. Similarly, in Bolivia and Paraguay, alliances involving peasants, coca growers (*cocaleros*), Indian communities, farmers and urban sectors (trade unions, civic groups) have cut highways and marched on the capital to confront the state.

The response of the state to these rural mobilizations has been substantially the same in each case: militarization of the countryside, extension and deepening of the presence of US military personnel and other federal policing agencies, and negotiations designed to defuse but not resolve basic demands. In Mexico, for example, massive urban support for the Zapatistas led to a process of "negotiations" and an agreement on which the government reneged immediately after the pressure lessened. Similarly, in Ecuador the government negotiated an agreement with CONAIE during the occupation of Quito and then, with the Indian withdrawal to the highlands, failed to comply with those parts of the agreement that came into conflict with earlier undertakings the government made with the IMF and World Bank.

Given the growth of international human rights concerns, US military missions have increasingly encouraged Latin American armies to work with paramilitary forces in order to carry out acts such as village massacres and assassinations of dissident trade unionists and human rights workers. In this way, Colombia is a replay of Vietnam. In 2000, Washington provided US$1.3 billion in aid to the Colombian government, and followed this with more than US$600 million the following year; further, Plan Colombia makes provision for the deployment in Colombia of more than a thousand US military advisers and subcontracted private mercenaries. Although presented as fighting the war against narcotics, the Plan is actually directed against suspected peasant sympathisers and peasant guerrillas linked to the Left. The use of paramilitary forces to repress civilians allows Washington and its military clients "plausible denial" (in fact, Washington even criticizes the "paras") while channelling arms, funds and protection via the Colombian military command.

In the last two decades, particularly with the introduction of neoliberal and neomercantilist policies, Latin American regimes have rejected land reform as a policy solution to rural poverty. Unlike the 1960s, when agrarian reform was perceived by some regimes as a method of pre-empting revolution, in recent decades the state has sought to reverse whatever reforms had taken place. Growing international linkages and markets, the re-colonization of the state, and a new Latin American "transnational capitalist" class are responsible for the rollback of these agrarian reforms as well as the growing impoverishment and militarization of the countryside in the interest of containing the growing rural insurgency. The rollback in the countryside is itself part of a general denationalization of industry and privatization of public services and enterprises. Nonetheless, the development of opposition has been uneven, with the urban working class lagging behind the advanced detachments of the peasantry and rural workers. Urban mass movements do exist such as the COB (Central Obrera Boliviana) in Bolivia, the CTA (Confederación de Trabajadores Agricolas) and the unemployed workers' movements engaged in mass roadblocks in Argentina (*Movimiento de Trabajadores Desocupados*), the CNT in Uruguay and the Frente Patriotico in Ecuador and Paraguay. However, in some cases, such as Argentina, Chile and Brazil (not to speak of the corrupt corporate unions of Mexico), the official trade union confederations are controlled by corrupt right-wing bureaucrats associated with neoliberal regimes (the Confederación General de Trabajo, or CGT, in Argentina, *Forza Sindical* in Brazil) or politically moderate officials (the Central Unica de Trabajadores [CUT] in Brazil, Colombia and Chile), who, while criticizing "neoliberalism," live off state stipends and have neither the incentive nor will to mobilize their followers. Given these adverse circumstances (state repression and laggard support), the demands and achievements of the rural movements are extraordinary. In Colombia, for example, the FARC–EP (Revolutionary Armed Forces of Colombia–People's Army), a movement of peasant-based guerrillas, has secured a demilitarized zone the size of Switzerland where social forums are held and noted scholars, government officials and others debate vital issues such as land reform and alternative cropping patterns. In addition, the guerrillas have major influence in more than one-third of the municipalities of the Colombian countryside (FARC–EP 2000).

The notion of territoriality is central to all of the indigenous peasant movements. For example, key Zapatista demands are legal recognition of Indian autonomy, and control by indigenous populations over the natural resources in their regions. Similarly, CONAIE in Ecuador, the Ayamara and Quechua nations in Bolivia and the Maya nation in Guatemala have all pressed their demands for national cultural autonomy and economic control — demands resisted both by the rulers of the client states and by US and EU extractive agribusiness enterprises. This issue of national autonomy grows out of increasing frustration with the neoliberal state, constant military incursions and massacres, and a growing reaffirmation of national cultural identity.

The second major advance made by contemporary peasant movements in Latin America is the anti-imperialist content of their struggles. US penetration of the Latin American state, and a desire to reassert control over important natural national resources, is the mainspring of resurgent anti-imperialism in rural areas. For example, the aggressive US anti-drug campaign involving direct roles for the Drug Enforcement Agency, the CIA and the Pentagon in destroying the livelihood of 40,000 coca farmers in Bolivia and more than 100,000 in Colombia has certainly fuelled anti-imperialist sentiment. US promotion and financing of sweeping fumigation programs that have adversely affected the health of the rural population in Colombia and destroyed traditional crops throughout the southern part of that nation have further heightened anti-imperialist consciousness. Similarly, Clinton's admission of US complicity in the genocidal war in Guatemala, where more than 250,000 — mostly Mayan Indian peasants — were slaughtered, has certainly not endeared US imperialism to the *campesinos*.

This combination of self-determination, anti-imperialism and opposition to neoliberalism is present in advanced detachments of all the Latin American peasant movements. Among rank-and-file activist peasants, however, the focus is on immediate local demands, particularly land reform, credits and prices and, in some regions, the right to cultivate coca. Leaders of the movements are only able to retain support on the basis of their militancy and honesty in sustaining the struggle for immediate demands. Not surprisingly, the Latin American state has not remained indifferent to this dual process of "from below" policy formulation and grassroots mobilization. Thus the government of Mexico under President Salinas Gortieri attempted to drive a wedge between the popular movement and its peasant constituency via a program (Pronasol) of poverty subsidies. In Brazil the Cardoso regime launched an agrarian bank to finance a commercial land-purchasing scheme in a failed attempt to draw peasant support away from the MST. Hitherto, these and other such moves on the part of the state against peasant movements of today have failed, unlike similar attempts made in the past against modern peasant organizations and movements, which, more often than not, succeeded in weakening or dividing them.

Conclusion

The history and present forms of peasant/state relations in Latin America underline the folly of ignoring or underestimating the instrumentality of the state and the class-based nature of its institutional agency. Claims about the "plurality" or "autonomy" of the state notwithstanding, it is clear that it has in the past acted on behalf of the capitalist class, either indigenous or external to Latin America, and continues to do so in the present. Arguments about whether the state is "strong" or "weak" miss the point, since it is the *politics* of the state — as embodied in its project and support — which is central. Insofar as the state is not merely the object but also the product (and producer) of conflict, therefore, it is both a cause of and participant in struggle. Much current non-Marxist — especially postmodern — analysis of the peasantry, however, either ignores the state altogether or recognizes its presence and impact but denies that its agency is based on class. The latter position gives rise to two equally problematic interpretations. One reproduces an epistemologically simplistic state/self dichotomy that, because it fails to analyze resistance to the state in terms of class, wrongly views all forms of grassroots resistance as necessarily progressive. The other focuses on the desirability of formal re-democratization, an outcome which similarly dissolves the contradiction between capital and labour that is present so long as accumulation and surplus extraction continue to be systemic imperatives. Whether the state discharges "good governance" within a liberal democracy or exercises "strong" government on behalf of neoliberal economic objectives is in the end irrelevant, since capitalism decrees that both forms lie on the same continuum. Sooner or later, therefore, the liberal democratic state in which peasants and workers attempt to realize their political interests electorally, and thus choose to be something other than that desired by national/international capital, *becomes of necessity, under capitalism,* a strong state administering a neoliberal economy.

The state in Latin America has played, and continues to play, a major role in shaping the agricultural economy, either following or setting an agenda that is for the most part directed against the peasantry. In a few specific contexts, the state has, for tactical reasons, supported an agrarian reform program, but such ostensibly pro-peasant interventions have been both time-bound and spatially limited, with little actual redistribution taking place. For its part, the peasantry has alternated between local struggles and broad confrontations with the state, at times playing a major role in challenging the governing class. Any positive achievements, such as securing land redistribution, tend to be counterbalanced by the incapacity of the peasant movement to shape the permanent institutions of the state and consequently prevent the reversal of reforms secured in periods of intense mobilization. This is not merely a debilitating factor of the past, but also a problem that persists to this day. For example, the Brazilian MST which, in the course of a protracted class struggle, managed to secure the expropriation of thousands of landed estates, has recently encountered a major setback in the form of a sharp reduction of credits, which has in turn bankrupted, or threatened to bankrupt, otherwise viable agrarian cooperatives.

The problem of breaking out of the constraints imposed by sectoral class struggles is not an easy one for contemporary peasant movements in Latin America. Today, unlike the past, many of the peasant leaders recognize that the financial system, the export regime and the macroeconomic policy directed by the state are all major obstacles to peasant-based development. Yet the construction of durable and consequential political alliances remains elusive. However, this weakness is not due to what happens in the agrarian sector alone. In most Latin American countries, the growth of informal and precarious forms of labour has led to the decline of urban-based industrial unions and a weakening of their capacity for collective action on anything but wage demands. Even where a potential for mass urban organization is present, however, there is the constant reality of state repression, hindering the deepening of any revolutionary urban-rural alliance. In Colombia, under the peace agreement of 1984–90 between the FARC and President Betancourt, for example, the Left attempted to organize a mass electoral party. Some four to five thousand activists and two presidential candidates were killed, and scores of municipal officeholders were murdered by military-backed death squads, forcing surviving militants to rejoin the guerrilla movement and to resume the armed struggle. In Central America (Guatemala, El Salvador), former guerrilla commanders were effectively incorporated into the electoral process, but only at the cost of their abandoning the peasant struggle and remaining a marginal force in the Congress.

Faced with this dilemma of co-optation or repression, Latin American peasant movements have responded in several ways. First, they have radicalized the struggle by engaging in sustained and extensive roadblocks, affecting the shipment of foodstuffs to the city and the transfer of primary materials for export. Second, they have brought the struggle to the city. The MST, for example, has organized national marches into Brasilia of more than 100,000 people, recruiting urban supporters as they march. In Mexico the Zapatistas marched to the national capital, mobilizing more than 300,000 in Mexico City itself. In Ecuador the CONAIE has occupied Quito and even "taken the Congress," establishing a short-lived "popular junta" with progressive junior military officers. Similar demonstrations and peasant marches have taken place in the Bolivian and Paraguayan national capitals, La Paz and Asunción. These demonstrations of force usually result in securing a negotiating session with the government, and not only generate a set of agreements that are honoured in the breach but also lead temporarily to demobilization. What all these examples underline is the centrality of both the urban sector and its state to the success or failure of agrarian movements.

However, mass show of force does serve peasant organizations as a negotiating tool, exerting pressure on the existing regime to modify its neoliberal agenda. Its revolutionary appearance notwithstanding, because of the subjective or objective realities it is in fact simply a reformist strategy. Many of the leaders of contemporary peasant movements, such as Antonio Vargas of CONAIE, have for almost a decade engaged in the cyclical ritual of mass protest/negotiation/agreements/broken promises/mass protest. It is clear that pursuit of mass pressure politics instead of revolutionary struggles for state power is a sign of ineffectualness rather than strength: in short, these tactics are dictated by the weakness in the cities, and/or limitations in the strategic thinking of peasant leaders concerning the nature of the state.

Compounding the complexity of the peasant struggles are divisions within peasant movements and weak coordination among peasant organizations, factors that play into the hands of divide-and-conquer strategies pursued by the state. In Bolivia the personal rivalry between Evo Morales of the *cocaleros* and Felipe Quispe of the peasant movements is a case in point. Similar divisions exist in Paraguay, and to a lesser degree in Brazil. The most striking case of fragmentation, however, is Mexico, where each state has its own independent militant organization, and sometimes as many as two or three, according to region. In this kind of situation, the state frequently offers agreements or concessions to one organization at the expense of others, driving a wedge among them.

Nonetheless, there have been a number of successes. Some efforts at forging tactical alliances between different rural organizations have paid off. In Colombia, for example, in August 2001 there was a successful agrarian strike (*paro agropecuario*) that included everyone from coffee growers to day labourers (*jornaleros*) and managed to paralyze major highways throughout the Colombian countryside. Similarly, a number of Indian organizations in Mexico have formed a national federation that articulates their collective interests and expresses their solidarity with the EZLN. Together with the growth of regional solidarity among peasant movements, these alliances and unified actions are a major step forward. However, the problem of confronting US-backed client states and their military forces remains a formidable challenge. The current efforts of the Zapatistas in Mexico and the MST in Brazil to build counterpart organizations in the cities have yet to be successful. While urban-based religious and human rights groups, leftist parliamentary deputies, academics and trade unionists do provide valuable support, they do not constitute an anti-systemic force that could aid revolutionary peasant movements in transforming the state. For one thing, unlike the peasant movements, they do not have an anti-systemic agenda. The most promising development in this regard is the barrio-based urban movement of the unemployed and underemployed in Argentina, and the community-based Coordinator of Popular Organizations (COPS) in the Dominican Republic. Both have demonstrated an ability to undertake coordinated national mass action that effectively paralyzes the urban economy, and this despite savage repression.

A current alternative to rural insurgency and the savage state repression it provokes has been what might be termed "passive grassroots agency," which takes the familiar form of rural displacement and mass overseas migration. More than two million Colombians have been displaced by the US-backed paramilitary/military scorched-earth policy, and today there are more El Salvadorians in the US and Mexico than in their home country. A massive exodus of peasants from Ecuador, Colombia, Central America and the Caribbean is the "passive/negative" response to the failed neoliberal experiment backed by state repression. Except for President Hugo Chávez in Venezuela, who speaks of a massive agrarian resettlement of rural migrants — a back to the countryside movement — no state in Latin America has the resources or the political will to reverse the current decline and crisis of agriculture and the peasant economy. Integrated into world markets and subordinated to Washington, the Latin American state has continued to pursue policies designed to "empty the countryside," confiscating fertile peasant lands and transferring them to big landowners and/or agribusiness enterprises, and then repressing those who dare to object to this process by taking part in the burgeoning mass movements. The dislike is mutual, and the element of standoff palpable: no mass peasant movement is currently aligned with any state in Latin America, and no state speaks for the peasantry. If nothing else, this situation underlines the importance of developing an accurate understanding of peasant/state relations.

8. Indigenous Peoples Arise

Ecuador on the Move

The 1980s saw a slow and relatively silent reorganization of indigenous peoples in Latin America, many of whom after years, and indeed centuries, of struggle had sought refuge and could still be found in what Subcomandante Marcos termed "*bolsillos de olvido*" (forgotten pockets) across the region. This organizational effort and resurgence was evident in regions dominated by communities of indigenous peasants in Bolivia, Peru, Ecuador, Guatemala and Mexico. It was also evident among indigenous populations in marginalized zones of the Amazonian tropical forests, which provided a refuge from Spanish conquest and colonization and had remained a refuge until the 1960s brought into the region religious missionaries and multinational capital bent on commercial exploitation of its abundant natural resources (Beltrán and Fernandez 1960). One striking and characteristic feature of this resurgence of indigenous peoples was the re-emergence of local ancestral identities and a bold assertion of pride in diverse ethnic and national cultures. José Bengoa (2000), an astute analyst of this re-ethnification process, sees the emergence of identity politics among indigenous peoples in Latin America as one of several unanticipated effects of the forces of globalization that have swept the region. Indeed, one of the ironies of these "forces" is that they have spread the ageless struggle for universal human rights and social justice, accentuated the myriad of local particularities and shaped the formation of new ethnic and national identities — and conflicts — across the world (see Macas 2000a, 2000b). Another irony is that, at the same time, cultural globalization has also tended to reduce ethnicity to the folkloric margins of an increasingly homogenous world society, especially because the mass media display little respect for ethnic, national or cultural differences and limits (Featherstone 1990).

In the 1990s the resurgence of the "indigenous question" took the form of widespread mobilization of the most diverse social forces organized over the previous decade, primarily in the struggle for land and opposition to exclusionary government policies. The decade began with a major uprising in May 1990 of indigenous peasants in the highlands of Ecuador, and within a few years, in January 1994, there occurred in Chiapas, Mexico, one of the most significant irruptions of indigenous struggle onto the stage of national and regional politics in Latin America. Indeed, the Zapatista uprising in Chiapas brought the struggles and social movements of indigenous peoples across Latin America onto the centre stage of world history, thereby extending the "short century" declared by the historian Eric Hobsbawm (1984) and giving the lie to his view that the indigenous question, like that of the peasantry, had disappeared into the dustbins of history. In subsequent years, from 1994 to the present, the uprisings of indigenous peasant farmers and communities in Ecuador and Mexico have become part of a broader movement. By the end of the decade and the turn of the new millennium, the indigenous question in Latin America had taken centre stage in a popular struggle against the forces of modernization and change, neoliberalism and global capitalism. In this chapter, the dynamics of this process will be briefly explored, as will the appearance of a new actor on the stage of world social change.

The Emergence of the Indigenous Question

The struggle of Latin America's indigenous peoples against "conditions of exclusion and adversity" is at least five hundred years old — 508 years, according to CONAIE (Ceriza et al. 2000: 7) — in some cases going back to the Spanish conquest and colonization. These conditions are widespread but are concentrated in countries, such as Bolivia, Ecuador, Peru, Guatemala and Mexico, with the largest indigenous populations. In each of these countries, as well as Brazil, Chile, Colombia and other countries with smaller concentrations, diverse groups and nations of indigenous peoples have maintained a virtually constant struggle to survive under conditions of exclusion and adversity generated by their relations with the dominant society. In this struggle, history is replete with wars of resistance, rebellions and periodic uprisings.[1] But it would seem that the 1980s saw specific conditions that would give rise to a major resurgence of the indigenous question across Latin America. The precise connection between these conditions and the latest irruption of the indigenous question requires further study, but there would seem to be at least four factors involved:

1. a deterioration in living standards for both the working classes and indigenous peoples in the region, reflected in the dramatic fall in the remuneration to labour and in national incomes; growing social

inequalities and inequities in the distribution of wealth and income; and the spread and deepening of conditions of absolute and relative poverty and associated immiseration, particularly for the indigenous population. (South American countries with the highest percentage of indigenous populations are also the poorest. Furthermore, the indigenous population, of every country with one, is the poorest group in society, in many cases with rates of poverty that exceed 80 percent.)

2. an accelerated process of capitalist development facilitated by neoliberal policies of sweeping reforms, a structural adjustment program designed to orient production towards the demands of the world market — to insert each economy into a capitalist globalization process; [2]
3. democratization in the form of a return to power of constitutionally elected civilian regimes, a movement to decentralize government and the emergence of a new civil society to occupy the spaces created by a retreating state; and
4. a marriage of strategic significance and convenience between the institutions of global capitalism and liberal democracy — free markets and open (electoral) politics (Domínguez and Lowenthal 1996).

In the 1970s, authoritarian-bureaucratic or military governments in Chile, Argentina and elsewhere in the Southern Cone of South America experimented with a program of sweeping reforms that in the 1980s, under conditions of a region-wide debt crisis, would arrest and reverse trends several decades in the making and re-establish the conditions for capital accumulation (Veltmeyer and Petras 1997). These reforms, pioneered by the "Chicago Boys" under the Augusto Pinochet regime, and adopted enthusiastically by José Martinez de Hoz in Argentina in 1976, included measures to (1) open up the economy to the forces of the world market, freed from the regulatory efforts of the nation-state; (2) liberalize the flow of goods and services, and capital markets, creating zones of free trade; (3) privatize the means of production by devolving state enterprises to the private sector; and (4) reduce the role of the state in the economy and increase reliance on "the market mechanism."

By the end of the decade these "structural" reforms were widely implemented, often as conditions attached to IMF and World Bank loans, with the exception of three major holdouts in the region: Brazil, Peru and Venezuela. However, within a few years, elected regimes in these countries also fell into line and installed some of the most extreme programs of structural adjustment to that date — in Peru under Alberto

Fujimori, Argentina under Carlos Menem, and in the latter half of the decade in Brazil under Fernando Enrique Cardoso. In both Venezuela and Ecuador the decade of the 1980s ended with governments committed to a radical program of IMF-mandated reforms and austerity measures. In Venezuela the result was an upheaval of political protest and repression that left in its wake a huge number of dead protestors — some three hundred by official count, unofficially many more. In Ecuador the conservative Sixto Durán-Ballen committed the government to an extension of the reform program initiated in the early 1980s.

By 1993, conditions in Ecuador had deteriorated to the point that the government launched a series of radical measures to stabilize the currency, balance accounts and adjust the economy, and concomitantly generated further resistance against these measures. The first mobilization of these forces of resistance and opposition occurred in June 1990 with an uprising of indigenous people that shook the government to its foundations within a highly inequitable ethnic and social structure.

By 1995 the government's neoliberal policies had created conditions for a popular movement that took the form of organized street protests against the government's austerity measures, marches on centres of public power from the countryside, mass demonstrations, occupations of public buildings, threats to disrupt production, a cutting off of highways and transportation arteries (*cortas de ruta*), direct pressures on the legislature and the executive, and, in concert with the labour movement, strike action. In the early to mid-1990s this popular movement was led by the Frente Unitario de Trabajadores (FUT), an organization of the country's largest unions, representing a membership in excess of 800,000, around 25 percent of the country's economically active population. By the second half of the decade, however, the National Confederation of Indigenous Peoples of Ecuador (CONAIE), a heterogeneous organization of regional associations of indigenous peoples and communities had, by and large, assumed this leadership role, being the only organization capable of large-scale mobilizations against the government's repeated efforts to implement its IMF-mandated program of "economic reform." (FUT has acknowledged its failures to bring about effective change or even to mobilize effectively against the government's neoliberal agenda. However, FUT is not alone. Across Latin America, organized labour has borne the brunt of structural adjustment programs and the offensives of the capitalist class against the working class.) CONAIE, however, was by no means the only organization involved in these mobilizations. Apart from a loose alliance of oil and electrical workers that joined CONAIE in its resistance against the government's privatization agenda, and a smattering of urban "social organizations" opposed to the government's neoliberal program, a recently constructed federation of indigenous communities, peasant farmers and Afro-Ecuadorians (FENOCIN, or National Confederation of Peasant, Indigenous and Black Organizations), with a social base of around 100,000 families, joined the fray.[3] As of the mid-1990s these mobilizations were coordinated with a newly formed directorate of diverse social movements called Coordinadora de Movimientos Sociales (MCS) that grouped together oil and electrical worker unions, indigenous peasants and Afro-Ecuadorians, and urban social organizations.

Towards the turn of the new millennium, the government's legislative reform programs came to be popularly known as TROLE I and TROLE II. The measures that made up these programs of economic reform — immediate increases in the price of basic services and the *canasta popular*, including fuel and electricity, and the imposition of a value-added tax (VAT) — led to the largest mobilization of the decade, orchestrated by FUT, CONAIE and CMS. In January 2000, and again in February, these popular forces were directed against the government, bringing about its collapse and preventing the implementation of its legislative program of structural adjustment measures that were designed in theory to "modernize the state" and establish macroeconomic stability but in practice had brought about "the globalization of misery" (*Boletín ICCI* August 1999; 20 February 2001).

The Indigenous Uprising: A Decade of Gains

The 1980s have been called "the lost decade" of socio-economic development. They witnessed a collapse of economic growth and a serious regression of living standards, including a 50–70 percent decline in wages; according to the Inter-American Development Bank (IDB 1998: 38), wages in Latin America in 1996 remained 50 percent below their 1980 indexed level. However, from the point of view of CONAIE, organized in 1986 in the throes of a region-wide debt and economic crisis, the decade was not lost; indeed, in the words of its leader at a national meeting (*encuentro*) of indigenous organizations organized in Quito on November 23, 1991, the 1980s represented a decade won for the Indians of Ecuador (quoted in Bebbington et al. 1992). In fact, the same could be said of the popular struggle waged by indigenous peoples elsewhere in Latin America, particularly in Mexico (Chiapas) and Bolivia, where the indigenous movement has undergone an almost parallel development to that in Ecuador — the 1980s involved a protracted period of silent political organization whose fruits would be realized in the 1990s. In the case of CONAIE, which, together with the Zapatistas in Chiapas, constitutes the most dynamic indigenous movement in the region, the level of organization was unprecedented, bringing together under one umbrella the three major groupings of indigenous peoples in the country: the Quechua of the Andean highlands, the Shuar nation of the eastern slopes of the Cordillera, and the indigenous nationalities of Amazonia. Until 1970 the Shuar lived in almost total isolation, but in defence of their "sovereign territory," a large area making up almost 70 percent of the largest province of the Oriente (Peru and Ecuador's Amazonian regions), they have had to form organizational alliances with the Huaorani, Siona, Secoya and Quechua. In the process the entire subregion has been transformed into a model of autonomy and self-government (Chiriboga 1992). In addition to these major groupings of indigenous peoples in the highlands and Amazonia, small clusters of the Chachis, Tshachilas and Awas formed several "areas of refuge" on the coast.

From the outset the struggle was directed against both the state and capital, pitting the movement against various governments of the day over government neoliberal policy and the demand for a pluri-national or multi-ethnic state, that is, "autonomy" within the Ecuadorian state. In the highlands the struggle in the 1960s and 1970s was between the landed oligarchy (*hacendados*) and the semi-proletarianized, near-landless *huasipungueros*. It was institutionalized within the political confines of Ecuador's developmentalist state and its land reform programs of 1964 and 1973, which, by most accounts, provided greater benefits to the *hacendados* than the *huasipungueros*. Legislation under these programs abolished the semi-feudal system of service land tenure (*huasipunguismo*) and other forms of unpaid labour, creating conditions for the capitalist transformation of production — the government's agenda, pursued against the not inconsiderable resistance of the big landlords who managed to block any effective implementation of the government's land reform program, including expropriation of underutilized farmland. In many cases, the big landlords divested themselves of relatively unproductive landholdings with sufficient compensation so as to allow them to modernize their own enterprises and build up their capital to invest in diverse areas of agro-production. The result was further concentration of land tenure and massive emigration of indigenous peasant farmers from their increasingly inadequate, small and poor landholdings. By November 2002 the lack of access to decent landholdings and credit, low productivity and meagre incomes were so bad that land reform had been placed on the back burner, most peasant farmers preferring, if not forced, to abandon their landholdings and emigrate (interview with Pedro de la Cruz, 31 November, 2002). In this context, which included the continued disintegration of the traditional peasant community, the capitalist transformation of agricultural production, an incipient but weak rural union movement, and recourse to legal institutions to advance the struggle for land, the indigenous movement failed to link the land struggle with the broader struggle for socialism in the countryside and cities.

However, in the same context the indigenous movement saw the growth of an increasingly complex form of socio-economic organization, from donor-sponsored and government-supported cooperatives to communalism, reflected in a startling increase in the number of legally recognized indigenous communities (Santana 1983). By 1993, the number of legally recognized communities in Ecuador had reached 2,400, with a total population of 1.4 million (IWGIA 1995). In the Amazonian region, diverse organizations of indigenous people confronted incursions of foreign multinational that wanted to extract petroleum and other natural resources from their homeland territory. Although this struggle occurred largely in the Oriente, it also spread to the isolated coastal zones where some indigenous people had sought refuge in post-colonial times.

The struggle waged by the indigenous peoples and communities in Ecuador against multinational corporations is part of a broad region-wide, and indeed worldwide, struggle. The International Working Group for Indigenous Affairs in Copenhagen has elaborated a record of this struggle (IWGIA 1995) that includes: in Ecuador, the fights of indigenous communities in the Oriente against Texaco's pollution of the environment, and against Arco; in Colombia, the battles of the Uwa against Occidental Oil and of Emberá Katio against Urra's hydroelecric dam; in Peru, the struggles of Ashuar against pollution by Texaco and the Achoa against Arco's oil exploration activity; in Bolivia, the fight of the Ayora, the Guaraníes and Chiquitos against the government's construction of a dam and gas pipes; in Chile, the Pechuenches against the energy corporation Endesa and the struggle of Aymara communities against mining activities and the construction of a cellullose plant; in Venezuela, the indigenous communities of la Gran Sabana Inataca and the Paragua against the government's building of an electric power grid connecting the country to Brazil, and the struggle of the Imataca against various mining ventures; in Brazil, the Xerente and Karajé communities' struggle against the building of dams and hydroelectric plants, and the fight of the Terena, Guató, Kavieawev and Parecí against Brazil-based Urucum. And this is only a partial list of ongoing conflicts between indigenous communities and TNCs across Latin America.

In Ecuador and elsewhere in Amazonia this struggle has almost taken on the dimensions and characteristics of a class and ethnic war. Issues in this war include:

1. the huge environmental and social costs of oil exploration and other resource extraction, pipeline building and road-clearing activities in the indigenous territories,
2. the demand to reclaim ancestral or traditional homeland in the Amazonian region, encompassing 90 percent of Pastaza, the largest province in the Oriente, and 70 percent of the area ceded to foreign companies for oil exploration,
3. control over oil exploration and extraction and any other resource-extractive activity in this and other regions populated by indigenous peoples,
4. the capacity for self-government to protect the ecosystem on which indigenous communities are dependent for their livelihoods and
5. the total withdrawal of the Ecuadorian state, of both the armed forces and the government, ceding autonomy to an indigenous form of government within a multi-ethnic state.

In this struggle the indigenous people have been pitted against both the government and the transnational corporations operating in the area and given large concessions for oil exploration and resource extraction. On behalf of the indigenous people in the Amazonian basin, in 1990, just months ahead of the June uprising, CONAIE demanded the creation of an independent autonomous territory governed solely by the Quechua, Shuara and Achuara nations. This demand was rejected out of hand as "unconstitutional," but by May 1992, after several years of hard struggle that involved threats to close down agricultural production and disrupt oil activities, cutting off road and highways around points of production, and large-scale marches on the city, street demonstrations and occupations of public buildings, the government gave in, forced to make some land concessions. These concessions led to the withdrawal of most foreign companies. As reported on May 16, 1992 (*Interpress Service* "Indians drive TNCs out of Ecuador"), the political risks of continued operation became simply too high for these companies to bear.

However, while the land struggle and the fight of CONAIE against the oil and other foreign companies in the Oriente subsided, struggles on other fronts continued to mount. In 1993 the conservative regime of Durán-Ballen announced a series of austerity measures and plans to modernize the state as part of a broader reform program.[4] The measures announced by the government, and in part implemented, included a major devaluation of the national currency; an automatic rise in the price of basic goods such as milk and bread, electricity, fuel and other basic services of anywhere from 35 to 50 percent; a decline of an estimated 50 percent in the standard of living of most consumers; and a reduction of state workers from 400,000 to 280,000.

The response of the popular movement to these measures was immediate. FUT, an amalgam of the country's most important trade union federations, organized the takeover of factories across the country and mobilized for a general strike. But, by all accounts (see official sources reported by *Interpress Service*, May 26, 1993) the government was more concerned with the response of the indigenous movement, which, through the agency of CONAIE, had taken the lead in the popular struggle against the government's neoliberal agenda. CONAIE responded to the call by the labour movement for concerted actions against the government with a threat to paralyze agricultural production and to close down most of the country's main roads and highways, a well-tried tactic more recently adopted by the movement of unemployed workers in the slum belts of Buenos Aires and elsewhere in the Southern Cone.

Class and Ethnic Identity and the Struggle Over and Against the State

The multi-ethnic nature of Ecuadorian society is clear: in a population of 10.5 million anywhere from 30 to 49 percent[5] belong to one of ten indigenous "nationalities" or ethnicities." As noted, these ethnic or national groups are generally found in three broad regions: the highlands, where the indigenous people, Quechua for the most part, have been involved in the long struggle of peasant farmers for land, land reform and release from the oppression and injustices of the *hacienda* system; Amazonia, which is occupied by small societies of diverse nationalities/linguistic/ethnic groups of indigenous people, fighting a long battle against the incursions of commercial capital seeking to extract oil and other natural sources; and several relatively isolated and marginalized coastal zones.

In the 1960s the indigenous question centred on a land struggle for access to and redistribution of land monopolized by a small class of *hacendados* or *latifundistas*, who, with the support of the political and church establishment had subjugated the indigenous peasant through gross exploitation, political oppression and social degradation. Under these conditions, a good part of the Quechuan peasantry was pressured to migrate to the cities and other populated centres in the search of wage employment and was integrated into the social structure of these centres under conditions of the worst gross class exploitation and ethnic discrimination;[6] another, larger part was converted into a huge semiproletariat, forced to subsist on meagre plots (*huasipungos*) and sell their labour part-year, generally on a seasonal basis, to the owners of commercial plantations or other capitalist enterprises; a third part continued to struggle on the land, directly against the landlords and indirectly under conditions of a government-led, USAID/Alliance for Progress–financed land reform program. In the 1970s this struggle increasingly took a less radical and a legal turn under conditions of liberal reform, with the actions of NGOs and outside donor agencies, and the organization of cooperatives and producer associations.

The results of these diverse struggles and processes included:

1. capitalist transformation of the traditional agrarian economic and social structure,
2. decomposition of the indigenous community, and social differentiation within both the peasantry and the indigenous population,
3. deterioration of standards of living and means of livelihood of the indigenous people, and the weakening and disappearance of traditional forms of social and economic organization and cultural practices,
4. the emergence of a developmentalist state with its politics of reform, and ideological control and co-optation of the indigenous population,
5. a weakening and increasing diversification and division of interests within indigenous organizations, and
6. a split between the politics of ethnic identity and the class demands of the peasantry, with the former being increasingly subordinated to the latter.

In the 1980s the indigenous movement acquired a new complexion and was given a somewhat new direction, with a greater focus on the questions of ethnic or cultural identity, and the struggle for a multi-ethnic or pluri-national state, that is, autonomous control of indigenous peoples over their own homeland territories. The indigenous movement has always had this dual character, being, on the one hand, a class struggle for land and against prevailing conditions of exploitation, oppression and social exclusion, and, on the other, a struggle to recover or gain respect for ancestral culture and traditions. However, in the 1980s, with the subordination of the peasant struggle for land reform to Ecuador's developmentalist state, the second aspect began to gain greater prominence.

The demands of the indigenous movement in the 1980s and 1990s for a multi-ethnic state can be viewed in the light of both dimensions of this struggle — for community control over the land and resources *and* for social justice based on respect for ancestral cultural traditions. However, as the land struggle was largely institutionalized via a system of legal and political reform, and the social forces mobilized in this struggle were constrained and subsequently demobilized, the ethnic and cultural issue became more and more salient (Santana 1983; Sylva 1986; Velasco 1979; Zamosc 1994).

By the late 1980s the politics of class increasingly gave way to the politics of cultural identity, leading some observers and analysts to construct a theory of the emergence of "new social movements."

Notwithstanding this development and the ensuing debate, in 1986 the two sides of the indigenous movement came together in the formation of the National Confederation of Indigenous Nationalities, which brought under one organizational umbrella the Confederation of Indigenous Nationalities of the Amazon (CONFENAIE), the Ecuarunari, which represented the land struggles of the highland Indians, and other federations of indigenous organizations and peasant communities. Over the next decade, CONAIE would become the primary organizational form of the indigenous movement in Ecuador, advancing both the class struggle for more land and social justice, mobilizing the forces of opposition and resistance against the government's neoliberal agenda, pressing the demand for cultural and political autonomy within a multi-ethnic state, and supporting the indigenous peoples of Amazonia in their struggle against Texaco and other agents of transnational capital. In these diverse conflicts, the class struggle against capitalist development *and* the popular struggle for political identity were both pursued, not without internal divisions. In fact, in the late 1990s the opposing and at times conflicting agendas involved in the indigenous movement have led to divisions that have threatened to tear it apart (Macas 2000b).[7]

Notwithstanding these divisions — and the formation of Pachakutik (Movimiento de Unidad Plurinacional Pachakutik Nuevo Patria), a political party formed for the purpose of contesting national elections — CONAIE continues to represent at a national level the most diverse groups and organizations of indigenous peoples, and to mobilize collective actions whenever called for. The indigenous uprising of January 21, 2000, like the earlier uprising of January 1, 1994, in Chiapas, provided an eloquent testimony to this mobilizing capacity, and to the dual nature of the struggle: politics of class and cultural identity.

January 21, 2000: *Golpe de Estado* or Indian Revolt?

January 21, 2000, in Ecuador represents like no other event in the long and protracted struggle of the country's indigenous people one of those rare historic periods in which relations between the past and present are condensed into a moment of transcendental significance: the indigenous people of Ecuador, through their own organizations and struggle, managed to displace from the presidential palace the elected representative of the traditional mestizo oligarchy which had controlled the levers of political power from the moment of the historic conquest some five hundred years earlier. For six hours, with the support of thousands of their kind, who breached a massive government security effort to march on the capital, Ecuador's indigenous people had captured the presidential palace on behalf of "the people," and with the support of the more broadly constituted Coordinadora de Movimientos Sociales. CONAIE provided the mass social base for the uprising and temporary capture of the state apparatus, but the supportive mobilizations orchestrated by the CMS, and its political activity within the armed forces at the operational level of disgruntled colonels and captains in charge of troops, was also a critical factor.

But the moment was short-lived. Within hours, under pressures from the US on the country's armed forces, the scions of the traditional establishment were back in power. However, as with the first ten days of the Zapatista uprising, after these six hours nothing would ever be precisely the same: a popular movement, dominated and led by indigenous peasants, could gain access to the seat of political power, thereby threatening the entrenched structure of relations between the dominant society and a subjugated people. In one swoop, the indigenous people of Ecuador gave the lie to a conceit popular in academic and policy-making circles, that the peasantry and indigenous peoples represented a numerically insignificant factor in the struggle against the forces of modernization and change — against history (Hobsbawm 1994).

By some, if not all, accounts, this historic event of January 21, 2000, although traceable to a long historic struggle against Creole domination, was triggered by a policy decision announced some ten days earlier by President Mahuad to adopt the US dollar as the national currency. In

August 1998 the exchange rate had been 5,000 sucres to one US dollar. This new policy implied an exchange rate of 25,000 sucres to the dollar in a country in which the minimum wage is barely $53, the cost of a monthly basket of basic goods was $200, and more than 70 percent of the population, and more than 90 percent of the indigenous population (49 percent, according to the World Bank 1999) lived below the World Bank's conservatively defined poverty line (World Bank 1999; Ceriza 2000: 6). In 2002, after several years of a dollarized economy, more than 50 percent of the population remains income-poor, even by the World Bank's conservative poverty measure of less than $2 a day; for the indigenous population this rate exceeds 80 percent.

CONAIE has led the popular struggle against the government's neoliberal policies of stabilization and structural adjustment measures — TROLE I and II — for close to a decade (Lluco Tixe 2000). It is clear that these policies have been directly responsible for the drastic if steady deterioration of the standard of living and the spread of poverty in the popular sectors of Ecuadorian society. But it seems that this latest twist in the government's insistent turn towards neoliberal capitalist development was the last straw for the popular movement. Within days, on the fifteenth of the month, CONAIE announced a planned march on Quito and the takeover of the government; within six days, hundreds of thousands of indigenous people had mobilized and managed to surround the legislature, judiciary and presidential palace, occupied by politicians accused of corruption and responsibility for the economic crisis.

The six days of active resistance and indigenous uprising involved a major intensification of a heated struggle that can be traced back to 1985, to the first attempts to implement a structural adjustment program.

Another round of neoliberal policy measures led to the indigenous uprising of June 1991 and the long march of indigenous peoples from the Oriente to Quito to press their demands for *autonomia*, recognition of their territories. The efforts of Abdalá Bucaram regime in 1997 to privatize social security and implement a series of neoliberal policies had disastrous consequences and generated protest actions across the country. After the efforts of the subsequent Mahuad regime in 1999 to privatize public sector enterprises and to adopt the US dollar as the national currency, these protests multiplied, bringing together in struggle diverse indigenous organizations, urban social organizations and the working class. By January 2001 the government's neoliberal agenda had created an explosive pre-revolutionary atmosphere (*Boletín ICCI*, February 1998–December 2000).

In response to CONAIE's announcement of another march on Quito, the Mahuad government, under a rapidly decreed law of national security, mobilized all of its repressive apparatus, including 100,000 operatives of the police and armed forces. However, like tropical rain the Indians from across the country circumvented the blockades and roadblocks, and massive efforts to detain trucks and other transports from the countryside, and began to arrive in small groups. On January 20 more than five thousand Indians were massed in Quito, forming a series of waves in a large sea of protesters. The armed soldiers guarding the palace could not, or did not, resist the sea of protest washing against the citadels of government power. Antonio Vargas, president of CONAIE, accompanied by army colonel Lucio Gutiérrez, appeared at the podium of the legislative assembly to announce the installation of a "People's Parliament" and the formation of a government of national salvation composed of Gutiérrez, Vargas and the ex-president of the Supreme Court. However, on the eve of the twenty-first, the newly formed triumvirate that addressed the masses from the balcony of the palace included not Gutiérrez, CONAIE's presidential candidate in 2000, but Gen. Carlos Mendoza Poveda, Chief of the Joint Armed Forces, who on the morning of the twenty-second dissolved the triumvirate, pronouncing himself in favour of a constitutional-legal solution to the crisis, thus opening up the road to the presidency of Gustavo Noboa Bejarano, the then vice-president (and the losing presidential candidate in the November 2002 electoral contest). The short-lived triumvirate of people power (the *Junta Cívica*) was dissolved and the immediate political crisis of the political establishment was over.

How to interpret this brief ascension to state power of "the people": as a *golpe de estado* or as an expression of a new political project, a new actor on Ecuador's messy political stage?

January 21, as an outcome of a popular uprising, represents a rupture in the democratization process, signaling a fundamental disrespect for the institutions of liberal democracy. On the other hand, it seems that the triumvirate of popular power was formed under conditions of political confusion, with an evident lack of any institutional mechanisms for establishing the legitimacy and functioning of the new government, and for channeling the grievances and demands of the indigenous movement. Apart from the obvious pressures placed by the US on the country's armed forces vis-à-vis the maintenance of constitutional procedures, and notwithstanding CONAIE's considerable mobilization capacity, the indigenous movement was not prepared to take over the government, nor was it able to circumvent the return to power of the traditional political class.

However, at the same time, the movement has drawn important lessons from this momentous political development of continuing symbolic significance. In the shadow of the long and protracted struggle of the indigenous people against capitalist development and for social justice, the future has caught up with the past. There is no reversing or holding back the struggle of indigenous people for social justice and systemic change. The future is upon them.

From 2000 to 2002: The Aftermath of January 21

January 21, 2000, presents a high point in the long march and protracted struggle for systemic change waged by Ecuador's indigenous peoples. But the events and developments in the subsequent two years illustrate some of the contradictory dynamics of the indigenous movement in Ecuador and elsewhere. For one thing, although the indigenous peoples, working through CONAIE, were the primary force in the uprising, they were by no means of one mind in their political project, nor did they act alone, or in a vacuum.

There were at least six major elements of this highly specific conjuncture of objective and subjective conditions that almost created a revolutionary situation. These conditions included: (1) implementation of a highly unpopular and regressive government program of austerity and structural adjustment policy measures, including a dollarization of the currency; (2) a serious deterioration of the economic situation for diverse groups and classes in the popular sector of society, and a serious crisis in the rural economy; (3) a highly mobilized mass of social forces within the highland indigenous peasantry; (4) serious divisions within the dominant and ruling political class, both the bourgeoisie and the oligarchy, unable to constitute a dominant bloc or formulate a coherent program, (according to Diego Delgado Jara (2000) the critical factor in the uprising were political machinations within the political class, divided between the supporters and opponents of President Noboa and the Guayaquil merchant mafia (mostly importers) and the exporting bourgeoisie); (5) a seriously disgruntled sector within the armed forces, concerned with the issue of poor salaries and low wages, and troubled about the institutional integrity of the armed forces; and (6) the coordination of diverse social movements, bringing together diverse sectors and groups in a common struggle against the government's neoliberal policies, its privatization agenda, dollarization of the currency and moves to open up the national economy to the forces of global capitalism.

It is difficult to determine precisely how these diverse factors combined to produce a "pre-revolutionary situation." It is equally difficult to precisely identify the missing conditions that could have converted this situation into an effective capture of the state apparatus by the popular movement. Undoubtedly, the US played a critical role in taking the military apparatus of the state out of play, through pressures exerted on the higher echelons of the armed forces. Also, the indigenous people, in the form of CONAIE, it would seem, were not prepared to assume the mantle of state power and form a government on the basis of a coherent program. In this sense, the momentary and highly tentative capture of the state apparatus could be viewed more as a symbolic act, which put the political class (and the country) on notice.

No doubt other conditions are also at issue. Be this as it may, the subjective conditions for revolution subsided, the moment was lost and the popular movement fragmented. In the subsequent thirty-two months, as a prelude to a massive popular campaign against the Free Trade Agreement of the Americas (FTAA), a regional expression of what Joseph Stiglitz (2002) dubbed the "fourth step towards hell" (the construction of a free trade zone), and to presidential elections in November 2002, a number of developments have transpired within the popular movement. These include a dispersion of the social forces of resistance accumulated within the indigenous movement. CONAIE itself has been riven by internal divisions and Pachakutik, its political instrument, has moved away from the Coordinora de los Movimientos Sociales and offered itself to Lucio Gutiérrez, sacrificing its program for radical change on the altar of his presidential campaign. CONAIE — and Pachakutik deputies — will undoubtedly be given some posts within the government (in exchange for a carte blanche to the Lucio Gutiérrez' regime), but, as Subcomandante Marcos argued several years ago, this form of "doing politics" will prove to be a dead end for the indigenous people, a mechanism for co-optation of its leadership without any substantial change in the structure of economic and political power. Real change can only come under the pressure of accumulated social forces mobilized against the government in direct collective action. In the conjuncture of electoral politics and the 2002 presidential campaign, CONAIE has given clear indications of having surrendered its project for societal transformation, the *sine qua non* for substantively changing the status of Ecuador's indigenous peoples. Where this will lead remains to be seen.

Conclusion

The socio-political movements formed by indigenous people and peasant producers in the Latin American countryside remain the most dynamic forces of opposition and resistance against the neoliberal policies of governments in the region and the globalization project that informs them.

Two features of these movements are of particular significance. One is the dual focus of their programmatic and political demands on both economic (class) and cultural (ethnic) issues. On the one hand, the indigenous movement is organized around issues that affect indigenous peoples as peasants. In this connection the central demands of the movement have always been connected to the question of land and land reform, and more broadly to the question of regional autonomy, that is, political control over their own territories. On the other hand, the indigenous movement is increasingly concerned to preserve and ensure respect for ancestral cultural values and traditions, and to recover the political identities of indigenous people. The formation of both CONAIE and Pachakutik reflect this growing concern for political and cultural identity. Unfortunately, enhanced cultural identity has come at the expense of substantive change in the class situation of Ecuador's indigenous peoples. Unlike cultural identity, this change cannot be accommodated by the existing system, as acknowledged by a significant sector of CONAIE that distanced itself from the Gutiérrez government at its February 2003 national assembly in Guayaquil on February 17–18, 2003. What is required is a revolutionary transformation of this system, a demand that Pachakutik abandoned in exchange for a few government positions for some of the movement's leaders.

The CONAIE assembly did not go so far as to entirely repudiate the Gutiérrez Pachakutik-MPD (Movimiento Patriótico Democrático) alliance.[8] However, it did resolve to distance itself from and reject its agreement with the IMF, and the government's proposed 2003–05 economic plan. Specifically, the assembly resolved to: (1) demand the derogation of the recently announced measures under this plan and the resignation of the economics minister and his team; (2) reject the neoliberal policies imposed by the IMF; (3) demand publication of the government's secret letter of intent with the IMF;[9] (4) not to pay the external debt; (5) extradite and sanction those charged by the Supreme Court for corruption; (6) increase the national budget in social areas such as health, education and local government;[10] (7) and immediately freeze gasoline, electricity and water rates.[11] More broadly, the assembly reiterated its opposition to a Free Trade Agreement of the Americas, seeing it as a form of neocolonial annexation and genocide. The CONAIE assembly also declared its opposition to the US military base in Manta, viewing it as "illegal," and to Plan Colombia, viewing it as simply one more form of US imperialism. Through its declarations and resolutions, CONAIE, in effect, signaled its intention to step back from its experiment in electoral politics and to engage a broader project of system transformation through the politics of class struggle.

This is probably the major lesson that CONAIE has drawn from the aftermath of January 21. Other lessons include the need for a new politics and the need to deepen and extend existing ties to like-minded and supportive organizations in the region and across the world. CONAIE had already come to this view early on in its struggle, as had the Zapatistas in Chiapas. One reflection of this view is the decision of CONAIE early in the 1990s to take the struggle from the countryside to the cities and to seek urban-centred allies in its struggle against the government and the state. Another reflection of this view is a pronounced tendency of CONAIE and other new socio-political movements in the region to reach beyond the national boundaries of the social formations in which they are enmeshed.

The indigenous movements in Ecuador and elsewhere, like the institution of capitalist economy and culture to which they are opposed, have to some extent gone global. An internal evaluation of the indigenous movement in the late 1990s by CONNAIE came to this conclusion, as had CLOC, the major regional association of peasants and indigenous organizations in the region. But where this might lead, however, is not clear. The Landless Workers Movement (MST) in Brazil has recommended the formation of a global directorate *(coordinadora)* of all the forces of opposition and resistance to the globalization project and the neoliberal model of capitalist development. The aim would be to amalgamate the rural struggles of indigenous peoples, peasants and landless workers into a broader popular movement that would have the capacity to confront the forces of reaction and to construct an alternative to the existing system.

9. Los Piqueteros

New Actors on the Political Stage

Latin America has witnessed three waves of overlapping and interrelated social movements since the late 1970s. The first wave, forming at that time and ebbing in the late 1980s, was largely composed of what have been termed "new social movements" (NSMs). These movements were concerned with, and organized around, issues of human rights, ecology, feminism, ethnic identity, social justice and "democracy" rather than class issues such as access to land and land reform, labour exploitation and changing the structure of labour-capital relations. These NSMs were formed with the agency of grassroots social organizations as well as NGOs and other expressions of an emerging "civil society." Despite the celebration of the grassroots, the leadership of these NSMs, for the most part, was constituted by lower middle class professionals whose politics revolved around challenging the military and civilian authoritarian regimes of the time.

The second wave of social movements was class-based, developing into a powerful political force from the mid-1980s to the present. It was largely composed of mass peasant and rural workers organizations engaged in direct action to promote and defend the economic interests of their supporters. To some extent, these movements were formed to revive similar movements that had dominated the political landscape of Latin America in the 1960s and early 1970s but were divided and ultimately defeated, because of fundamental divisions at the levels of strategy and tactics reform, and rural development and political reform versus social transformation and political revolution. The composition, demands and tactics of these rural movements varied, but they were united in their opposition to neoliberalism and imperialism (dubbed "globalization"). The most prominent of these movements included the Zapatistas of Mexico (the EZLN), the rural landless workers of Brazil (MST), the *cocaleros* and peasants of Bolivia, the National Peasant Federation in Paraguay, the FARC (Revolutionary Armed Forces of Colombia), and the peasant-Indian CONAIE in Ecuador.

These movements were led by peasants or rural workers and struggled for agrarian reforms (redistribution of land), national autonomy for Indian communities, and against US intervention, including coca-eradication programs, colonization of territory via military bases, penetration of national police and military institutions, and militarization of social conflicts, such as Plan Colombia and the Andean Initiative. The centrepiece of their struggles was the neoliberal economic regime and the growing concentration of wealth in the hands of local and foreign elites.

The third wave of social movements is centred in the urban areas. It includes the barrio-based mass movements of unemployed workers in Argentina, the unemployed and poor in the Dominican Republic, and the shantytown dwellers who have flocked to the populist banner of Venezuelan President Hugo Chávez.

In addition to these urban movements, new multi-sectoral movements engaged in mass struggles that integrate farm workers and small and medium-sized farmers have emerged in Colombia, Mexico, Brazil and Paraguay. The nature, mode of operation and style of political action of these movements challenge many of the stereotypes and assumptions of conventional liberal social science thinking and post-Marxian orthodoxies. For example, "new social movement" writers have declared the end of class politics and the advent of cultural and "citizen-based" civic movements concerned with democracy, gender equality and identity politics. However, the subsequent demobilization of the so-called "issue-and-identity-oriented" NSMs and the explosion of peasant-based and urban-based class movements of unemployed workers in pursuit of land, jobs and/or political power, as well as opposition to government policy and the system, has shattered these illusions of disconnected intellectuals. The notion that the advent of economic and political liberalism would lead to an end of mass ideological struggles evaporated before the emergence of the Zapatistas in Chiapas, Mexico, the FARC in Colombia and CONAIE in Ecuador. Each in its own way was expanding territorial influence and deepened political participation. The elite and authoritarian civilian electoral systems, dubbed "democracies" by liberal ideologues, were challenged by popular assemblies from below that defined a new, substantive form of direct democracy.

After decades of abusive, corrupt and reactionary rule by elite selected executives and congresspeople, the urban poor, rural working class and peasants turned toward direct action to realize their legislative goals of jobs, land, credit, housing and public services. The centrality of direct action struck at the centre of the organized systems of exploitation, pillage, wealth and state power, frequently paralyzing the production and circulation of commodities essential to the reproduction of the neoliberal regime. While some discursive theorists like Eric Hobsbawm (1994) have used specious demographic arguments to dismiss the centrality of peasant movements in contemporary political struggles, others have argued that the mass of urban poor, engaged in marginal employment or divorced from the means of production, are incapable of challenging established political power.

Hobsbawm's thesis was refuted by the splendid display of political power embodied in the Indian takeover of the Ecuadorian parliament in the year 2000, the FARC's formidable influence in almost half the municipalities of Colombia and the MST's show of force in twenty-three of Brazil's twenty-four states. In addition, the development of a mass unemployed urban workers movement in Argentina challenges the concept of an atomized, impotent urban poor and is a situation worth exploring for its innovative features and explosive possibilities for the rest of urban Latin America.

Theoretical Issues: The Unemployed

One of the major arguments of orthodox Marxists when asserting that the industrial working class is central to any social transformation is this class's strategic location in the productive process. Despite the enormous growth of underemployed, unemployed and informal or marginal urban workers, it was argued that their fragmented job structure atomized them, and their relative isolation from the main sectors of the economy undercut their capacity to undermine the accumulation process. It was further argued that this urban mass was a benefit to capitalism because it kept wages down and lowered the demands of employed workers, via job replacement.

More recently, mainstream social scientists and NGOs have emphasized micro-activities, subsistence economies and reciprocal exchanges among the urban poor as a solution and not a problem. The absence of stable employment, declining living standards, growing social discontent, increasingly violent outbursts and the enormous rise of illicit economic activities emanating from the barrios called into question the idyllic picture painted by mainstream ideologues of "self-help."

In August 2001 a nationwide mobilization of highly organized unemployed groups, numbering more than 100,000 people, shut down more than three hundred highways in Argentina, paralyzing the economy. In the previous months and weeks, five *piqueteros* had been killed and more than three thousand had been arrested by federal police in violent clashes throughout the country. At the same time, the organized unemployed were able to pressure and secure thousands of minimum-wage temporary jobs from the state, food allowances and other concessions, while retaining their independent organization. By September 2001 the unemployed were able to organize massive highway blockages throughout the capital of Buenos Aires and a successful general strike in association with sectors of the trade unions, blocking government activity and the entrances of all the major private industries.

Several key factors account for the success of unemployed workers organizations and activities:

1. organization at the point of habitation in the suburban barrios, where there was a high concentration of unemployed industrial workers and never-employed young people and female heads of household;
2. the strategy of cutting highways, the functional equivalent of workers downing the tools of production, paralyzed the circulation of inputs for production and outputs destined for domestic or overseas markets;
3. the massive-assembly style of direct representation, decision-making and allocation of benefits prevented personalistic and opportunistic leaders from being bought off during individual negotiations;
4. the presence in the barrios of unemployed industrial workers with organizational experience and awareness of the advantages of collective, assembly-style democracy in carrying out a consequential struggle; and
5. the prolonged nature of the crises, and chronic impoverishment and its devastating effect on households, led to a disproportionate number of women among the most militant *piqueteros*.

Absence of prior work experience and their bleak future prospects of employment activated a large number of adolescents, especially young women, to become activated and engaged in direct action politics and willing to confront federal police. Previous, half-hearted attempts by trade unions to organize unemployed workers had failed, even in the case of "militant unions." Despite programmatic demands to organize the unemployed, all unions concentrated efforts on their dues-paying members and sectoral struggles. Where unemployed workers were organized, they frequently served as auxiliary partners in one-day demonstrations and had very little impact on the economy and securing reforms. Likewise, political parties, whether rightist, populist or leftist, organized the unemployed in a clientelistic manner, providing payoffs for their votes or a few jobs to vote hustlers.

The success of the unemployed movement in Argentina today is due to the fact that it learned from experience how to avoid pitfalls of the past by organizing independently from within the barrios, autonomous of electoral parties, trade union bureaucracies and state apparati.

These organizations overcame the occupational diversity of informal workers, and the insecurities of precariously employed or temporary workers and the unemployed by organizing at points of concentration in the barrios and engaging in action on proximate highways. They organized prolonged mass road blockages, rather than forming the tail of symbolic trade union marches in downtown plazas.

The Unemployed Workers Movement

Several factors facilitated the organization of the unemployed in Argentina:

1. the high concentration and density of the unemployed in quasi-segregated, relatively homogeneous barrios, distant from the centres of lower middle class influence;
2. The massive firing of factory workers with some trade union experience and downward mobility;
3. The privatization of mineral and energy centres, accompanied by a massive closure of certain installations and discharge of workers, creating virtual ghost towns in which all socio-economic sectors were adversely affected; and
4. The relative proximity of major highways supplying and transporting goods and commuters to and from the major cities and across national frontiers.

The road blockages of unemployed workers draw on a long history of working class picketing intended to prevent employers from using scabs to undermine strikes. The *piquetero* is thus a respected figure within popular culture and even among sectors of the Argentine middle class.

The unemployed workers' application of road-blockage tactics and mass picketing began in two towns of the interior, Cutral Co. and Plaza Huincul, on the twentieth and twenty-sixth of June 1996, and again in April 1997. These demonstrations mobilized thousands in protest against job cuts and plant shutdowns resulting from the privatization process. By the late 1990s, massive route blockages occurred in the working class suburbs of Buenos Aires, protesting the high rates of privatized light and power companies and the cutoff of unemployed consumers unable to pay their exorbitant bills. By the year 2000, mass demonstrations had taken place in the cities of Neuquen and General Mosconi, which had previously been relatively prosperous oil-producing centres. Privatization led to the closure of work sites and massive expulsions of the labour force, while the state and federal government failed to comply with its promises to finance alternative employment, largely because of budget cuts to meet IMF fiscal requirements.

Municipal, state and federal governments refused or were unwilling to heed the petitions and demands of the unemployed, and ignored their peaceful demonstrations. The irate workers and unemployed turned on state and municipal office buildings, occupying and occasionally torching them. The federal government responded with force.

The unemployed demonstrations drew support from a wide swath of citizens and social classes: local merchants threatened with bankruptcy as consumer power declined precipitously; thousands of provincial and municipal employees who had not been paid for months or were paid in "funny money"; unemployed public employees and professionals fired as part of budget-reduction and fiscal austerity programs; pensioners suffering a reduction in payments; and public health workers and school teachers suffering pay cuts and worsening work conditions. In the ghost towns, the "industrial cemeteries," privatization policies had a devastating effect.

The speculative economy financed by foreign borrowing, the sell-off of lucrative public enterprises and the movement by the Argentine bourgeoisie of more than $130 billion overseas (equivalent to Argentina's public debt) led to a chronic recession that began in 1997 and deepened into a full-blown depression by 2001. Unemployed and underemployed workers varied from 30 to 80 percent depending on the location. In greater Buenos Aires, official unemployment figures of 16–18 percent were multiplied by two, as most employed workers in the urban suburbs held temporary or precarious (part-time, occasional) employment. In the big working-class suburbs, unemployment reached 30–50 percent and underemployment 40–50 percent as the great majority of households fell below the poverty line.

These economic and social conditions converged with favourable opportunities for mass organization.

Political Conditions

In the post-dictatorial period, the mass of the working class, employed and underemployed had been denied their most elementary social economic demands. Presidents Rául Alfonsin, Carlos Menem and Fernando de la Rua had each in his turn aggressively pursued a political economic agenda that totally reversed existing social legislation, exonerated military officials responsible for thirty thousand deaths and disappearances, and handed over the country's "family jewels" to Argentine and foreign capitalists at prices far below market value.

To pacify growing discontent among the burgeoning army of impoverished and unemployed workers, the two major parties, the Radicals and the Peronists, organized clientelistic electoral machines that distributed occasional food baskets and employment to their loyal followers. With the deepening crises, these patronistic relationships were totally inadequate to contain rising discontent. The barrios, immersed in "passive poverty," crime, disorganization and clientelistic manipulation, began to organize.

Fundamental to the new organization of the unemployed is their rejection of the clientelistic patronage politics of the electoral party bosses and trade union bureaucrats. The Unemployed Workers Movement (MTD) began and continues as a grassroots movement organized and led by members of the barrio and the municipality. The organization of the MTD is very decentralized. Each municipality has its own organization based on the barrios within its frontiers. Within each barrio, every few blocks has its own informal leaders and activists, and each municipality is organized by a general assembly where all active members participate. Policy is decided in assembly; for example, the demands and organization of road blockages are decided collectively in assembly. Once a highway or principal artery is designated, the assembly organizes support within the barrios. Hundreds and even thousands of women, men and children participate in the blockage, setting up tents and soup kitchens at the side of the road. If the police threaten, hundreds more pour in from adjoining shantytowns. If the government decides to negotiate, the movement demands that negotiations take place with all the *piqueteros* at the blockage. Decisions are made at the site of the action by the collected assembly.

From experience, the *piqueteros* distrust sending delegates — even militant local people — to individually negotiate in government offices because, as one *piquetero* leader put it, "They buy them off with a job." Once the demands — mostly a quota of state-funded temporary jobs — are secured, the distribution of jobs takes place by collective decision according to prior criteria of family needs and active participation in the blockages. Jobs are allocated on a rotating basis when there are fewer jobs than unemployed.

Piqueteros have learned from experience that when individual leaders negotiate and distribute jobs, they tend to favour family members, friends and others, turning themselves into *caudillos* (personalistic leaders) with a patronage machine that corrupts the movement.

The organization and activities of the MTD has had an electrifying effect on the unemployed. From passive victims of poverty, social disorganization and clientelistic manipulation, they have become active in a powerful solidarity movement engaged in autonomous grassroots social organization and independent politics.

The early success of the MTDs in Salta, Juijuy and Matanzas led to the rapid extension of new MTDs throughout the poverty-stricken suburban belt surrounding Buenos Aires, Cordoba and Rosario, as well as in "ghost towns" of the interior. The multiplier effect was evidenced in late 2001 when two major national congresses with more than two thousand delegates met in Matanzas and La Plata to discuss a common platform for national struggle.

The success of the movement in mobilizing tens of thousands of unemployed workers, energizing thousands of trade union activists and securing (limited) concessions from the regime is the principal reason for the expansion of the movement at the local, regional and national level. The strength of the movement, however, continues to lie principally at the local level, based on neighbourhood ties, mutual trust and concrete demands.

The success of the *piqueteros* has spread into the central cities, drawing support from public employees facing major wage cuts and massive firings. Human rights groups, especially the Madres de Plaza de Mayo, school teachers, health workers and university and secondary students, have joined in blocking major intersections in downtown Buenos Aires.

In the first major nationally coordinated action, more than three hundred major highway and city thoroughfares were blocked by more than 100,000 *piqueteros*. All the major cities, including the former petroleum towns, were affected, causing the bourgeoisie endless delays and monstrous traffic tie-ups, and effectively paralyzing economic activity in many sectors, including the hitherto invulnerable financial sector.

On the picket lines and in mass assemblies are a disproportionate number of women, estimated at 60 percent of the participants, and young people, including numerous adolescents with no job prospects.

The attraction of the MTD is that it catalyzes action in a society exhausted by endless structural adjustment policies, budget cuts, multiple low-paid jobs, corruption and impotence on the part of Congress and an authoritarian and elitist execute branch. The trade unions, particularly the CGT in both variants, has been run by a venal group of high-paid, repressive bosses closely aligned with the Menem regime and unwilling to confront the De la Rua regime or its regressive policies. The occasional denunciation and even general strike is understood by everyone, regime and workers, as a meaningless symbolic ritual to blow off steam and gain submission. Given the coincidence of the two parties in perpetuating the neoliberal regime, in sharing the spoils of office and keeping the working majority on a downward spiral, and given that the mass of employed industrial workers are subject to the control of millionaire trade-union bosses, the unemployed workers are the only pole for opposition. The MTD has the only effective tactics: direct action, the prolonged blocking of highways until minimum demands are met.

The immediate demands of the MTD centre on state-funded jobs to be administrated by local unemployed workers associations. Second, they demand distribution of food parcels, the freeing of hundreds of jailed unemployed militants and a host of public investments in water, paved roads, health facilities etc. The demands for employment go beyond subsistence temporary work and include stable employment with a living wage. In General Mosconi, the leaders of the movement have formulated more than three hundred projects, some of which are successfully operating, to provide food and employment, including a bakery, organic gardens, water purifying plants and first-aid clinics in the barrios. The town is *de facto* ruled by the local unemployed committee, as local municipal officials are marginalized.

The leaders in General Mosconi, Pepino, Hippie and Piquete are local workers who have most forcefully articulated the demands of the community. These grassroots leaders are those least fearful in speaking out and making demands. The general populace is supportive but fearful of speaking out and losing their slot in the work plans. However, they become massively involved in supporting the road blockages and preventing the police from arresting their leaders.

The power of the unemployed in some working class suburbs has led to quasi-liberated zones, where the power of mobilization neutralizes or is superior to that of local officials and is capable of challenging the state and federal regimes on the issues being raised. The emergence of a parallel economy on a limited scale in General Mosconi sustains popular support between struggles and offers a vision of the capabilities of the unemployed to take command of their lives, neighbourhoods and livelihoods.

Beyond the local and immediate demands, the national meetings of unemployed in August and September of 2001 called for an end to debt payments and austerity programs, a reversal of the neoliberal model and the re-emergence of state-regulated and state-financed economic development.

The most promising national organizational development was the convocation of two meetings of unemployed groups from around the country in Matanza and La Plata on September 5, 2001. These meetings drew more than two thousand delegates from dozens of unemployed, trade-union, student, cultural and NGO groups. Their purpose was to coordinate activities, share ideas and forge a national program and plan of struggle. The assembly of delegates in La Plata agreed to six immediate demands:

1. derogation of the structural adjustment, zero-deficit policies and judicial process against arrested and other activists;
2. the withdrawal of the austerity budget;
3. extension and defence of public employment schemes and food allocations to each unemployed worker over sixteen years of age, and the establishment of a massive register of unemployed under the control of the unemployed workers organizations meeting in the assembly;
4. one hundred pesos (one peso=$1) per hectare for small and medium-sized farms so farmers could seed their fields;
5. prohibition of firings; and
6. immediate withdrawal of *gendarmería* (police) from the town of General Mosconi.

The assembly convoked two nationwide road blockages in September to back up their demands. In addition to the immediate demands, the assembly embraced five strategic goals:

1. non-payment of the illegitimate and fraudulent foreign debt;
2. public control of pension funds;
3. re-nationalization of banks and strategic enterprises;
4. forgiveness of the debts of small farmers and sustainable prices for their products; and
5. ousting of the hunger-provoking regimes and all reshuffled politicians.

The assembly ended by calling for a thirty-six-hour general strike and the formation of a national committee to coordinate activities with the dissident trade-union confederation, the CTA (Confederación de Trabajadores Argentinos).

Social Alliances: Uneasy Allies

As the unemployed movement grew in numbers and capability for action, it attracted allies from university students, dissident trade unions, human rights groups and small leftist parties. The most numerous and significant tactical alliances were forged with the public employees unions the ATE, or Asociacíon de Tradajadores Estatates and with local teachers unions. The Madres de la Plaza de Mayo gave moral support and mobilized their supporters, as did a number of leftist university student organizations.

Throughout the joint activities, especially with the trade unions, the unemployed movements jealously guarded their hard won autonomy and freedom of action. They rejected demagogic interventions by conventional politicos who sought to capitalize on the unemployed movements' growing power.

State Repression in General Mosconi, Salta

Early on the De la Rua regime turned to violent repression to destroy the movements: five *piqueteros* were killed, dozens were wounded by gunfire and thousands were arrested. The town of General Mosconi, where three *piqueteros* were killed, was taken over by hundreds of national *gendarmería* in the best style of military dictatorship. This "development" was repeated in a number of towns in the industrial (deindustrialized) belt, particularly in the northern province of Salta.

In order to impose harsh austerity policies, including massive firings and a 12 percent cut in the salaries of public employees, measures proposed by the IMF and supported by US and European private bankers, the regime criminalized collective action among the unemployed. The failure of the regime to stem the slide into economic depression, and its pending debt default, only hardened its resolve to impose new austerity measures in hopes of attracting speculative funding from Wall Street and a new bailout from the IMF.

The increasing militancy of the unemployed movements, as evidenced in the expansion and frequency of mass road blockages, was a desperate response in the face of the regime's policy of replacing nutrition with coercion. As malnutrition spread, the workers' anger deepened as they watched trainloads of grains and beef being shipped to export markets overseas.

Contradictions: New Challenges for the Unemployed Workers Movement

The dynamic and unprecedented growth of the unemployed movement and its success with using road blockages to paralyze the movement of commodities was accompanied by robust discussions on how to proceed. Several basic issues arose within the movement debates.

Localism

The continuing strength of the movements is based on their close ties to communities, barrios and neighbours. Yet as repression and cutbacks proceed, it is evident to many movement activists that only collective action at the national level will provide the leverage to weaken state violence and secure concessions from the regime. Yet some of the leaders who have been most successful in consolidating popular participation resist and are distrustful of national meetings and organizations. The movement in General Mosconi is a case in point: they refused to formally participate in the two national meetings in early September 2001.

Competing Groups

The decentralized origins of the movement have been a necessary and important element in promoting local initiatives and leadership and guarding the autonomy of the various movements. But in several cases political and personal differences have emerged which could undermine future unity of action. While most unemployed movements reject electoral politics, a few leaders have been offered a place on the lists of leftist parties, particularly a new formation called the "Social Pole." Other differences relate to the relationship with the established dissident trade unions. While few unemployed leaders would object to tactical cooperation, many are fearful that the CTA and ATE will eventually dominate the action and manipulate the movement to fit the moderate agenda of progressive trade-union officials. For example, in one of the national days of action in August, under the influence of ATE, the *piqueteros* allowed alternate roads to remain clear while they blocked main arteries. The purpose of this concession was to "win over" middle-class commuters and to present a goodwill gesture to the minister of labour. Many unemployed activists rejected the "alternate route" strategy as effectively undermining the purpose of road blockages and opening the door to the demoralization of the unemployed and the demise of the movement in favour of traditional trade-union wheeling and dealing to secure the approval of electoral politicians.

Penetration by Politicians

The powerful thrust of the movement comes from its autonomy of action and rejection of patronage and clientelistic politics. As successful mobilization accelerated, conventional, opportunistic politicos from the nominally "opposition" parties (Peronist and other) attempt to take up some of the movement's demands, offering to "mediate" between the *piqueteros*, secure jobs, gain a section of the movement, divide the movement and rebuild their depleted ranks. However, the movement retains its power of convocation and capacity to mobilize against repression and has successfully resisted the blandishments of these opportunistic demagogues. But, if repression becomes more severe and basic needs are not met, the stark choice will be either further political radicalization or the temptation to accept "mediation" by the old political bosses.

Students: Allies and Dangers

The September 7–8 national assembly was convoked by unemployed workers. In addition to this movement, a large number of student, cultural and even self-help groups turned up, diluting the social composition of the conference. The long and often tedious presentations of student orators did not add a great deal of clarity to the movement's future. While the unemployed movements' delegates did maintain control and welcomed student and other participation, there was concern that students could introduce ideological rifts that might paralyze action. A genuine search among some student groups to "articulate" with the unemployed movement was counterbalanced by a student harangue to the assembly on why globalization inevitably condemned the movements to failure. The unemployed delegates unanimously rejected this type of intervention and proceeded to outline a practical series of immediate and strategic demands. The unemployed movement of Lanus called attention to the pressures of unholy alliances following mass demonstrations and for retention of leadership by autonomous unemployed workers movements.

These contradictions point to new challenges that face the movement. The important point is not that there are problems, but that these are open assemblies at the local, regional and national level where the unemployed can debate and resolve issues.

Conclusion

One debate about the declining power of the labour movement focuses on the issue of the proliferation of precarious work, growth of the informal sector and increase in the number of unemployed. When questioned, trade union leaders constantly cite the difficulty of organizing the unemployed and the unemployed's lack of leverage over the economic system or interest in collective action. The massive growth of the organization of the unemployed in Argentina calls into question many of these assumptions and raises new questions. It demonstrates that unemployed workers can be organized, will engage in collective action, possess leverage to paralyze the economic system and are capable of negotiating and securing concessions, in a manner that organized labour unions have not been able to accomplish in recent years.

This all suggests that the decline of labour has less to do with the nature of unemployed and informal workers and more to do with the structure, approach and leadership of the trade unions. The unemployed movement organizes from the bottom up, through face-to-face recruiting in the barrios. Trade union bureaucrats ignore non-dues-paying workers and, when organizing, send professionals in, usually failing to gain the confidence of the unemployed. Furthermore, the unemployed movement has a horizontal structure in which leaders and supporters come from the same class and discuss and debate as equals in open assemblies; trade unions are vertical structures built around personal loyalties to their top bureaucrats, many of whom draw salaries comparable to CEOs. The unemployed movement engages in sustained direct action and collectively negotiates demands in open assemblies; trade union elites engage in symbolic protests and then negotiate with the state or employers behind closed doors, reaching agreements that may ignore workers' key concerns, and then "sell" the agreements to union members or simply impose them. As a result, unemployed movement leaders have the confidence and support of their constituents, while trade union bosses are viewed with distrust, if not as active collaborators with employers and an austerity-minded state.

The problem, then, is the subjective and organizational nature of the trade unions not the condition of the labour market. The "labour market," the large pool of unemployed, presents a challenge to the conventional way of top-down organizing, automatic dues check-off and formal organization. No trade union boss is willing to trudge through the muddy unpaved roads of shantytowns organizing, attending meetings in icy or sweltering improvised meeting places amidst crying children and women militants demanding food now or unemployed young men bored by long-winded lectures on globalization and unemployment. No trade union leaders stand behind barricades of burning tires with slingshots, blocking highways and facing live ammunition. They prefer to secure a half-hour appointment in the offices of the minister of labour in order to form a tripartite committee to discuss how to cushion the austerity program and secure governability. The fact is that almost all trade unions as they are organized today are only concerned with their electoral ties to official parties and are totally irrelevant, if not a major obstacle, to organization of the unemployed.

Through initiative, social inventiveness and trial and error, the unemployed have found a way to gain some leverage over the economic system by cutting the highways that link markets and production sites. The early success of road blockages by unemployed petroleum workers in the ghost towns of Neuquen in 1996 has spread throughout the country.

Road blockages have become a tactic of exploited and marginalized groups throughout Latin America. In Bolivia, tens of thousands of peasants and Indian communities have blocked highways, demanding credit, infrastructure, freedom to grow coca, increased spending on health and education etc. In Ecuador, massive street blockages protest the dollarization of the economy, the absence of public investments in the highlands etc. In Colombia, Brazil and Paraguay, road blockages, marches and land occupations have been combined in pursuit of immediate demands, redistributive policies and an end to neoliberalism and debt payments.

What all these movements have in common is that they represent non-strategic economic groups acting on strategic areas of the economy. The banks and mineral, petroleum and certain manufacturing sectors are the principal foreign-exchange earners and revenue and profit producers for the elite. Food is imported, as are manufactured intermediary and capital goods. From the perspective of the elite accumulation process, the activities of the peasants, unemployed, Indians, farmers, local merchants and small manufacturers are superfluous, expendable and irrelevant to the main economic activities — exports, financial transactions and imports of luxury goods. But these flows of goods and capital require free passage across roads to reach their markets. This is where marginal groups can become strategic actors whose direct actions interfere with elite circuits and disrupt the elite accumulation process. Road blockages by the unemployed are a functional equivalent of industrial workers stopping their machines and production lines: one blocks the realization of profit, the other the creation of value. Mass organization outside the factory system is a viable strategy when it takes place outside of the electoral party/

bureaucratic trade-union structure. Autonomous organization is the key in Argentina and the rest of Latin America. Experience demonstrates that the new mass movements of unemployed workers, peasants and Indians can sustain struggles, resist violent repression and secure temporary and immediate concessions. The formation of a national coordinating committee of unemployed organizations in Argentina and similar national organizations among peasants and small farmers throughout Latin America demonstrates that local movements can unite to confront the state.

Many questions remain unanswered. Is it possible for these new movements to unify into a national political force and transform state power? Can links be forged with employed urban industrial workers and the downwardly mobile middle class to create a power alliance to transform the economy? Can local meetings become the basis for a new assembly-based socialism?

In Argentina the success of the Unemployed Workers Movement has opened up new perspectives for advancing the struggle for justice in the face of a prolonged depression. With similar direct-action movements growing throughout Latin America, it is not difficult to imagine the convergence of marginal groups and classes into a formidable challenge to the US empire and its regional collaborators.

10. The Dynamics of Anti-Globalization

From Development to Globalization

Within the confines of the world order set up after the Second World War, several strategic geopolitical and geo-economic projects were launched: "development" (or "modernization," "industrialization"), "revolutionary transformation and socialism," "globalization" and "imperialism" (McMichael 1996).

This world order included a system for promoting free trade, currency-exchange mechanisms, financial architecture to regulate the movement of capital, means to resolve temporary imbalances in international payments, and a funding mechanism for the economic reconstruction and development of Europe first, and then the new nations liberated from colonial rule and vulnerable to the lure of communism. At the national political level, the "system" included social contracts between capital and labour whereby the latter might participate in productivity gains, and the state was committed to ensuring employment, social welfare and health and education. At the international level, the United Nations, with its General Assembly, Security Council and agencies, and NATO, a military alliance of nations committed to "freedom, democracy and free enterprise" (to cite the national security report presented by George W. Bush to the US Congress in September 2002), were set up to ensure that no nation would dream of world domination or act unilaterally to bend the world to its political will and national interests. This was in the early 1950s, in the context of an emerging east-west ideological and military divide, when the US was not as secure in its own power and did not have hegemony over the system.

Within this institutional framework and historic context, the first major project to strategically control and direct the productive resources of the world system was based on the idea of "development." This project was launched in 1946 by Harry Truman in his "four-point program" to provide assistance to backward nations so they might defend themselves against the siren of communism. For some twenty-five years, this project directed the government policies of the rich industrialized states, each of which established an agency for international development and a program of overseas development assistance (ODA) to supplement the resources made available by multilateral agencies such as the World Bank. This ODA, or "foreign aid," became the largest stream of resource flow between the "developed" societies of the North and the "developing" societies of the South. In the 1970s, however, other forms of resource transfers came on stream — bank loans extended by US, and then European and Japanese commercial and investment banks; foreign direct investments by TNCs and investments made by a host of financial institutions in government bonds and other portfolio funds (on the political dynamics of these international resource transfers and the surrounding debates, see Petras and Veltmeyer 2002). By the mid-1970s the crisis of the world capitalist system, already apparent in the late 1960s when labour launched what turned out to be its last great offensive, led to a serious rethinking of the entire development project and to a major counteroffensive of the capitalist class against the incursions of the state into "private property."

A small group of countries in the South was in the process of successful transition from "economic backwardness" or "underdevelopment" to "economic development," transforming themselves into "newly industrializing countries" (NICs). More generally, however, the North-South gap had grown and there was a divergence rather than convergence in the fortunes and prospects of the industrialized and the non-industrialized countries still caught up in the exploitative international division of labour that political economists in the radical stream of development thought termed "the old imperialism."

In the context of an emerging crisis the "development project" fragmented, leading to its involution within the mainstream of development thought and practice, and, on both the Right and the Left, to its abandonment. In the mainstream there was, first of all, a strong push towards reform, orienting development away from an economic growth-first policy towards meeting the basic needs of the world's population, one-quarter of which were discovered to be "poor" (World Bank 1973).

A second response within the mainstream was to search for "another development," initiated *from below* and *within* (rather than *from above* and *outside*), and based on "appropriate technology," that is participatory, human in scale and form, equitable, socially inclusive and sustainable in terms of both the environment and livelihoods (Goulet 1989; Liamzon et al. 1996; Veltmeyer and O'Malley 2001). In the 1980s this search led to a paradigmatic shift and a global movement for "alternative development."

A third response was to abandon the development project altogether or, rather, to replace it with another: "globalization." Pioneered by the "Chicago Boys" of Chile in the 1970s, who engineered what was described by McKinnon (quoted in *El Mercurio*, 18 October 1983: C14), one of the architects of the "new economic model" (or "neoliberalism"), as "the most sweeping reforms in history," the globalization project was widely implemented in the 1980s in the form of what became known as "structural adjustment programs," series of measures to reorient the domestic economic and social policies of nation-states in the direction of a global economy based on free trade and a free flow of capital. By the end of the decade, based on this move to create an integrated global economy driven by the principles of "freedom, democracy and private enterprise" (to use George W. Bush's terminology), a majority of countries in the developing world had been economically restructured, having introduced bold reforms and epoch-defining changes in their internal organizational structures and external relations. By the end of the 1990s and the beginning of the new millennium, "holdout" countries such as Brazil completed the "transition" and were brought into the fold with a new set of macroeconomic policies and emerging forms of governance (Petras and Veltmeyer 2003). The "globalization project" had successfully integrated most countries, North and South — and Russia and other "countries in transition" — into the new world order. Globalization, as a template of prescribed policies and unavoidable changes, had become an irresistible reality.

However, neither the "transition" nor the path towards globalization has been smooth and easy. In fact, like "development," "globalization" has been, and remains, heavily contested, generating widespread discontent with the outcome (prosperity for the few, poverty for the many) among diverse groups and organizations all over the world, discontent that has been mobilized into forces of opposition and resistance. In the case of "development," these forces of opposition have led to a widespread search for a "new paradigm," alternative forms of development ranging from proposals for reform ("structural adjustment with a human face," "productive transformation with equity," a "New Social Policy") and more radical, if somewhat involuted, proposals for "societal transformation" (community-based or local forms of participatory development) to a rejection of the whole development project as a misbegotten enterprise (Sachs 1993).

In practice, many organizations in the popular sector have rejected the "development option," whether initiated "from above and outside" or "from within and below." Social movements have opted instead for direct and collective action oriented against government policies in the immediate context and towards "social transformation" (or socialist forms of organization) in the longer term. This is the case, for example, for each of the "new peasant social movements" that now dominate Latin America's political landscape — the MST, CONAIE, FARC and the EZLN, among others (Petras 1997).

From Globalization to the New Imperialism

Both "development" and "globalization" can be viewed not only as geopolitical class projects but as theoretical models used to direct the forces of change in a broader class struggle waged by capital against labour. One of the first campaigns in this war was launched in the context of the 1973–74 crisis, as part of a broader counteroffensive against the advances of labour in its struggle for higher wages and better working conditions. Both "development" and "globalization" can be viewed as means of advancing the agendas of what Sklair (1997) and others define as the "transnational capitalist class." In a similar way, it is possible to view the emergence of what could be termed "the new imperialism" as a project led by forces initially under the command of US President George W. Bush to advance the economic, geopolitical and security interests of the United States and re-establish hegemony over the system, if not world rule. Unlike development and globalization, this project relies not so much on economic institutions and agents such as multinational corporations, the IMF and the World Bank as on the projection of naked military power. In this form, imperialism has had a long history and inglorious pedigree, but since the latter half of the twentieth century has for the most part served as an adjunct to other favoured institutions and mechanisms. However, in the context of the 1980s and 1990s — economic crisis at home within the United States itself and serious losses of influence at the centre as well as the margins of empire — the imperialist project has emerged as the principal institutional approach towards renovating and securing a new world order — and US hegemony. In fact the emergence of international terrorism and the persistence of "rogue states" unwilling to bend to the will of the US administration have been very functional for the imperialist project. With the collapse of the USSR-led socialist bloc and the vaunted victory of the forces of "freedom, democracy and free enterprise" (i.e., capitalism), the US was in desperate need of an enemy to engage and justify its adventures and interventions.

The "Cold War" against "international communism" had served this purpose for more than thirty years. But al-Qaeda and the purported new threat to the United States posed by international terrorism provided a pretext needed for unilateral action, first against Afghanistan and then Iraq, although in the case of this latter member of the "axis of evil," the pretext could not be sustained and had to be changed to the production and presumed willingness to use "weapons of mass destruction" (nuclear, chemical and biological weapons). Only a few years earlier, no US president could have engaged in such unilateral military action geared to curb the threat of international terrorism, even under a pre-emptive strike policy. But the events of 9/11 have radically changed the context for launching the imperialist project, and George W. Bush and his cronies were not disposed to let the opportunity slip.

The changed political climate has been tested with a series of trial balloons and probing declarations that in earlier contexts would have been viewed as irrational right-wing craziness, if not suicidal. Voices in support of a "new imperialism" have risen on both sides of the Atlantic. While the political Left is caught up in the anti-globalization struggle and nurses fanciful notions of an emerging "empire without imperialism," that is, without a single state seeking world rule (Hardt and Negri 2000), the political Right openly and stridently argues the need to revert to rougher methods of an earlier era: the use of force, pre-emptive attacks, deception, whatever is necessary to deal with those in the premodern world of developing countries who still live in the nineteenth-century world of every state for itself (Cooper 2002b: 7). As explained by Robert Cooper (2002b), foreign policy advisor to Tony Blair, "among ourselves [in the postmodern states of Europe and North America] we keep the law, but ... in the jungle we must also use the laws of the jungle." Very few have stated the justification for a new imperialism as forthrightly and clearly as Cooper, but on the other side of the Atlantic similar sentiments have been voiced by the Bush administration.

In this connection, the writings of *Financial Times* economic columnist Martin Wolf (10 October 2001: 13) have been used to point towards the need for a new, more direct form of imperialism that does not hesitate to use force whenever and wherever necessary. In Wolf's words, "To tackle the challenge of the failed state [in the impoverished third world], what is needed is not pious aspirations but an honest and organized coercive force." This is precisely the view that George W. Bush and his regime incorporate into their national security doctrine, which includes a right to take unilateral military action and make pre-emptive first strikes against the threat of "international terrorism" and "weapons of mass destruction."

The Dynamics of Anti-Globalization and Anti-Capital

Just as the development project generated a search for alternatives, as well as forces of opposition and resistance, the idea — and project and thus process — of globalization and the new imperialism have given rise to movements of resistance and forces of opposition. These proposals for alternative forms of globalization, and associated forces of opposition and resistance, are part of what has become known as the "anti-globalization movement" (AGM).

The dynamics of this movement, part of an effort to construct a "global civil society," are not that well understood despite the multiplicity of recent efforts to document and analyze them. Is the AGM the juggernaut that it is frequently made out to be, able to mobilize, if not unite, the forces of resistance into an effective movement to derail the agenda of corporate capital? Or should it be viewed as a "jalopy," susceptible to breakdown and not likely to run the course? This question, raised by Adam Morton (2003), is not yet settled. Despite the broad range of studies that have emerged to describe developments within the AGM, its dynamics require a closer look. Nevertheless, we can make several theoretical points.

The first is that the neoliberal model of capitalist development and globalization, in reality, is simply a dummy target, advanced in the contested terrain of world development as if in a game of "go," to force the opposition to waste energy in attacking a position that has already been abandoned. Hardly any of the many apparent apologists and defenders of the new world order are prepared to defend neoliberalism. Indeed, one and all have acknowledged the need for fundamental reform, for an alternative form of development/globalization sustained by new forms of international governance. For example, key members of the Council on Foreign Relation, one of several nodes in the global network set up by the self-appointed guardians of the new world order, have argued that the North-South gap is too deep to sustain no matter what system of governance is put into place (Kapstein 1996). They argue that the resulting poverty will generate a social discontent that will be inherently destabilizing and too easily mobilized into movements of opposition. Others, (Soros 2000; Stiglitz 2002), have pointed towards the need for a new financial architecture to regulate volatile movements of productive and speculative capital. Carlos Slim, the richest man in Mexico, a multibillionaire who has benefited immensely from his country's insertion into the new world order, goes so far as to say that the neoliberal agenda that drives "globalization" is nothing more than a form of "neocolonialism" that generates excessive social inequalities, non-functioning markets and political instability. The system, he says, simply does not work.

A second point that can be made about the AGM is that to a considerable extent its member organizations and leading activists have been in practice manipulated by the self-appointed guardians of the new world order, who have tried to limit opposition and direct proposals for alternative design and action, to keep them within acceptable limits, as a form of controlled dissent. To analyze the ways in which this is done is beyond the scope of this book, but the point can be illustrated by an analogy. The parasitic wasp of the genus *Hymenoepimecis*, unknown to the spider it targets, lays its eggs in the abdomen of the spider, which then goes to work spinning a pupal cocoon that it does not need but is necessary for the larvae, unwittingly serving the interests of the parasite. Similarly, the World Bank, as an agency of the "development" and "globalization" projects, has turned to non-governmental organizations, of what used to be viewed as "the third sector" but in current discourse is known as "civil society," as a partner institution, thus making the NGOs unwitting agents of a project they are in fact opposed to in principle. Together with other institutions at the disposal of the "transnational capitalist class," the World Bank seeks to ensure that the forces of opposition and resistance are contained within acceptable limits or channelled towards reform of the existing system, reform to which it is itself committed. Funding is one way to control dissent. Indeed, it seems that a good part of the organizational efforts and protest activities orchestrated by the AGM is in fact made possible by funding from governments and international organizations that espouse the activities to which they are opposed (Okonski 2001). In this and other ways the AGM in fact helps the guardians of the new world order to realize their agenda. For one thing, the AGM serves as a repository of ideas for improving and reforming the system, to secure its sustainability and "good governance."

A third critical issue in the political dynamics of anti-globalization is the split within the movement between the mass oriented towards reforming the system — changing the form taken by globalization, accepting its positive features as well as its inevitability but rejecting its current neoliberal form and its negative effects — and the number of groups and organizations that are against capitalism in all of its forms. The differences between these two streams of thought within the AGM are not only strategic (with regard to the ends of the struggle) but tactical (with regard to its proposed actions). The two sides differ over whether to favour direct action to the point of violent confrontation or a more pacific and controlled form of action and dialogue. However, the way this internal division plays out in the context of actual struggle is not clear. This too needs a closer look, and further study. But for the most part the institutional mechanisms of controlled dissent have appeared to be working, even at, for example, the greatest mobilizations of the AGM to date, at the Anti-G-8 Summit in Genoa in summer 2001 and at the World Social Summit in Porto Alegre in February 2002.

However, at a number of more recent protest actions, including the European Social Forum (ESF), which brought together close to forty thousand protesters from five hundred organizations in 105 countries, the two streams of the AGM have tended to converge, allowing for, if not leading to, a concertation of diverse strategies and tactics, as well as a more radical vision of the road ahead. This development was captured very well in the following assessment by Ramón Montovani, a Communist Renewal deputy, of the debate within and outside the anti-globalization movement (on this movement and its efforts to construct a new world with the agency of a "global civil society," see Cox [1999] and Seoane and Taddei [2001]):

> There are those who think that neoliberal globalization can be reformed and those, that we believe to be in the majority, who think that there is no negotiation with neoliberalism, that something new has to be created. Any attempt to reform [the system] and humanize it is useless; it just serves to legitimize it. Today neoliberalism is war and destruction … this is the capitalism we have today. For this reason the forces of the Left have to understand that globalization is an attack on humanity and life itself, and that therefore the game has to be abandoned, and to create something new from below. The parties of the Left have to approach the [anti-globalization/anti-capital] movement with humility and learn from it, not pretend to direct it. (*La Jornada*, 11 November 2002: 24)

This appears to be a fairly accurate assessment of where the majority of the Left finds itself: caught between diverse political positions that have served to advance, on the one hand, the struggle for state power and, on the other, the construction of a new, all-encompassing socio-political movement capable of bringing the system down and creating something new.

It is too early to tell where this all may lead. Boris Kagarlitsky (2001: 16–19), for example, insists that "what is needed is for the [anti-corporate, anti-capital] struggle that was born in the streets to expand both in breadth and in depth.... Our main field of battle must not be in elections ['Such a move would be suicidal'] but in the factories." Kagarlitsky argues this point on the basis of the struggle in Quebec, where "corporate chiefs openly acknowledged that while they were not especially afraid of street protests, they were very concerned that the spirit of the streets might penetrate the workplaces." He adds: "We need to bring about precisely such a development of events." His final conclusion, which, it must be said, opens up a rather broad debate, is that

> History has shown that workplace strikes are always more effective than street demonstrations and that street actions are frequently more effective than motions made in parliament — not to speak of the fact that it is impossible to buy off and corrupt thousands of activists, while with parliamentarians this happens quite often. A revolution begins ... when the "streets" in these circumstances resonate with the factories. (Kagarlitsky 2001: 18)

These and other such reflections on the anti-globalization, i.e., anti-corporate, movement have opened up a debate on the political dynamics of the struggle involved. For one thing, the diverse theatres, forms and conditions (objective or structural, and subjective or political) of this struggle reach beyond the parameters of the elections, streets and factories identified by Kagarlitsky. These parameters undoubtedly involve some, if not most, of the major forms of this struggle, but, as we have argued, the major dynamics of anti-systemic struggle today need to be analyzed in the broader context of the economies and societies that are in crisis on the "periphery" of the system, on the south of a growing divide within the neoliberal world order. In this context, we have drawn attention to assemblies held by indigenous peasant communities in Ecuador and Chiapas; *cocaleros* (coca-producing peasants) in Bolivia; and unemployed workers — the *piqueteros* — in Argentina. These assemblies are also found in and around factories and industrial plants as well as in open and closed spaces in working-class neighbourhoods in Argentina, Brazil and elsewhere. They are the source of some of the most innovative and effective forms of anti-systemic struggle exhibited by the AGM today. Many of these struggles take place in the streets but are not just limited to street protests at meetings or forums of the WTO, the G-8 and other institutions of the capitalist world order. The forms of struggle are diverse and often combined, including negotiations with government officials and private sector representatives, street marches and protest actions, popular assemblies and occupations of public buildings and factories, hunger strikes, blockades and *cortas de ruta*, strikes and pitched battles behind barricades.

Towards A Conclusion

June 2002 marked a critical turning point in the movement against corporate globalization. On the long road from Seattle to Genoa and Quebec City the AGM had been divided both as to its ultimate goals and its tactics of struggle. On the one side were diverse voices and a complex of non-governmental organizations, including significant elements of the labour movement, pushing for pacific or non-violent forms of confrontation, dialogue and cooperation that are directed towards moderate reform of the system. On the other side were the anti-capitalist proponents of direct action, pushing for confrontationalist politics and radical changes in social and economic forms of organization, not towards reform but rather a dismantling of the new world order.

This division is not new. It was evident from the beginning, in the confrontation with the WTO in Seattle in 1989 and in the successful derailing of its agenda to impose the Multilateral Agreement on Investment (MAI), a new set of globally applicable rules for securing the property rights of investors. However, in the aftermath of 9/11 this division seriously deepened, creating a fundamental rift within the AGM, with an increasing intolerance for radical change and confrontationalist politics. Events from September 2001 to June 2002 within the movement provided increasing evidence of this rift. But at the same time there was some evidence of efforts to mend fences within the movement and to heal the rift between the two wings.

This last point is illustrated by developments within the Canadian AGM. In Canada, demonstrations were organized in two cities to express opposition to the G-8 meetings in remote Kananaskis. The demonstrations evidenced a push for cooperation and concerted action against an admittedly distant common enemy. In this context, the more radical, direct-action wing of the Canadian AGM, led by Montreal's Anti-Capitalist Convergence (CLAC) and the Toronto-based Ontario Coalition Against Poverty (OCAP), organized two days of marches in Ottawa. Meanwhile, the labour movement and more moderate forces of anti-globalization such as the Council of Canadians joined local Alberta activists in organizing a week of events (including a People's Summit) in Calgary, the nearest city to Kananaskis.

Taken together, these various actions provide a moderately successful challenge to the G-8, especially considering the efforts of the governments involved to not only "control" dissent and protest but to prevent it altogether by locating meetings in remoter places, such as Qatar or Kananaskis. In Canada, not only did the government host the G-8 in a remote location where five separate checkpoints prevented anyone getting anywhere near the assembled dignitaries and leaders, but it paid off an Alberta farmer who had rented out land to protesters near the summit site, convincing him to withdraw this invitation (Judy Rebick, "All we are saying is give protests a chance," *Globe and Mail*, 3 July 2002: A11).

The particular forms taken by the protests reflected several months of deep discussion among individuals in the two wings of the AGM about the most appropriate tactics of struggle. Anarchist groups, opposed to any form of hierarchy and committed to notions of individual autonomy, insisted that an agreement to use only non-violent tactics at demonstrations was "authoritarian" and divisive. Echoing previous irruptions of the protest movement in the 1960s, 1970s and even earlier, they argued that only the principle of "diversity of tactics" would allow everyone to participate and ensure the growth and unity of the movement — "diversity within unity." At the same time, the refusal of the "anarchists" and other groups to exclude tactics of direct action and violence, to limit action to pacific forms of protest, deepened their split from the labour movement and the NGOs, exacerbating the cultural and political differences between the two. Marxist-oriented political groups within the labour movement, perhaps more accustomed to top-down decision-making and internal discipline, were only too happy to organize their own actions without having to deal with the unruly anarchists. Most "anti-corporate globalization" protesters could be found somewhere in between.

After the end of June 2001, the Canadian and European wings of the movement seemed to reach a critical turning point. In Canada, for example, although proponents of direct action were unwilling to compromise with more moderate elements in the labour movement for the sake of unity, they agreed to the principle of non-violence to ensure the involvement of immigrant and refugee communities. For whatever reason, demonstrations in both Ottawa and Calgary were surprisingly free of violence, in part the result of this agreement and in part the result of a new strategy by the forces of law and order. In Calgary, police on bicycles even distributed water to protesters, a far cry from the tactics adopted by these forces in Seattle, Paris, Melbourne, Barcelona and Genoa.

The question is: What, if anything, does this development within the AGM mean? What conclusions, if any, can be drawn from it? On the one hand, anti-capitalist organizers claimed victory for their ability to successfully mobilize and broaden the movement from university youth, non-governmental organizations and unionists to include immigrant communities and people of colour. On the other hand, the demonstrations and protests, albeit peaceful, were decidedly smaller than previous protests. While Calgary had probably never seen 2,500 anti-corporate protesters on its streets before, the march was modest by movement standards elsewhere in the world. But even the much larger meetings of the AGM in Porto Alegre managed to confine actions to public lectures, workshop discussion and peaceful marches, containing the dispositions of more radical elements of the movement towards direct action and violent confrontation.

Because the threat of violence at demonstrations has been at the root of divisions within the AGM, the peaceful nature of protest actions in both Calgary and Ottawa has led some to see a basis for movement convergence. As Judy Rebick (*Globe and Mail*, 3 July 2002: A11), for example, mused: "Imagine what could be accomplished if both wings came back together, respecting their differences but working in concert to build the kind of mass challenge to corporate globalization and war as their colleagues in Europe and Latin America." However, Rebick, publisher of *rabble.ca*, an interactive independent news magazine, here begs a question she has clearly not examined: What is behind the mass challenge represented by the AGM in Europe and Latin America? Is it convergence or is it a commitment to employ a diversity of tactics within a broader movement? Does the latter imply the former? Even if it does, what are its likely ramifications? What is the impact on the capacity of the AGM to mobilize forces of opposition and resistance and bring about substantive change? Is change in this context oriented towards, and limited to, reform of the system, creating a more humane form of capitalist development and globalization ("another world")? Or can the anti-capital forces of opposition and resistance thereby secure the conditions of revolutionary transformation, an alternate or new "system"?

These questions remain unanswered. One thing is clear, however. Any successful transformation of the system of capitalist development and globalization will necessarily entail a combination, and "concertation" of the diverse forms of struggle exhibited by the AGM with the broader class struggle of indigenous peasants in Bolivia, Ecuador, Mexico and elsewhere; of unemployed workers in Argentina and elsewhere; of the labour movement in its diverse forms, particularly in the streets and factories of countries in the "developing world" or "in transition." All of these and other forms of struggle have to be combined, if not concerted and led, in a massive mobilization of diverse oppositional forces, particularly those in a strategic position vis-à-vis the system (being able to close down or cut access to the production apparatus), taking advantage of the objective conditions generated by the contradictions of a system in crisis. The system has many diverse points of vulnerability and its crisis is generating both objective (structural) and subjective (political) conditions for anti-systemic action. This is to say, as Marx said in an earlier and very different context, capitalism in its current global projection is "creating its own gravediggers." The Left has the responsibility and historic mission to understand and actively support this process.

Endnotes

Chapter 1: The Dynamics of Systemic Crisis

1. The poverty estimates by the UN Commission for Latin America (Campos 2002) are conservative, given that the cited figure for Argentina is only 30.3 percent (20 percent just two years ago), whereas even the government has acknowledged that more than 50 percent of Argentina's population today are below the poverty line. Similarly, while CEPAL places the percentage of the poor in Mexico at 42.3 percent (36.5 percent in 1981), a poverty survey carried out by the government placed the poor at more than 50 percent of the population (Cortés et al. 2002). In Central America even CEPAL placed the poor at more than 79 percent in Honduras and 67 percent in Nicaragua. Of course, CEPAL, like the World Bank, attributes this growth of poverty to an unexplained economic crunch rather than the economic policies that most of the countries in the region have been pursuing since the mid-1980s. This issue is elaborated upon in Chapter 4.
2. In the academy there is an ongoing debate as to how best to view problems such as poverty, low incomes and unemployment — the result of a process of exploitation (extracting unpaid labour time from the worker and direct producer) or as a pillar of social exclusion, an issue on which there is a voluminous literature (on this in the Latin American context see, inter alia, Veltmeyer 2002).
3. The literature on this ecological crisis is too voluminous to cite, let alone review, but see Sachs (1999).
4. It is in this context that we can place and understand the agenda of the operational agencies of the UN system and the association of overseas development associations (ODAs) to incorporate the private sector (i.e., the global corporations) into the development process. The UNDP, to the surprise and disgust of many watchdogs and critics, has assumed the role of broker in this strategic marriage on the basis of a plan formulated in 1989 and giving rise, some years later, to a global compact between the UN and those transnational corporations (TNCs) who signed on guidelines for ethical behaviour and corporate responsibility vis-à-vis the environment and popular participation — the incorporation of women etc. On the UN's new global compact with "the private sector" (global corporations), see, inter alia, Utting (2002) and UN (1998).
5. This partnership is predicated on a new model that is based, according to Micheld Camdessus (quoted in *La Jornada*, 16 March 1996: A4), former executive director of the IMF, on three pillars: the invisible hand of the market, the visible hand of the state, and solidarity of the rich and poor. Within this model both the state (governments) and the private sector (the TNCs) are assigned roles. The latter is to provide the engine of growth and the drivers of this engine; undertake the responsibilities of property, viz. the functions of investment, entrepreneurship, management, and marketing; and to create conditions of economic development — "employment [and those conditions that come with] royalties, foreign currencies

and taxes" (Aria 2002: 47–48).

6. In countries like Argentina the external debt, in fact, was contracted by private firms. But the government assumed responsibility for this debt, converting the private debt into a public debt. This paralleled the bailout of the private banks in the region that were on the brink of collapse. In the case of Chile, this bailout, engineered by the neoliberal economic regime of Augusto Pinochet, was equivalent to 3.5 percent of the country's GNP.
7. Slim has since come out against neoliberalism, regarding it as a dysfunctional form of neocolonialism — it simply doesn't work, he notes (although he himself has done very well by it) (Global Progress Commission 1999).
8. These defenders of capitalist development have become equally well-known for their criticism of a system in which financial capital is allowed too free a hand in determining the rules of the game (making money, lots of it) and in roaming the world in search of profit, scavenging whatever productive system in the real economy fuels their insatiable appetites and greed (Laxer 1998: 93–94).
9. This loss of nerve (and self-confidence) is reflected in the inversion of the question raised by Dudley Seers (1972) at the beginning of the decade: Why do visiting economists fail (in their planning missions)? At the end of the decade the question, raised by Paul Streeten, was: 'Why do failed economists (continue to) visit?
10. On this point Michel Camdessus, formerly executive director of the IMF, clarified that the IMF's policies were not based on a neoliberal order, but rather on three pillars: the invisible hand of the market, the visible hand of the state, and solidarity between the rich and the poor.
11. For an analysis and critique of this form of post-structuralist analysis, see Veltmeyer (2001b).
12. For an analysis of these intellectual and political dynamics, see Petras and Veltmeyer (2001a).

Chapter 4: Argentina

1. Interview of Mario Xiques, bank worker and trade union delegate, 10 May 2002.
2. Published by MTD Solano. Also see interview with Simeca (Sindicato Independiente de Mensajeros y Cadetes) 20 April 2002; Eduardo Lucita, *"La rebellion popular en Argentina,"* and "*Argentina: La nueva rebellion Porteña*" (email, 25 December 2001).
3. Interviews in Solano with Padre Alberto, 21 April 2002.
4. For background on recent social protests prior to the uprising of 19/20 December 2001, see *Observatorio Social de America Latina,* Clasco, Buenos Aires, September 2001. For detailed accounts of the neighbourhood assemblies, see *Argentina Arde*, from February 2002 on; Asamblea, *Popular Parque Lezama*, 1 January 2002, through no. 11.
5. Interviews with participants in Parque Centenario in April 2002. See also *Argentina Arde* 1, no. 3, 15 February 2002.
6. Interviews with Hebe Bonafini on 11 April 2002 and the *Motoqueristas* (motorcycle messengers) on 19 April 2002.
7. "*Zanon: Una fabrica tomada donde sus trabajadores estan produciendo algo mas que ceramica*," interviews by Juan Carlos Cena of three leaders of Zanon (Raul Godoy, Carlos Acuna and Alejandro Lopez), to be published in *Maza,* no. 3, July–August 2002.
8. Plan Fenix was published in its entirety in *Enoikos,* no. 19, November 2001; it was

written in September 2001.
9. The essays are individually authored and reflect the various specializations of each economist.
10. See "*Hacia el Plan Fenix, Diagnostico y propriestas. Documento Final,*" *Enoikos*, no. 19, November 2001, 19–29.

Chapter 6: Cod

1. Even in recent years fishing in the cold waters of the North Atlantic is one of the most dangerous "occupations," with notoriously harsh working conditions and high rates of accidents and deaths from drowning. On this see Kurlansky (1997: 115–17).
2. With regard to the "virtual population" method of analysis (VPA) used to measure stock, see Chantraine (1992: 33).
3. In the 1920s, protests by inshore fishers had forced the Canadian government to prohibit further expansion of the dragger fleet.
4. A study by Anthony Davis (1984) showed that communities of fishers are much better managers of the commons and its resources than the government. In addition, he showed that not only were the fishing practices of inshore fishers more sustainable, but in economic terms the smaller production units of the inshore were more efficient in their use of labour and capital than the large, vertically integrated companies that operated offshore.
5. Total food fish supply for human and other forms of consumption has been growing at a rate of 3.6 percent per annum since 1961, while the world's population has been expanding at 1.8 percent per annum. The proteins derived from fish, crustaceans and molluscs account for between 13.8 and 16.5 percent of the animal protein intake of the human population. In regards to the commercial fishery, 36 percent of world fisheries production was marketed as fresh fish, the remainder undergoing some sort of processing — freezing, curing or canning (FAO 2000: 21–22).

Chapter 8: Indigenous People Arise

1. With the onset of the indigenous uprising of June 1990, Mercedes Jiménez (*Hoy*, 25 June 1990) reminded everyone that the uprising was by no means the first; indeed, she pointed out, it was the sixth major uprising since 1578, the date of the first.
2. Structural adjustment programs (SAPs) have been introduced all across the region (see Veltmeyer and Petras 1997) in two basic modalities: heterodox and orthodox. On the difference, see Meller (1988).
3. Fenocin is neither as strong nor as representative of indigenous people as CONAIE. According to Pedro de la Cruz, the president of Fenocin, around 60 percent of its membership — and around 20 percent of CONAIE's membership — is composed of indigenous communities and families, and these are found in eighteen of the country's twenty-two provincial jurisdictions. Around 25 percent of its membership is composed of diverse mestizo groups, primarily peasants, and 15 percent are Afro-Ecuadorians from Esmeraldas and Guyas provinces, also peasants and small producers in the main (Interview, November 31, 2002). In 1995, in the context of an economic downturn and political crisis, Fenocin was restructured (at its Sixth National Congress in Ibarra), taking a 180 degree turn to the left, with a clear class understanding of its situation. In this situation, Fenocin joined CONAIE and other labour and social organizations in a popular movement against the government's

neoliberal agenda. As one result, the government's privatization agenda was halted in its tracks, one of the few successful anti-privatization struggles in the region.

4. This program had been introduced as early as May 1982, under the government of Osvaldo Hurtado, in the form of a plan to stabilize the economy by controlling inflation. In March 1983, in the context of a region-wide debt crisis, a second structural adjustment program was introduced. Leon Febres Cordero moved beyond IMF stabilization measures to open up the economy to the world market and foreign capital. In August 1986 the government signed a standby agreement with the IMF, and in January 1988 it signed a fourth IMF agreement, setting the stage for the heterodox "National Economic Emergency Plan" of the new social democratic regime. In September 1989 the government entered into its fifth agreement with the IMF in the context of a plan to change the role of the state, allowing the country to insert itself into the process of global capitalism. In August 1992, with assumption of state power by Durán-Ballená, the SAP in Ecuador was given a new twist in a series of rigorously orthodox measures that matched the severity of those introduced by Menem in Argentina and Fujimori in neighboring Peru. This SAP was introduced, measure by measure, over the next four years, bringing about a radical change in the relationship of the state to private capital, and an equally radical growth of a broad popular movement in the urban centres. Over the next four years both the SAP and this oppositional movement grew in tandem, each government measure leading to further protest actions. In 1997 the government of Abdalá Bucaram was forced out of office over government plans to privatize social security, and the government of Jamil Mahuad was brought down by the popular movement led by CONAIE. The context for these developments was a series of efforts by the government to privatize up to 160 public enterprises, dollarize the economy and introduce some of the most stringent SAPs to date.
5. According to the International Working Group for Indigenous Affairs (IWGIA 1995), indigenous people account for around 30 percent of the national population, even though the World Bank (1995) writes of an increase in the 1990s to 49 percent. It is likely that this latter figure includes all sorts of indigenous peoples who no longer live in the indigenous community, having migrated to various urban centres, becoming by dominant cultural definition "mestizo," and thus, strictly speaking, no longer "indigenous."
6. This 'development' has been repeated, with numerous permutations but the same pattern, all across Latin America, both in countries with large ethnic or indigenous populations and those in which they are numerically insignificant.
7. Lucas (2001) warns of a division between the social movement represented by CONAIE and the political movement represented by Pachakutik and its project to participate in the electoral system of the Ecuadorian state. According to Lucas, this division reflects the dilemma of a movement caught between the Scylla of a class-oriented old Left and the Charybdus of a new Left oriented towards cultural issues of political identity. The issue: Should the Pachakutik movement transform itself into an other centre-left political party with its political base among the indigenous community and urban poor, and with the support of social organizations and NGOs of Ecuador's civil society contest national and local elections? In effect, should the indigenous movement seek to transform the Ecuadorian uni-national state into a pluri-national one from within or via the agency of an independent social movement?
8. After resolving to repudiate the government's economic policies, the assembly gave

an opportunity for Miguel Lluco, the national coordinator of Pachakutik, to speak. Being well aware of the mood of the assembly vis-à-vis the government's policies, Lluco limited his intervention to the virtue and necessity of supporting Gutiérrez as the lesser of various evils that would otherwise ensue, particularly the resurgence of the political Right. He also recommended an evaluation of government policies at the national and provincial levels and frequent meetings of CONAIE to ensure transparency.

9. The letter of intent requires the adoption of neoliberal policy measures that include a commitment (1) not to incur any further arrears in debt repayment; (2) to not impose any restrictions on international trade; (3) to maintain the US dollar as the national currency; (4) to effect a 35 percent increase in the price of fuel to generate US$400 million (1.5 percent of GNP); (5) to end the subsidy on gasoline; (6) to privatize the Banco del Pacifico; (7) to ensure the administration of the telephone and electrical utilities by foreign companies; (8) to freeze pensions; and (9) to implement fiscal, tax and labour reforms (implying an increase of taxes on workers with low and medium incomes).
10. The budget proposals sent by the government to the IMF assigns 35.7 percent to debt service versus 19.5 percent for social programs in the areas of health, education, housing and welfare. The share of education in this budget would be 11.2 percent (versus 12.5 percent in 2002).
11. The government's letter of intent put together by the IMF entails an increase of at least 35 percent.

Bibliography

Amador, F. 1990. *Un siglo de lucha de los trabajadores en Nicaragua*. Managua: Centro de la Investigación de la Realidad de América Latina.

Amalric, Frank. 1998. "Sustainable Livelihoods, Entrepreneurship, Political Strategies and Governance." *Development* 41, no. 3.

Angel, J.R., D.L. Burke, R.N. O'Boyle, F.G. Peacock, M. Sinclair, and K.C.T. Zwanenburg. 1994. *Report of the Workshop of Scotia-Fundy Groundfish Management from 1977 to 1993*. Canadian Technical Report. Fish. Aquatic Science. Ottawa.

Arias, Dario. 2002. "Hidrocarburos, protección ambiental y seguridad juridical en Bolivia." *Petróleo y Gas* no. 26.

Arias, Durán. 1996. *El proceso social de la participación popular: problemas y potencialidades*. La Paz: SNPP.

Atlantic Development Board (ADB). 1969. *Fisheries in the Atlantic Provinces*. Ottawa: ADB.

Azpiazu, Daniel, et al. 2001. *Privatizaciones en la Argentina, Penegociación permanente, consolidación de privilegios ganancias extraordinarias y captura institucional*. Buenos Aires: Flasco.

Azpiazu, Daniel, and Eduardo Basualdo. 2001. "Concentración económico y renegociación de los servicios publicos." *Enoikas* no. 19 (November).

Azpiazu, Daniel, and Martin Schorr. 2002. "Desnaturalización de la regulación públicos y ganancias extraordinarias." *Realidad Economica* no. 184.

Barraclough, S. 1973. *Agrarian Structure in Latin America, A Resumé of the CIDA Land Tenure Studies*. Lexington: Lexington Books.

Barrett, Gene. 1984. "Capital and the State in Atlantic Canada: The Structural Context of Fisheries Policy between 1939 and 1977." In C. Lamson and A. Hanson (eds.), *Atlantic Fisheries and Coastal Communities: Fisheries Decision-making Case Studies*. Halifax: Dalhousie Ocean Studies Program.

Barrow, Clyde W. 1993. *Critical Theories of the State*. Madison, Wis.: University of Wisconsin Press.

Bartra, Roger. 1976. "¡Si los campesinos se extinguen!" *Historia y Sociedad* 8.

Basualdo, Eduardo. 2001. *Concentración y centralización del Capital en la Argentina durante la década del noventa*. Buenos Aires: Universidad de Quilmes.

Basualdo, Eduardo, and Daniel Azpiazu. 2002. "El proceso de privatización en Argentina." *Página 12* (Buenos Aires), April.

Basualdo, Eduardo, and Claudio Lozano. 2000. "Entre la dolarización y la devaluación: La crises de la convertibilidad en la Argentina." *Realidad Económica* no. 73: 60–66.

Bauer, Arnold J. 1975. *Chilean Rural Society from the Spanish Conquest to 1930*. Cambridge: Cambridge University Press.

_____. 1979b. "Reply." *Hispanic American Historical Review* 59, no. 3.

Bebbington, A., et al. 1992. *Actores de una década ganada: Tribus, comunidades y campesinos en la modernidad*. Quito: Comunidec.

Beckman, Björn. 1982. "Whose State? State and Capitalist Development in Nigeria." *Review of African Political Economy* no. 23.

Beltran, Fausto, and José Fernández. 1960. *¿Donde Va la reforma Agraria Boliviana?* La Paz: Talleres Gráficos Bolivianos.

Benasayag, Miguel, and Diego Sztulwark. 2000. *Política y situación: de la potencia al contrapoder.* Buenos Aires: Ediciones Mano en Mano.

Bendix, Reinhard. 1964. *Nation-Building and Citizenship: Studies of Our Changing Social Order.* New York: John Wiley & Sons.

Bengoa, José. 2000. *La emergencia indígena en América Latina.* México and Santiago: Fondo de Cultura Económico.

Berger, Guy. 1992. *Social Structure and Rural Development in the Third World.* Cambridge: Cambridge University Press.

Best, Lloyd, and Kari Levitt. 1975. *Pure Plantation Economy.* Mimeo. St. Augustine, Trinidad: Institute of International Relations.

Black, Conrad. 1995. "Post-Election Prospects in Canada." In Frederic Jackman et al. (eds.), *The Empire Club of Canada Speeches, 1993–1994.* Toronto: Empire Club Foundation.

Bordegaray, Soledad, and Toti Flores, eds. 2001. *1o Foro Social Mundial desde los desocupados.* Argentina: MTD Editora — Movimiento de Trabajadores Desocupados de la Matanza.

Bowser, Frederick P. 1974 *The African Slave in Colonial Peru, 1524–1650.* Palo Alto, Calif.: Stanford University Press.

Brass, Tom. 1991. "Moral Economists, Subalterns, New Social Movements and the (Re) Emergence of a (Post) Modernised (Middle) Peasant." *Journal of Peasant Studies* 18 no. 2.

_____. 1999. *Towards a Comparative Political Economy of Unfree Labour: Case Studies and Debates.* London and Portland, Ohio: Frank Cass.

_____. 2000. *Peasants, Populism and Postmodernism: The Return of the Agrarian Myth.* London: Frank Cass.

Bromley, D., and M. Cernea. 1989. *The Management of Common Property Resources.* Washington: World Bank.

Bruton, M. 1995. "Have Fishes Had Their Chips? The Dilemma of Threatened Fishes." *Environmental Biology of Fishes* 43.

Brzezinski, Zbigniew. 1997. *The Grand Chessboard: American Primacy and Its Geostrategic Imperatives.* New York: Basic Books.

Campos, Roberto. 2000. "Desigualdades y asimetrias en el orden global." In Ernesto Ottone (ed.), *La modernidad problemático: cuatro ensayos sobre el desarrollo.* Santiago: CEPAL.

Canada. 1928. *Report of the Royal Commission on the Quebec and Maritime Fisheries.* Ottawa: Queen's Printer.

Canadian Council on Rural Development (CCRD). 1977. *Canadian Atlantic Fisheries in Transition.* Ottawa: CCRD.

Cancian, Frank. 1987. "Proletarianization in Zinacantan 1960–83." In Morgan Maclachan (ed.), *Household Economies and Their Transformation.* Lanham, Md.: University Press of America.

Cashin, Richard. 1993. *Charting a New Course: Toward the Fishery of the Future.* Ottawa: Minister of Supply and Services.

Castells, Manuel. 1976. *Movimientos sociales urbanos en América Latina: tendencies históricas y problemas teóricos.* Lima: Pontífica Universidad Católica.

Castillo, Leonardo. 1982. "Chile's Three Agrarian Reforms: The Inheritors." *Bulletin of Latin American Research* 1, 2.

Ceriza, Alejandra, et al. 2000. "Análisis de casos: la revuelta indígena en Ecuador." *OSAL*

— *Observatorio Social de América Latina* (June). Buenos Aires: CLASCO.

Chambers, Robert, and Gordon Conway. 1998. "Sustainable Rural Livelihoods: Some Working Definitions." *Development* 41, no. 3 (September).

Chantraine, Pol. 1992. *The Last Cod-Fish: Life and Death of the Newfoundland Way of Life.* Montreal/Toronto: Robert Davies.

Chevalier, François. 1963. *Land and Society in Colonial Mexico: The Great Hacienda.* Berkeley, Calif.: University of California Press.

Chilcote, Ron, and Dale Johnston, eds. 1983. *Theories of Development.* Beverley Hills, Calif.: Sage.

Chiriboga, Manuel. 1992. "Movimiento Campesino e indígena y participación política en Ecuador: la construcción de identidades en una sociedad heterogenea." *Sintesis* (AIETI), January/April.

Chopra, K., G. Kadekodi and M. Murty. 1990. *Participatory Development.* London: Sage.

CIDA. 1966. *Chile: Tenencia de la tierra y desarrollo socio-económico del sector agrícola.* Santiago de Chile: Talleres Gráficos Hispano Suiza.

Clarke, Simon, ed. 1991. *The State Debate.* London: Macmillan.

Cockcroft, James D. 1968. *Intellectual Precursors of the Mexican Revolution, 1900–1913.* Austin, Texas: University of Texas Press.

_____. 2001. *América latina y Estados Unidos: historia y política país por país.* México DF: Siglo Veintiuno Editores.

Cohen, Jean L., and Andrew Arato. 1992. *Civil Society and Political Theory.* Cambridge, Mass.: MIT Press.

Cole, Jeffrey A. 1985. *The Potosí Mita, 1573–1700: Compulsory Indian Labor in the Andes.* Palo Alto, Calif.: Stanford University Press.

Colectivo Situaciones de Buenos Aires. 2001. *Contrapoder: una introducción.* Buenos Aires: Ediciones de Mano en Mano.

Collier, David, ed. 1979 *The New Authoritarianism in Latin America.* Princeton, NJ: Princeton University Press.

CONAIE (National Confederation of Indigenous Peoples of Ecuador). 1990. *Resoluciones del Primer Encuentro Continental de Pueblos Indígenas.* Quito.

_____. 1991. *Violencia, derechos humanos y pueblos indígenas.* Puyo.

Cooper, Robert. 2002a. "The Post-Modern State." *Reordering the World: The Long Term Implications of September 11.* Foreign Policy Centre, info@fpc.org.uk.

_____. 2002b. "The New Liberal Imperialism." *Observer Worldview, The Guardian,* April 7.

Copes, P. 1977. *Canada's Atlantic Coast Fisheries: Policy Development and the Impact of Extended Jurisdiction.* Burnaby: Simon Fraser University.

_____. 1978. *Rational Resource Management and Institutional Constraints: The Case of the Fishery.* Burnaby: Simon Fraser University.

Cortés, Fernando, Daniel Hernández, Enrique Hernández Laos, Miguel Székely and Hadid Vera. 2002. "Evolución y características de la pobreza en México en la última década del siglo XX." *Serie Documentos de Investigación* no. 2 (Agosto), México DF: Sedeso.

Cotler, Julio. 1978. *Clases, estado y nación en el Perú.* Lima: Instituto de Estudios Peruanos.

Coull, James R. 1993. *World Fisheries Resources.* London: Routledge.

Cox, Robert. 1999. "Civil Society at the Turn of the Millennium. Prospects for an Alternative World Order." *Review of International Studies* 25.

Crouch, C., and A. Pizzorno. 1978. *Resurgence of Class Conflict in Western Europe Since 1968.* London: Holmes & Meier.

Dandler, Jorge. 1969. *El Sindicalismo Campesino en Bolivia.* México: Instituto Indigenista Interamericano.

Davis, Anthony. 1984. "'You're Your own Boss:' An Economic Anthropology of Small Boat Fishing in Port Lameron Harbour, Southwest Nova Scotia." PhD dissertation.

Davis, Diane E. 1994. "Failed Democratic Reform in Contemporary Mexico: From Social Movements to the State and Back Again." *Journal of Latin American Studies* 26, no 2.

De Janvry, Alain. 1981. *The Agrarian Question and Reformism in Latin America.* Baltimore, Maryland: Johns Hopkins Press.

De Rivero, Oswaldo. 2001. *The Myth of Development: The Non-Viable Economies of the 21st Century.* London and New York: Zed Press.

De Walt, Billie, and Martha Ress, with Arthur Murphy. 1994. *The End of Agrarian Reform in Mexico: Past Lessons and Future Prospects.* San Diego: Center for US-Mexican Studies.

Delgado Jara, Diego. 2000. *Atraco bancario y dolarización.* Quito: Gallo Rojo.

Department of Fisheries and Oceans (DFO). 1982. *Northern Cod: A Fisheries Success Story.* Ottawa: DFO.

_____. 1988. *Resource Prospects for Canada's Atlantic Fisheries, 1989–1993.* Ottawa: DFO.

_____. 1989. *DFO Fact Book.* Ottawa: Minister of Supply and Services.

_____. 1994. *Report on the Status of Groundfish Stocks in the Canadian Northwest Atlantic.* Ottawa.

Desmarais, Annette-Aurélie. 2002. "The Via Campesina: Consolidating an International Peasant and Farm Movement." *Journal of Peasant Studies* 29, no 2.

Domínguez, Jorge, and A. Lowenthal. 1996. *Constructing Democratic Governance in Latin America and the Caribbean in the 90s.* Baltimore, Maryland: Johns Hopkins University Press.

Duggett, Michael. 1975. "Marx on Peasants." *Journal of Peasant Studies* 2, no. 2.

Duncan, Kenneth, Ian Rutledge and Colin Harding, eds. 1977. *Land and Labour in Latin America: Essays on the Development of Agrarian Capitalism in the Nineteenth and Twentieth Centuries.* New York: Cambridge University Press.

Dunkerley, James. 1984. *Rebellion in the Veins: Political Struggle in Bolivia, 1952–82,* London: New Left Books.

_____. 1992. *Political Suicide in Latin America.* New York: Verso.

Durrenberger, E.P., and G. Palsson. 1987. "The Grass Roots and the State: Resource Management in Icelandic Fishing." In B. McCay and J. Acheson, (eds.), *The Question of the Commons.* Tucson: University of Arizona Press.

Edelman, Marc. 1998. "Transnational Peasant Politics in Central America." *Latin American Research Review* 33, no. 3.

Esteva, Gustavo, and M.S. Prakash. 1998. *Grassroots Postmodernism.* London: Zed Books.

FARC-EP. 2000. *Historical Outline — International Commission, Revolutionary Armed Forces of Colombia Peoples Army.* Toronto: Fuerzas Armadas Revolucionarias de Colombia-Ejército del Pueblo, International Commission.

Featherstone, Mike, ed. 1990. *Global Culture: Nationalism, Globalization and Modernity.* London: Sage.

Feder, Ernest. 1971. *The Rape of the Peasantry: Latin America's Landholding System.* New York: Doubleday.

Finlayson, A.C. 1994. *Fishing For Truth: A Sociological Analysis of Northern Cod Stock Assessment from 1977 to 1990.* St. John's: Institute of Social and Economic Research.

Fisheries and Marine Service. 1976. *Policy for Canada's Commercial Fisheries.* Ottawa:

Department of the Environment.

Fletcher, H.F. 1977. *Toward a Relevant Science: Fisheries and Aquatic Scientific Resource Needs in Canada.* Ottawa: Ministry of Supply and Services.

Florescano, Enrique, ed. 1975. *Haciendas, Latifundios y Plantaciones en América Latina.* México, DF: Siglo XXI.

Fogel, Ramon Bruno. 1986. *Movimientos Campesinos en el Paraguay.* Asunción: Centro Paraguayo de Estudios Sociologicos (CPES).

Food and Agriculture Organization (FAO). 1998. *World State of Agriculture and Food: Brazil.* Rome.

_____. 2000. *The State of the World Fisheries and Aquaculture.* http://www.fao.org/DOCREP/003/X8002E/X8002E00.htm.

_____. 1998. *Yearbook.* Vol. 51. Rome: FAO.

Foster, John Bellamy. 1999. *Ecology Against Capitalism,* New York: Monthly Review Press.

Foweraker, Joseph W. 1978. "The Contemporary Peasantry: Class and Class Practice." In Howard Newby (ed.), *International Perspectives in Rural Sociology.* New York: John Wiley and Sons.

Fox, J., ed. 1990. *The Challenge of Rural Democratization.* London: Frank Cass.

Frank, André Gunder. 1969 *Capitalism and Underdevelopment in Latin America.* New York: Monthly Review Press.

Furedi, Frank. 1994. *The New Ideology of Imperialism.* London: Pluto Press.

Gavaris, S. 1988. "Abundance Indices from Commercial Fishing." In D. Rivard (ed.), *Collected Papers on Stock Assessment Methods.* CAFSAC Resource. Document 88/613–15.

Ghimire, Krishna B., ed. 2001. *Land Reform and Peasant Livelihoods: The Social Dynamics of Rural Poverty and Agrarian Reform in Developing Countries.* London: ITDG.

Gilly, Adolfo. 1971. *La revolución interrumpida. México 1910–1920: una Guerra campesina por la tierra y el poder.* México: El Caballito.

Global Progress Commission. 1999. "Outlook for Latin America and the Caribbean in Relation to Globalization." Synthesis of meeting, Mexico City, March 22–23.

Goldsmith, Edward. 2002. "Poverty — The Child of 'Progress.'" CCPA *Monitor* 9, no. 4 (September).

Góngora, Mario. 1975. *Studies in the Colonial History of Spanish America.* Cambridge: Cambridge University Press.

Goodman, David, and Michael Watts, eds. 1997. *Globalising Food: Agrarian Questions and Global Restructuring.* London: Routledge.

Gould, Jeffrey. 1983. "El trabajo forzoso y las comunidades indígenas nicaragüenses." In Hector Pérez Brignoli and Mario Samper (eds.), *El café en la historia de Centroamérica.* San José: FLASCO.

Goulet, Denis. 1989. "Participation in Development: New Avenues." *World Development* 17, no. 2: 165–78.

Greenpeace Foundation. 2002. "Canadian Atlantic Fisheries Collapse," http://www.greenpeace.org/comms/cbio/cancod.html.

Grindle, Merilee S. 2000. *Audacious Reforms: Institutional Invention and Democracy in Latin America.* Baltimore, Maryland: Johns Hopkins University Press.

Gunther, R.E., and J.R. Winter. 1978. *Fisheries Rationalization, Employment and Regional Economic Policy.* Wolfville: Acadia University.

Gutelman, Michel. 1971. *Réforme et mystification agraires en Amérique latine: Le cas du Mexique.* Paris: François Maspero.

Gwynne, Robert, and Cristóbal Kay, eds. 1999. *Latin America Transformed.* New York: Oxford University Press.

Haagh, Louise. 2002. *Citizenship, Labour Markets and Democratization: Chile and the Modern Sequence.* Oxford: Palgrave.

Haché, J.E. 1989. *Scotia-Fundy Groundfish Task Force.* Ottawa: Minister of Supply and Services.

Hall, Anthony L. 1989. *Developing Amazonia.* Manchester and New York: Manchester University Press.

Hanrahan, Maura, with Dave Simms, Alton Hollett and Annette Stuckless. 1986. *Statistical Overview of the Newfoundland Fisheries.* Background report. St. John's: Royal Commission on Employment and Unemployment, Newfoundland and Labrador.

Hardin, G., and J. Baden. 1977. *Managing the Commons.* San Francisco: Freeman.

Hardt, Michael, and Antonio Negri. 2000. *Empire.* Cambridge, Mass.: Harvard University Press.

Harris, Leslie. 1989. *Independent Review of the State of the Northern Cod Stock.* Harris Report. Ottawa: Department of Fisheries and Oceans.

Harris, Richard L. 1992 *Marxism, Socialism, and Democracy in Latin America.* Boulder, Colo.: Westview Press.

Harris, Richard L., Anthony Winson, Florencia Mallon, Rosemary Galli, Alain de Janvry and Lynn Ground, and Roderigo Montoya. 1978. "Peasants, Capitalism, and the Class Struggle in Rural Latin America (Part II)." *Latin American Perspectives* 5, no. 4.

Hart, John Mason. 1987. *Revolutionary Mexico: The Coming and Process of the Mexican Revolution.* Berkeley: University of California Press.

Hartlyn, Jonathan. 1998. *The Struggle for Democratic Politics in the Dominican Republic.* Chapel Hill, N.C.: University of North Carolina Press.

Harvey, Neil. 1994. *Rebellion in Chiapas: Rural Reforms, Campesino Radicalism and the Limits to Salinismo.* San Diego: Centre for U.S.–Mexican Studies.

_____. 1995. "Rebellion in Chiapas: Rural Reforms and Popular Struggles." *Third World Quarterly* 16, no. 1.

Held, David, ed. 1993. *Prospects for Democracy: North, South, East, West.* Cambridge: Polity Press.

Hernandez, Virgilio. 2001. "Reflexiones preliminares sobre el levantamiento de los bases indigenas y campesinas." *Boletín ICCI 'RIMAY'* no. 3 (February).

Hobsbawm, Eric J. 1959. *Primitive Rebels.* Manchester: Manchester University Press.

_____. 1994. *The Ages of Extremes: The Short 20th Century, 1914–1991.* London: Michael Joseph.

Holloway, John. 2001. "Doce Tesis sobre el Anti-Poder." *In Colectivo Situaciones de Buenos Aires, 2000, Contrapoder: una introducción.* Buenos Aires: Ediciones de Mano en Mano.

Holloway, John, and Sol Picciotto, eds. 1978. *State and Capital: A Marxist Debate.* London: Edward Arnold.

Hood, P.R., R.D.S. Macdonald and G. Carpentier. 1980. *Atlantic Coast Groundfish Trawler Study.* Ottawa: Department of Fisheries and Oceans.

House, Douglas, Maura Hanrahan and David Simms. 1986. *Fisheries Policies and Community Development: Proposal for a Revised Approach to Managing the Inshore Fisheries in Newfoundland.* Background report. St. John's: Royal Commission on Employment and Unemployment.

Huizer, Gerrit. 1973. *Peasant Rebellion in Latin America.* London: Penguin.

Hunt, Diana. 1989. *Economic Theories of Development.* Hemel, Hempstead, Herfordshire:

Harvester Wheatsheaf.

Hutchings, J.A., and Ranson A. Myers. 1994. *What Can Be Learned from the Collapse of a Renewable Resource? Atlantic Cod, Gadus Morhua, of Newfoundland and Labrador.* St. John's: Science Branch, Department of Fisheries and Oceans.

Instituto Nacional de Colonização e Reforma Agrária (INCRA). 1999. *Balanço da Reforma Agraria e da Agricultura Familiar 1995–99.* Brasilia: Ministério do Desenvolvimiento Agrário.

Inter-American Development Bank (IDB). 1998. *Economic and Social Progress in Latin America: Facing Up to Inequality.* Washington, D.C.

International Commission for the Northwest Atlantic Fisheries (ICNAF). 1996. *Annual Statistical Bulletin* no. 426: 1954–76.

International Labour Organization (ILO). 2002. *Panoramo Laboral [Employment Panorama] 2002.* Geneva.

International Working Group for Indigenous Affairs (IWGIA). 1995. "The Indigenous World, 1993–1994." iwgia@iwgia.org.

Jackson, Moana. 1993. "Indigenous Law and the Sea." In J. van Dyke, D. Zaekle and G. Hewison (eds.), *Freedom for the Seas in the 21st Century: Ocean Governance and Environmental Harmony.* Washington, D.C.: Island Press.

Jessop, Bob. 1990. *State Theory: Putting Capitalist States in Their Place.* Cambridge: Polity Press.

Jorgenson, Dale, and Kevin Stiroh. 1999. "Information Technology and Growth." *American Economic Review* (May).

Joseph, Gilbert M., and Daniel Nugent, eds. 1994. *Everyday Forms of State Formation: Revolution and Negotiation of Rule in Modern Mexico.* London and Durham, N.C.: Duke University Press.

Kagarlitsky, Boris. 2001. "The Road to Genoa." *Social Policy* 32 no. 1 (Fall): 16–19.

Kapstein, Ethan. 1996. "Workers and the World Economy." *Foreign Affairs* 75, no. 3 (May–June).

Katz, Friedrich, ed. 1988. *Riot, Rebellion, and Revolution: Rural Social Conflict in Mexico.* Princeton, N.J.: Princeton University Press.

Katz, Jorge, and Giovanni Stumpo. 2001. "Producción tecnologico y competitividad internacional." *Enoikas* no. 19 (November).

Kautsky, Karl. 1988. *The Agrarian Question.* 2 vols. London: Zwan.

Kay, Cristobal. 1977. "The Development of the Chilean Hacienda System, 1850–1973." In Kenneth Duncan, Ian Rutledge, and Colin Harding (eds.), *Land and Labour in Latin America.* New York: Cambridge University Press.

_____. 1981. "Political Economy, Class Alliances and Agrarian Change in Chile." *Journal of Peasant Studies* 8, no. 4: 485–513.

_____. 1982. "Achievements and Contradictions of the Peruvian Agrarian Reform." *Journal of Development Studies* 18, no. 2: 141–70.

_____. 1998. "Latin America's Agrarian Reform: Lights and Shadows." *Land Reform* 2.

_____. 1999. "Rural Development: From Agrarian Reform to Neoliberalism and Beyond." In Robert Gwynne and Cristobal Kay (eds.), *Latin America Transformed.* New York: Oxford University Press.

Kearney, Michael. 1996. *Reconceptualizing the Peasantry.* Boulder, Colo.: Westview Press.

Kirby, M.J.L. 1983. *Navigating Troubled Waters: Report for the Task Force on the Atlantic Fisheries.* Ottawa: Minister of Supply and Services.

Klein, Herbert S. 1986. *African Slavery in Latin America and the Caribbean.* New York: Oxford University Press.

Knight, Alan. 1985. "The Mexican Revolution: Bourgeois? Nationalist? Or Just a Great Rebellion." *Bulletin of Latin American Research* 4, no. 2.

_____. 1986. *The Mexican Revolution. Volume I: Porfirians, Liberals and Peasants.* Cambridge: Cambridge University Press.

Koeller, RA. 1980. "Biomass estimates from Canadian research vessel surveys on the Scotian Shelf and in the Gulf of St. Lawrence from 1970–79." CAFSAC *Resource.* Document 80/18.

Koeyu Latinoamericano. http://www.koeyu.com.

Kovel, Joel. 2002. *The Enemy of Nature: The End of Capitalism or the End of the World?* New York: Zed Books.

Kirlansky, Mark. 1997. *Cod.* New York: Penguin.

Lamson, C., and A. Hanson, eds. 1984. *Atlantic Fisheries and Coastal Communities: Fisheries Decision-Making Case Studies.* Halifax: Dalhousie Ocean Studies Program.

Landsberger, Henry A., ed. 1969. *Latin American Peasant Movements.* London and Ithaca: Cornell University Press.

_____. 1974. *Rural Protest: Peasant Movements and Social Change.* London: Macmillan.

Latin American Bureau. 1980. *Bolivia: Coup d'Etat.* London: LAB.

Laxer, James. 1998. *The Undeclared War: Class Conflict in the Age of Cyber Capitalism.* Toronto: Viking.

Lee, Marc. 2002. *The Global Divide: Inequality in the Global Economy.* Ottawa: CCPA.

Lehmann, David. 1978. "The Death of Land Reform: A Polemic." *World Development* 6, no. 3.

Lenin, V.I. 1964. "The Development of Capitalism in Russia." *Collected Works*, vol. 3. Moscow: Foreign Languages Publishing House.

Liamzon, Tina, et al., ed. 1996. *Towards Sustainable Livelihoods.* Rome: Society for International Development (SID).

Lichbach, Mark. 1994. "What Makes Rational Peasants Revolutionary? Dilemma, Paradox and Irony in Peasant Collective Action." *World Politics* 46, no. 3.

Lievesley, Geraldine. 1999. *Democracy in Latin America: Mobilization, Power and the Search for a New Politics.* Manchester: Manchester University Press.

Llorens, C. Javier, and Marion Cafiero. 2002. "Por que se Quiere Derogar La Ley de Subversion Economica." Mimeo. Buenos Aires.

Lluco Tixe, Miguel. 2000. "La aplicación tortuosa del modelo neoliberal en el Ecuador." *Boletín ICCI 'RIMAY'* 2 (January).

Lora, Guillermo. 1964. *La Revolución Boliviana.* La Paz: Difusión SRL.

_____. 1967–70. *Historia del Movimiento Obrero Boliviano.* 3 vol. 1848–1900, 1900–23, 1923–33. La Paz: Editorial Los Amigos del Libro.

_____. 1970. *Documentos Políticos de Bolivia.* La Paz: Editorial Los Amigos del Libro.

Loveman, Brian. 1976. *Struggle in the Countryside: Politics and Rural Labor in Chile, 1919–1973.* Bloomington: Indiana University Press.

_____. 1979. "Critique of Arnold J. Bauer's 'Rural Workers in Spanish America: Problems of Peonage and Oppression.'" *Hispanic American Historical Review* 59, no. 3.

Lucas, Kintto. 1991. "El levantamiento indígena visto por los protagonistas." In lleana Almeida et al. (eds.), *Indios: una reflexion sobre el levantamiento indígena de 1990.* Quito: Logos.

_____. 1999. "Los desafíos del movimiento indígena." *Boletín ICCI* 1, no. 1 (April).

_____. 2000. *La rebelión de los indios.* Quito: Abya Yala.

_____. 2001. "A propósito del ultimo levantamiento indígena: Divorcio entre movimiento politicio y movimiento social." *Boletín ICCI 'RIMAY'* 3, no. 23 (February).

Macas, Luis. 2000a. "Diez años del levantamiento del Inti Raymi de Junio de 1990: un balance provisional (Ten Years of the Inti Raymi Uprising of June 1990: A Provisional Assessment)." *Boletín Mensual* Quito: Instituto Científico de Culturas Indígenas, June 15.

_____. 2000b. "Movimiento indígena Ecuatoriano: Una evaluación necesaria *Boletín ICCI 'RIMAY'* 3, no. 21 (December).

MacDonald, Martha, and Patricia Connelly. 1983. "Class, Gender in Nova Scotia Fishing Communities." In C. Leys, B. Fairley and J. Sacouman (eds.), *Restructuring and Resistance in Atlantic Canada.* Toronto: Garamond Press.

Macdonald, R.D.S. 1984. "Canadian Fisheries Policy and the Development of Atlantic Coast Groundfisheries Management." In C. Lamson and A. Hanson (eds.), *Atlantic Fisheries and Coastal Communities: Fisheries Decision-Making Case Studies.* Halifax: Dalhousie Ocean Studies Program.

MacEwan, Arthur. 1999. *Neo-Liberalism or Democracy? Economic Strategy, Markets, and Alternatives for the 21st Century.* London: Zed Books.

Maddison, Angus. 1995. *Monitoring the World Economy, 1820–1992.* Paris: OECD Development Centre.

Mahoney, James. 2001. *The Legacies of Liberalism: Path Dependence and Political Regimes in Central America.* Baltimore, Maryland: Johns Hopkins University Press.

Mainwaring, Scott, Guillermo O'Donnell and J. Samuel Valenzuela, eds. 1992. *Issues in Democratic Consolidation: The New South American Democracies in Comparative Perspective.* South Bend, Ind.: University of Notre Dame Press.

Mallon, Florencia. 1983. "Murder in the Andes: Patrons, Clients, and the Impact of Foreign Capital, 1860–1922." *Radical History Review* no. 27.

_____. 1992. "Indian Communities, Political Cultures and the State in Latin America, 1780–1990." *Journal of Latin American Studies* 29, supplement.

_____. 1994. "The Promise and Dilemma of Subaltern Studies: Perspectives from Latin American History." *American Historical Review* 99, no. 5: 1491–1915.

_____. 1995. *Peasant and Nation: The Making of Postcolonial Mexico and Peru.* Berkeley: University of California Press.

_____. 1999. "Time on the Wheel: Cycles of Revisionism and the 'New Cultural History.'" *Hispanic American Historical Review* 79, no. 2: 331–51.

Malloy, James M., and Richard S. Thorn, eds. 1971. *Beyond the Revolution: Bolivia Since 1952.* Pittsburgh, Pa.: Pittsburgh University Press.

Marsh, Cabot. 1992. *No Fish and Our Lives: Some Survival Notes for Newfoundland.* St. John's: Creative Publishers.

Matthews, David Ralph. 1993. *Controlling Common Property: Regulating Canada's East Coast Fishery.* Toronto: University of Toronto Press.

McCay, B., and J. Acheson. 1987. *The Question of the Commons.* Tucson: University of Arizona Press.

McEwan, Arthur. 1981. *Revolution and Economic Development in Cuba: Moving Towards Socialism.* New York: St. Martin's Press.

McMichael, Philip. 1996. *Development and Change: A Global Perspective.* Thousand Oaks, Calif.: Pine Gorge Press.

Meier, Gerald. 1976. *Economic Development: Theory, History, Policy.* New York: Wiley.

Meillassoux, Claude. 1981. *Maidens, Meal and Money.* Cambridge: Cambridge University Press.

Meller, Patricio. 1988. "Revisión de los enfoques teóricos sobre ajuste externo y su relevancia para América Latina." *Notas CIEPLAN* no. 109.

Mendes, Chico. 1992. "Chico Mendes — The Defence of Life." *The Journal of Peasant Studies* 20, no. 1.

Midlarsky, Manus, and Kenneth Roberts. 1995. "Class, State and Revolution in Central America: Nicaragua and El Salvador Compared." *Journal of Conflict Revolution* no. 29 (June).

Miliband, Ralph. 1969. *The State in Capitalist Society*. London: Weidenfeld and Nicolson.

Miliband, Ralph, and John Saville, eds. 1974. *The Socialist Register 1974*. London: Merlin Press.

Mittleman, James. 2000. *The Globalization Syndrome: Transformation and Resistance*. Princeton: Princeton University Press.

Moore, Barrington, Jr. 1966. *Social Origins of Dictatorship and Democracy: Lord and Peasant in the Making of the Modern World*. New York: Beacon Press.

Morton, Adam David. 2003. "The Juggernaut or Jalopy of Globalization? The Travelling Circus of Anti-Globalization Resistance." In H. Veltmeyer (ed.), *The Dynamics of Antiglobalization*. London: Ashgate.

Munck, Ronaldo. 1984. *Revolutionary Trends in Latin America*. Montreal: Centre for Developing Areas.

_____. 1997. "Social Movements and Latin America: Conceptual Issues and Empirical Applications." Paper presented to the Latin American Studies Association, Guadalajara, April 17–19.

Munro, Gordon. 1980. *A Promise of Abundance: Extended Fisheries Jurisdiction and the Newfoundland Economy*. Hull, Que.: Canadian Government Publishing Centre.

Negri, Toni. 2001. "Contrapoder." In *Colectivo Situaciones de Buenos Aires. Contrapoder: una introducción*. Buenos Aires: Ediciones de Mano en Mano.

Neiss, Barbara. 1993. "Flexible Specialization: What's That Got To Do with the Price of Fish?" In J. Jenson, R. Mahon and M. Bienefeld (eds.), *Production, Space, Identity: Political Economy Faces the 21st Century*. Toronto: Canadian Scholars Press.

Newby, Howard, ed. 1978. *International Perspectives in Rural Sociology*. New York: John Wiley and Sons.

Nieboer, H.J. 1910. *Slavery as an Industrial System*. The Hague: Martinus Nijhoff.

Nudler, Julio. 2002. "Imperialismo para poner orden." *Página 12* (April 13).

Nugent, Daniel, ed. 1998. *Rural Revolt in Mexico: US Intervention and the Domain of Subaltern Politics*. London and Durham, N.C.: Duke University Press.

O'Connor, James. 1998. *Natural Causes: Essays in Ecological Marxism*. New York: Guilford Press.

O'Donnell, Guillermo. 1979. "Tensions in the Bureaucratic-Authoritarian State and the Question of Democracy." In David Collier (ed.), *The New Authoritarianism in Latin America*. Princeton, N.J.: Princeton University Press.

_____. 1988. *Bureaucratic Authoritarianism: Argentina, 1966–1973, in Comparative Perspective*. Berkeley: University of California Press.

_____. 1992. "Transitions, Continuities, and Paradoxes." In Scott Mainwaring, Guillermo O'Donnell and J. Samuel Valenzuela (eds.), *Issues in Democratic Consolidation*. South Bend, Ind.: University of Notre Dame Press.

Okonski, Kendra. 2001. "Riots Inc: The Business of Protesting Globalization." *Wall Street Journal* editorial, August 14.

Ommer, Rosemary. 1991. *From Outpost to Outport: A Structural Analysis of the Jersey-Gaspé Cod Fishery, 1767–1886*. Montreal and Kingston: McGill-Queen's University Press.

Orlove, Benjamin S., and Glynn Custred, eds. 1980. *Land and Power in Latin America: Agrarian Economies and Social Processes in the Andes*. New York: Holmes and Meier.

Ortega, M. 1990. "The State, the Peasantry and the Sandinista Revolution." *Journal of Development Studies* 26, no. 4.

Ostry, Silvia. 1990. *Government and Corporations in a Shrinking World: Trade and Innovation Policies in the US, Europe and Japan.* New York: Council on Foreign Relations.

Pachano, Simon. 1996. *Democracia sin sociedad.* Quito: ILDIS.

Paige, Jeffery M. 1975. *Agrarian Revolution: Social Movements and Export Agriculture in the Underdeveloped World.* New York: Free Press.

Palacios, Jorge. 1979. *Chile: An Attempt at 'Historic Compromise.'* Chicago: Banner Press.

Palmer, Craig. 1992. "The Northwest Newfoundland Fishery Crisis." *ISER Report* no. 6, Memorial University of Newfoundland.

Panayotou, Theodore. 1982. *Management Concepts for Small-scale Fisheries: Economic and Social Aspects.* Rome: FAO.

Parsons, L.S. 1993. *Management of Marine Fisheries in Canada.* Ottawa: National Research Council.

Passet, René. 2002. "Una crisis bursátil que viene de lejos." *Le Monde Diplomatique* 1, no. 2 (November).

Patel, Surendra. 1995. "In Tribute to the Golden Age of the South's Development." *World Development* 20, no. 5: 767–71.

Pearse, Andrew. 1975. *The Latin American Peasant.* London: Frank Cass.

Pearse, P.H. 1982. *Turning the Tide: A New Policy for Canada's Pacific Fisheries.* Vancouver: The Commission on Pacific Fisheries Policy.

Petras, James. 1997. "Latin America: The Resurgence of the Left." *New Left Review* 1, no. 223: 17–47.

_____. 2002. "Community Organizing: Unemployed Workers' Movement in Argentina." *Social Policy* 32, no. 3.

Petras, James, and Morley Morris. 1995. *Empire or Republic.* New York: Routledge.

Petras, James, and Henry Veltmeyer. 2001a. *Globalization Unmasked: Imperialism in the 21st Century*, London: Zed/Halifax: Fernwood.

_____. 2001b. *Brasil de Cardoso: expropriação de un pais.* Petrópolis: Editorial Vozes.

_____. 2001c. "Are Latin American Peasant Movements Still a Force for Change? Some New Paradigms Revisited." *Journal of Peasant Studies* 28, no. 2.

_____. 2002. "The Age of Reverse Aid: Neoliberalism as a Catalyst of Regression." *Development and Change* 33, no. 2 (April).

_____. 2003. *Cardoso's Brazil: A Land for Sale.* Boulder: Rowman & Littlefield.

Pinkerton, E., ed. 1989. *Co-operative Management of Local Fisheries.* Vancouver: University of British Columbia Press.

Polanyi, Karl. 1944. *The Great Transformation.* New York: Reinhart.

Pross, A.P., and S. McCorquodale. 1987. *Economic Resurgence and the Constitutional Agenda: The Case of the East Coast Fisheries.* Kingston: Queen's University.

Quintero, Rafael. 2000. "El alzamiento popular del 2I de enero y sus consecuencias para la democracia en el Ecuador." Mimeo. Ponencia presentada en el VI Congreso Nacional de Sociologia y Ciencias Políticas, Guayaquil.

Reyeros, Rafael. 1949. *El Pongueaje: La Servidumbre personal de los Indios Bolivianos.* La Paz: Empresa Editora Universo.

Robinson, William I., and Jerry Harris. 2000. "Towards a Global Ruling Class: Globalization and the Transnational Capitalist Class." *Science and Society* 64, no. 1 (Spring): 11–54.

Robles, Wilder. 2001. "Beyond the Politics of Protest: The Landless Rural Workers Movement of Brazil." *Canadian Journal of Development Studies* 22, no. 2.

Rogers, Raymond. 1995. *The Oceans Are Emptying: Fish Wars and Sustainability*. Montreal: Black Rose.

Romero, Jose Luis, and Luis Alberto Romero. 2000. *Buenos Aires: Historia de Cuatro Siglos*. Buenos Aires: Altamira.

Roseberry, William, Lowell Gudmundson and Mario Samper Kutschbach, eds. 1995. *Coffee, Society, and Power in Latin America*. Baltimore, Maryland: Johns Hopkins University Press.

Rout, Leslie B., Jr. 1976. *The African Experience in Spanish America: 1502 to the Present Day*, Cambridge: Cambridge University Press.

Rowe, J.W.F. 1932. *Studies in the Artificial Control of Raw Material Supplies — Brazilian Coffee*. London: Royal Economic Society.

Ruiz, Ramón Eduardo. 1980. *The Great Rebellion: Mexico, 1905–1924*. New York: Norton.

Sachs, Wolfgang, ed. 1993. *Global Ecology*. London: Zed.

_____. 1999. *Planet Dialectics: Explorations in Environment and Development*. London: Zed.

Salbuchi, Adrian. 2000. *El cerebro del mundo: la cara oculta de la globalización*. Córdoba: Ediciones del Copista.

Sánchez, Gonzalo, and Donny Meertens. 2001. *Bandits, Peasants and Politics*. Austin: University of Texas Press.

Sandbrook, Richard. 2000. *Closing the Circle: Democratization and Development in Africa*. London and New York: Zed.

Santana, Roberto. 1983. *Campesinado indígena y el desafío de la modernidad*. Quito: Centro Andino de Acción Popular (CAAP).

Saul, John S. 1974. "The State in Post-Colonial Societies: Tanzania." In Ralph Miliband and John Saville (eds.), *Socialist Register 1974*. London: Merlin Books.

_____. 1976. "African Peasantries and Revolutionary Change." In Joseph Spielberg and Scott Whiteford (eds.), *Forging Nations*. Ann Arbor: Michigan State University Press.

Saxe-Fernandez, John. 2002. *La compra-venta de México*. México DF: Plaza & Janés editores.

Saxe-Fernandez, John, James Petras and Henry Veltmeyer. 2001. *Globalización, Imperialismo y Clase Social*. Buenos Aires/Mexico City: Editorial Lumen.

Sbattella, Jose. 2001. "El Excedente economico en la Republic Argentina." *Realidad Economico* no. 181.

Schvarzer, Jorge. 2000. "La Implantacion Industrial." In Jose Luis Romero and Luis Alberto Romero (eds.), *Buenos Aires: Historia de Cuatro Siglos*. Buenos Aires: Altamira.

Scott, J.C. 1976. *The Moral Economy of the Peasant: Rebellion and Subsistence in Southeast Asia*. London and New Haven: Yale University Press.

_____. 1985. *Weapons of the Weak: Everyday Forms of Peasant Resistance*. London and New Haven: Yale University Press.

_____. 1990 *Domination and the Arts of Resistance*. London and New Haven: Yale University Press.

_____. 1998. *Seeing Like a State: How Certain Schemes to Improve the Human Condition Have Failed*. London and New Haven: Yale University Press.

Seers, Dudley. 1972. "The Meaning of Development." In N. Uphoff and W. Ilchman (eds.), *The Political Economy of Development*. Berkley: University of California Press.

_____. 1979. "The Birth, Life and Death of Development Economics." *Development and Change* 10, no. 4 (October).

Semo, Enrique. 1978. *Historia Mexicana: economía y lucha de clases*. México City: Ediciones Era.

Seoane, José, and Emilio Taddei, eds. 2001. *Resistencias mundiales [de Seattle a Porto Alegre]*.

Buenos Aires: CLACSDO.

Silva Herzog, Jesús. 1959. *El agrarismo méxicano y la reforma agraria: Exposición y crítica.* México, D.F.: Fondo de Cultura Económica.

Simbaña, Floresmilo. 1999. *Boletín ICCI* 1, no. 7 (October).

Simpson, Eyler N. 1937. *The Ejido: Mexico's Way Out.* Chapel Hill: University of North Carolina Press.

Sinclair, P.R. 1985. *The State Goes Fishing: The Emergence of Public Ownership in the Newfoundland Fishery.* St. John's: Memorial University.

Sinclair, W.E. 1977. *Management Alternatives and Strategic Planning for Canada's Fisheries.* Ottawa: Fisheries and Marine Services.

Sklair, Leslie. 1997. "Social Movements for Global Capitalism: The Transnational Capitalist Class in Action." *Review of International Political Economy* 2, no. 3.

Soros, George. 2000. *Open Society: Reforming Global Capitalism.* New York: Public Affairs.

South American Indian Information Center (SAIIC). 1993. "Organizing to Save the Amazon: An Interview with Valerio Grefa, New Coordinator of COICA." *Abya Yala News* 7, no. 1–2: 12–14.

Spielberg, Joseph, and Scott Whiteford, eds. 1976. *Forging Nations: A Comparative View of Rural Ferment and Revolt.* Ann Arbor: Michigan State University Press.

Stavenhagen, Rodolfo. 1970. *Agrarian Problems and Peasant Movements in Latin America.* New York: Anchor Books.

_____. 1994. "Indigenous Peoples: Emerging Actors in Latin America." Paper presented at the symposium "Ethnic Conflict and Governance in Comparative Perspective," Woodrow Wilson Center, Washington, D.C., November 15.

_____. 1997. "Indigenous Organizations in Latin America." *CEPAL Review* (August) 63–75.

Stedile, Joao Pedro. 2000. Interview with James Petras, May 14.

Stein, Stanley J. 1985. *Vassouras: A Brazilian Coffee County, 1850–1900.* Princeton, N.J.: Princeton University Press.

Stiglitz, Joseph. 1998. "More Instruments and Broader Goals: Moving Toward the Post-Washington Consensus." 1998 WIDER Annual Lecture. Helsinki: UN University, World Institute for Development Economics Research.

_____. 2002. *Globalization and its Discontents.* New York: W.W. Norton.

Streeten, Paul, et al. 1981. *First Things First: Meeting Basic Needs in Developing Countries.* New York: Oxford University Press.

Sullivan, Kathleen. 1995. "Rural-Urban Restructuring Among the Chamula People in the Highlands of Chiapas." In June Nash et al. (eds.), *The Explosion of Communities in Chiapas.* Copenhagen: International Working Group for Indigenous Affairs (IWGIA).

Sylva, Paola. 1986. *Gamonalismo y lucha por la tierra.* Quito: Abya Yala.

Tannenbaum, Frank. 1968. *The Mexican Agrarian Revolution.* New York: Archon Books (first published in 1929).

Task Group on Newfoundland Inshore Fisheries. 1987. *A Study of Trends of Cod Stocks off Newfoundland and Factors Influencing their Abundance and Availability to the Inshore Fishery.* Ottawa: Department of Fisheries and Oceans.

Taussig, Michael. 1986. *Shamanism, Colonialism, and the Wild Man.* Chicago: University of Chicago Press.

Teichman, Judith A. 1995. *Privatization and Political Change in Mexico.* Pittsburgh, Pa.: University of Pittsburgh Press.

Thorner, Alice. 1982. "Semi-Feudalism or Capitalism? Contemporary Debate on Classes and Modes of Production in India." *Economic and Political Weekly* 17 nos. 49–51.

Thorpe, Andy et al. 1995. *Impacto del ajuste en el agro Hondureño*. Tegucigalpa: Posgrado Centroamericano en Economia de la Universidad Nacional Autónoma de Honduras.

Tocancipá-Falla, Jairo. 2001. "Women, Social Memory and Violence in Rural Colombia." *Journal of Peasant Studies* 28, no. 3.

Toye, John. 1987. *Dilemmas of Development: Reflections on the Counter-Revolution in Development Theory and Policy*. Oxford: Basil Blackwell.

Traven, B. 1974. *The Rebellion of the Hanged*. New York: Hill and Wang.

_____. 1981. *The Carreta*. London: Allison & Busby.

_____. 1982. *March to the Monteria*. London: Allison & Busby.

_____. 1994, *Trozas*. London: Allison & Busby.

United Nations (UN). 1998. "The UN and Business: A Global Partnership." June. http://www.globalpolicy.org/reform/un-bus.htm.

United Nations Development Programme (UNDP). 1996, 2002. *Human Development Report*. New York: Oxford University Press.

United Nations Economic Commission for Latin America (CEPAL). 1990. *Productive Transformation with Equity*. Santiago de Chile: CEPAL.

_____. 2002. *Panorama social de América Latina, 2001–2002*. Santiago, Chile: CEPAL.

United Nations Research Institute for Social Development (UNRISD). 2000. *Civil Society Strategies and Movements for Rural Asset Redistribution and Improved Livelihoods*. Geneva: UNRISD.

Utting, Peter. 2002. "UN-Business Partnerships: Whose Agenda Counts?" UNRISD News no. 23 (Autumn–Winter).

Velasco, Fernando. 1979. *Reforma agraria y movimiento campesino*. Quito: Editorial El Cagnejo.

Veltmeyer, Henry. 1979. "The Underdevelopment of Atlantic Canada." In R. Brym and J. Sacouman (eds.), *Underdevelopment and Social Movements in Atlantic Canada*. Toronto: New Hogtown Press.

_____. 1983. "Surplus Labour and Class Formation on the Latin American Periphery." In Ron Chilcote and Dale Johnston (eds.), *Theories of Development*. Beverly Hills, Calif.: Sage.

_____. 1990. "The Regional Problem and Development." In C. Leys, B. Fairley and J. Sacouman (eds.), *Restructuring and Resistance in Atlantic Canada*. Toronto: Garamond Press.

_____. 1997a. "Class and Identity: The Dynamics of New Social Movements in Latin America." *Journal of Peasant Studies* 25, no. 1: 139–69.

_____. 1997b. "Decentralisation as the Institutional Basis for Participatory Development: The Latin American Perspective." *Canadian Journal of Development Studies* 18, no. 2.

_____. 1999. Labour and the World Economy." *Canadian Journal of Development Studies* 20 (special issue).

_____. 2000. *América Latina: capital global y la perspectiva del desarrollo alternativo*. Zacatecas, Mexico: UAZ, UNESCO.

_____. 2001a. "Civil Society and Social Movements in Latin America: The Dynamics of Intersectoral Linkages and Alliances." Thematic paper, UNRISD, Geneva.

_____. 2001b. "The Politics of Language: Deconstructing Postdevelopment Discourse." Paper presented as keynote address at meeting of the Canadian Association for the Study of International Development (CASID), Quebec City, May 27.

_____. 2002. "Social Exclusion and Rural Development in Latin America." *Canadian*

Journal of Latin American and Caribbean Studies.

Veltmeyer, Henry, and Anthony O'Malley. 2001. *Transcending Neoliberalism: Community-Based Development.* West Hartford, Conn.: Kumarian Press.

Veltmeyer, Henry, and James Petras. 1997. *Neoliberalism and Class Conflict in Latin America.* London: Macmillan Press/New York: St. Martin's Press.

_______ 2000. *The Dynamics of Social Change in Latin America.* London: Macmillan Press.

Via Campesina. 1996. "Managua Declaration, 1992." *The Proceedings of the II International Conference of Via Campesina.* Brussels: NCOS Publications.

Vilas, Carlos. 1995. *Between Earthquakes and Volcanoes: Market, State and Revolutions in Central America.* New York: Monthly Review Press.

Walker, Thomas, ed. 1997. *Nicaragua Without Illusions: Regime Transition and Structural Adjustment in the 1990s.* Wilmington, Del.: Scholarly Resources Press.

Warren, Kay. 1998. *Indigenous Movements and Their Critics.* Princeton, N.J.: Princeton University Press.

Weber, Peter. 1993. *Abandoned Seas: Reversing the Decline of the Oceans.* Washington: Worldwatch paper no. 116.

Weeks, E., and L. Mazany. 1983. *The Future of the Atlantic Fisheries.* Montreal: Institute for Research on Public Policy.

Wheelock Román, Jaime. 1975. *Imperialismo y dictadura: crisis de una formación social.* Mexico City: Siglo Veintiuno Editores.

Whetten, Nathan. 1948. *Rural Mexico.* Chicago: University of Chicago Press.

Wolf, Eric R. 1969. *Peasant Wars of the Twentieth Century.* London: Faber & Faber.

_____. 1982. *Europe and the People Without a History.* Berkeley: University of California Press.

_____. 1999. *Envisioning Power: Ideologies of Dominance and Crisis.* Berkeley: University of California Press.

World Bank. 1973, 1989. World Development Report. New York: Oxford University Press.

_____. 1995. *Ecuador Poverty Report.* Vol II. Washington, D.C.

_____. 1996. *World Development Report: From Plan to Market.* New York: Oxford University Press.

_____. 1999. *World Development Report: Knowledge for Development.* New York: Oxford University Press.

_____. 2002. *Global Economic Prospects and the Developing Countries.* http://www.worldbank.org.

World Commission on Environment and Development (WCED). 1987. *Our Common Future.* New York: Oxford University Press.

Wray, Natalia. 1987. *Constitución del mouimiento étnico nacion.* Quito.

Zamosc. León. 1994. "Agrarian Protest and the Indian Movement in the Ecuadorian Highlands." *Latin American Research Review* 29, no. 3.

Zeitlin, Maurice. 1967. *Revolutionary Politics and the Cuban Working Class.* Princeton, N.J.: Princeton University Press.

Ziemann, W., and M. Lanzendörfer. 1977. "The State in Peripheral Societies." In Ralph Miliband and John Saville (eds.), *Socialist Register.* London: Merlin Press.

Index